TURN RIGHT AT ISTANBUL

A walk on the Gallipoli Peninsula

TONY WRIGHT

ALLEN&UNWIN

Allen & Unwin
83 Alexander Street
Crows Nest NSW 2065
Australia
Phone: (61 2) 8425 0100
Fax: (61 2) 9906 2218
Email: info@allenandunwin.com
Web: www.allenandunwin.com

National Library of Australia
Cataloguing-in-Publication entry:

Wright, Tony.
Turn right at Istanbul: a walk on the Gallipoli Peninsula.

ISBN 1 86508 830 7.

1. Backpacking—Turkey—Gallipoli Peninsula—Anecdotes.
2. Travellers' writings. 3. Gallipoli Peninsula (Turkey)—Description and travel. I. Title.

915.6204

Pictures courtesy of Richard and Julia Butler, Peter Macinnis and Gregg Sonnenburg
Maps by Ian Faulkner
Set in 11 on 14.5pt Garamond Three by Midland Typesetters, Maryborough
Printed by McPherson's Printing Group

10 9 8 7 6 5 4 3 2

CONTENTS

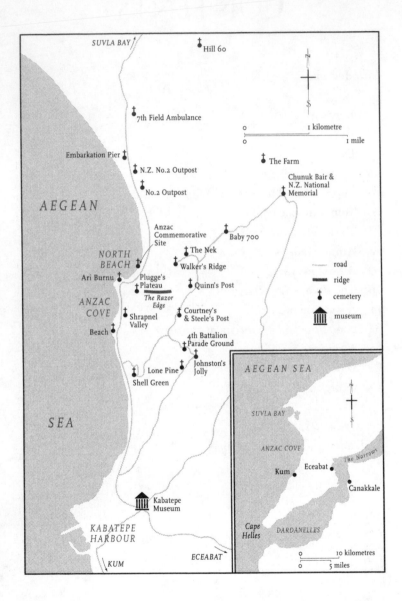

SUVLA BAY

Hill 60

7th Field Ambulance

Embarkation Pier

N.Z. No.2 Outpost

No.2 Outpost

The Farm

Chunuk Bair &
N.Z. National
Memorial

AEGEAN

Anzac
Commemorative
Site

Baby 700

The Nek

NORTH
BEACH

Walker's Ridge

Ari Burnu

Plugge's
Plateau

Quinn's Post

The Razor
Edge

road

ridge

ANZAC
COVE

cemetery

Courtney's
& Steele's Post

museum

Shrapnel
Valley

Beach

4th Battalion
Parade Ground

Johnston's
Jolly

Lone Pine

Shell Green

AEGEAN SEA

SEA

SUVLA BAY

ANZAC COVE

The Narrows

Kum   Eceabat

Canakkale

Kabatepe
Museum

KABATEPE
HARBOUR

Cape
Helles

DARDANELLES

KUM

ECEABAT

0   1 kilometre
0   1 mile

0   10 kilometres
0   5 miles

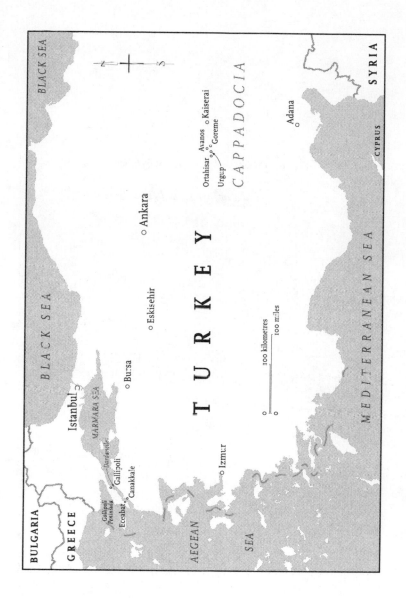

To my parents, who taught me to wander and wonder.

And Tim, who couldn't be there.

INTRODUCTION

There were weeks when I thought this book should not be completed. It was the period after 12 October 2002, when 88 Australians, and 114 Balinese, Britons, Europeans, New Zealanders and others had their lives blown away by terrorist bombs in Kuta, Bali. Most of those people were young, enjoying a carefree night out in a place that had a whiff of the exotic about it.

I remembered a night in a bar on the Gallipoli Peninsula, Turkey. It was a day or two before Anzac Day, and the bar, perched at the edge of the Dardanelles in the township of Eceabat, was crowded with young Australians and New Zealanders. One of the young revellers shouted in my ear that it was as if we were in Kuta north, but minus the surf. This observation echoed around my head as the televised pictures of the horror in Kuta were screened again and again in the days following 12 October. Here I was, writing a book celebrating a trip across the world to a place where thousands of Australians and New Zealanders gather, just as they did in Bali. Was it right any more, or responsible, to endorse such behaviour? Perhaps not, yet the alternative seemed worse. We could hardly sit petrified within our borders simply because evil might lurk out there in the shadows.

Every journey, anyway, begins before the traveller takes the first step. The journey to Gallipoli began before most of us were born, and hundreds of thousands of feet have tramped the path before us, beating it into the map of the Australian and New Zealand soul. For all that, everyone who makes the trip claims personal ownership of it, for it becomes a journey of the heart into a place of the mind. We take away from it a pebble from

Anzac Cove and the knowledge of emotions we hardly knew existed, and we each leave a part of ourselves there.

Every year now, thousands of Austalians and New Zealanders make the trip to Gallipoli. Or, rather, call it a pilgrimage, for there is something of the sacred quest in it. None of the travellers are old soldiers returning to the battlefield of their youth. They are all gone, but the care of Gallipoli has been turned over to new generations who have taken to it with an enthusiasm that defies all the predictions of a decade or so ago. That it is Australians and New Zealanders who make the trek in the greatest numbers is striking. Our countries are more distant from the Gallipoli Peninsula than those of all the other allied nationalities that took part in the campaign of 1915, British, French, Indian, Nepalese, Senegalese, Newfoundlanders, Poles and Russians.

It is well, however, to remember that vastly more Britons and Turks died at Gallipoli than did Australians and New Zealanders. This book does not detail the exploits and battles of those from other allied nations, and little of the travails of the Turks, but this is meant as no slur—I have limited myself to the Anzac area from an Australasian perspective and do not even cover the whole of that.

That it is in large part *young* Australasians who come to Gallipoli is even more striking. Most of them are not tracing the steps of their fathers, or even their grandfathers. They are walking a track taken by their great-grandfathers, or their great-great uncles, or they have no familial link to the place at all. But it is not only the young who make the trek. Veterans of World War II, Korea and Vietnam mingle with elderly men and women whose fathers were at Gallipoli, or whose mothers were nurses on the hospital ships and islands nearby. Families who simply want a glimpse of history wander the graveyards around and above the Cove. What each of them finds is that though the place is far from home, it is part of it. The light, the scrubby heath, the very essence of the Gallipoli Peninsula sings with long acquaintance.

Happily, the trip to Gallipoli is also a journey to Turkey. This is a country that might not be a nation at all if Turkish soldiers had not successfully defended their land in 1915. They were soldiers like our own: farmers, villagers, teachers, lawyers, boys hardly out of short pants, intellectuals and shopkeepers. They died and were wounded in roughly the same numbers, perhaps many more, because records were not accurate then, as the massed troops of all the allied nations that came on to the peninsula that had seen warriors marching across it for thousands of years. Gallipoli gave to the Turks their most revered leader, Mustafa Kemal Ataturk, who created from the ashes of the Ottoman Empire the republic we now call Turkey.

Most Antipodean travellers thread into our journeys to Gallipoli a wider sweep of this extraordinary country. In doing so, we do honour to the Turks, and we do ourselves a favour. Consider the Aegean coast, where much of Hellenic history resides in crumbling temples and hilltop cities that inspired Homer and the authors of the Bible; Cappadocia, where a dozen civilisations burrowed into the earth to escape another dozen civilisations sweeping by; the south-east, where ancient ethnic feuds bubble still and where Turkey meets the Middle East, the Black Sea coast, where the Georgian Caucasus rises into what was the USSR; Ankara, the modern capital and, most of all, Istanbul, the city that was Constantinople—fabulous Byzantium.

This book attempts to take you there, but it is not a book of history. All the good histories of Gallipoli have been done. It is a journey.

I

LEAVING

'Always sleep on the top bunk (bedwetters!),' she warned. 'If the place looks flea infested, it is. If someone looks like they want to knock your bag off, they will!! Jeans will not dry on the heater overnight, no matter how hard you try, and you will have chafing the next day.'

Gallipoli had long occupied an elusive place in my mind. There was an old man who shuffled around the edges of my childhood, half his face gone, who scared us kids but was saved from taunting because our parents whispered that he had 'been on Gallipoli'. As a knobbly-kneed Boy Scout, I would shiver on Anzac mornings before the obelisk standing outside our little school, half hearing the address by a shire president or an RSL man or a pastor who would always mention the dawn landing at Gallipoli. 'In the morning and in the evening, we will remember them,' we intoned. Remember what, exactly? I could not quite grasp where Gallipoli actually was. It sounded Italian, but hadn't we been fighting the Turks? And why? It was as insubstantial as the wind.

Even when I eventually found the place, it continued to evade me. A few years ago, a mate and I breezed in, took a car around the famous places—Anzac Cove, Lone Pine, The Nek, Chunuk Bair—and stood among the thousands at the dawn service on

North Beach, rendered mute as the sound of a didgeridoo echoed out across the empty sea.

'It's the paradox that affects everyone who comes to Anzac Cove: the peace of the place, easy as a cliché,' I wrote for my newspaper at the time. 'The gentle waters of the Aegean Sea lap the shore, and the great cliffs look down, bleak and ageless and unconcerned.'

The thousands of pilgrims, Australians and New Zealanders, my yarn continued, 'stood in the shadow of those cliffs, moved across the world by their nations' deepest and most enduring shared myth, hypnotised by the sense of place and the knowledge of old events here, both hideous and grand'.

All very well. In fact, I still knew little of that small patch of land called Anzac on the Gallipoli Peninsula. I had not walked it. I had not discovered the secret places. All I knew was a cliché.

It gnawed at me, and I hardly knew why. There was something else, too. I had been an observer at the dawn service, but I had not been a real part of that crowd of mostly young travellers. What did they feel, why were they there? Did the experience change them?

I had to go back.

It was five o'clock in the morning and I was bashing out a book review for my magazine, Australia's old bible of the bush, *The Bulletin*.

A soft April rain fell in the darkness outside. I was in Sydney, in the terrace cottage my university student daughter Jessica had chosen as the first modest step on her road to personal sovereignty.

Once, all the terraces around here were occupied by the families of workers and wharfies who did it tough, and sometimes I wondered how many children were born and lived and occasionally starved in the four tiny rooms—two up, two down— that now housed my daughter and her flat-mate. How many fathers and sons, almost a century ago, might have escaped the narrow streets and straitened lives and the daily grimy grind of factories and wharves and bawling babies and lit out for a uniform, six bob a day and a mysterious glory waiting far away? And how many might not have come home, leaving families existing on hand-outs, or come back strangers, busted in body and mind, to roar and rant in the six o'clock closers or to drift silently around the alleyways, chewed up by their adventuring?

There is no one left to say. They are all dead now, those young fellows who became old, and the shops nearby tell you that ordinary working families no longer live around here. Restaurants and cool delicatessens and bookshops bang up against organic vegetable markets and a cinema that shows nothing but art-house movies. Old Australia has moved out and university students and double-income, no-kids couples have shifted in. Where urchins once played in the streets, BMWs and students' clunkers jostle for parking spaces in the evenings.

Jessica was upstairs asleep, but I had robbed myself of the right to such comfort.

Naturally, there was a dinner earlier in the night. Naturally, there was too much wine. And now I was behind deadline, with a plane to catch in a few hours and an ache marching into my head.

It seems always to be like this. The business of setting out on a journey ought to be planned so the leaving is a calm thing. I tap-tapped at my keyboard, despairing as the rain ceased and birds in the trees outside began chirruping at the dawn.

I was writing a review of a book with a deceptively lovely name, *White Butteflies*, a story about a boy, Colin McPhedran, and his mother, brother and sister who fled their Burmese hill station as the Japanese advanced during World War II. It is a story of a long journey, of hardship and death and aching loss and eventually, a melancholy redemption.

There was a symmetry here, for I was about to visit a place on a different continent that echoes those themes from an earlier war. First, though, I had to find a way to send the story to my magazine. I needed a phone line so I could plug in the computer's modem but my daughter, a mobile phone girl, had no such thing.

There was a bakery next door with a team of bleary-eyed workers packing muffins for Sydney's breakfasts. I begged the baker for the use of his landline. 'No worries, mate,' he said. As the story flashed away down his phone wire, the baker told me he had wanted to travel to Gallipoli for years. He leaned against his flour-dusted bench and wondered aloud why so many young people took the trek these days. Dozens of friends and acquaintances had wondered the same thing when they heard where I was going. It was, I said, precisely what I wanted to find out for myself.

'Have a great trip,' this good bloke waved as I bolted into the morning, juggling computer and a bag of blueberry muffins, and there was something in his eyes that had become familiar— the resigned envy of those who are shackled while others fly away.

Is there an Australian who does not look skyward as a jumbo jet lumbers by, thinking of places a long way away? We are wanderers. Always have been. The geography that has stranded us on our big empty island continent has made us so. It used to be the sails of ships that set the restless heart a-bump. A long time before that, the original inhabitants of this place spent much of their lives roaming.

I had already said predictably inadequate farewells in Canberra to my wife Fiona and youngest daughter, Georgina, before flying to Sydney. I had phoned my eldest daughter Melanie and my parents, all of them in distant western Victoria, where the roots of all sides of my family have been dug deep into the soil for a century and a half.

My childhood outside Heywood, a township in the far south-west of that state where the few streets vanish quickly into farmland, was blessed with the freedom of cantering on my horse around my parents' wide paddocks, dreaming.

The thing about Heywood, snug in a river valley, is that it has a highway going through and a railway line too, and the thing about highways and railways is they stretch away, both ways. Just down the road is Portland, where ocean-going ships berth and shelter and sail away. One of my favourite pastimes was to watch the departure of ships from the wharves there—the hurrying of tugboats, the wharfies releasing ropes, the beat of big motors and the sudden boiling of propeller-thrashed water. A ship does not simply leave—it is a ponderous, majestic process, and the import of it is sealed by the farewell blast from the vessel's horn.

There is nothing but the ocean between this edge of Australia and Antarctica. On the still nights of my youth, when storms set waves smashing powerfully into the cliffs, it was possible to hear the percussion of it from our farm. It was the sound of beyond. The lonely whistle of a train and the restless movements of trucks and cars along the highway, the boom of the sea and the moan of a ship's foghorn were sounds to infect dreams with wanderlust. They meant that you could leave, and I did. I have been leaving places ever since.

Jessica was awake and grumpy with the morning (I had used all the hot water trying to wash away my hang-over) as I stuffed my backpack and tightened its straps, repeating the process three times as I spied bits and pieces I had left out. A guidebook to Istanbul, a tube of toothpaste, a map I had spread out on the dinner table the evening before, tracing the route I would take through Turkey. A sleeping bag, crushed small by compressor straps, still seemed too big to fit anywhere comfortably. The old warning to pack light is never quite possible. The bag was heavy. I had played with the idea of purchasing one of those little palm-held computers with a feather-light fold-out keyboard with which to record the thoughts of this trip, but it seemed inappropriate. The men who went to Gallipoli committed their thoughts by pencil to diaries, and all these years later they remain heirlooms, growing in value to their descendants as well as to historians and to the national fabric. You can go to the Australian War Memorial any day and find people bent over desks, burrowing through these old diaries as intently as a geologist might brush away the dust from a hieroglyphic chiselled by an artisan from an ancient civilisation.

And so I had purchased a small pile of journals, their lovely white pages bound within sturdy black covers. They were heavy, but the words that would be jotted within them would not flit airily into the ether that swallows and discards history committed to computers.

They would fit snugly next to a very old diary—that of George Reuben Moore. George was my father's mother's brother—my great-uncle. He was also an Anzac.

On 22 August 1914, just twelve days after recruiting for World War I began in Australia, he saddled up his horse and rode 15 miles (24 kilometres) from the hilltop property on which he worked outside Heywood to the seaside at Portland and signed up with the Australian Imperial Force. He was given the regimental number of 1440.

He was designated as a driver in the ammunition column of the 2nd Field Artillery Brigade of the First Division of the AIF, which means his job was to ride the lead horse of a team dragging ammunition wagons into battle.

I can only imagine he was assigned to this unit instead of the more glamorous Light Horse because he not only knew horses, but as a station hand he was a specialist in driving carts with teams of heavy animals. Perhaps he joined the artillery because he was struck by the power of large cannons that sat on the headland above Portland, still known as Battery Point. The guns were put there during the Crimean War when Australian authorities were consumed by the absurd fear that the Russian fleet might try to invade Britain's southern colony.

As it turned out, there wasn't much call for an artillery column driver on the cruel steep ridges and the exposed gullies of Gallipoli. George spent his time there carrying boxes of ammunition up from the beach at Anzac Cove to the trenches by hand, dodging snipers and hoping a spray of shrapnel did not kill him, and hauling—with teams of other men and sometimes mules—howitzers and great shells to the artillery batteries that rained hell on the Turkish defenders.

When I decided to set off for Gallipoli, I knew I had to take something of George's with me. But I had met him only a few times, and I had no idea that he might have left something behind. The homestead in which his parents lived had burned down in the Black Friday bushfires that cremated Victoria in 1939, and my father's opinion was that any letters George might have sent from Gallipoli would have been incinerated then.

Almost everyone in George Moore's family lived long lives, but now there is just one of his siblings left, his sister and my great-aunt Eileen Bell who is 95. She still lives in Heywood.

I phoned her before my departure to Turkey, inquiring whether there might be some fragment remaining that would link her brother George to his time at Anzac Cove.

She was delighted to assist. 'What's your fax number?' she asked, as if a facsimile machine was the sort of thing everyone had at their right hand. Astonished, I told her the number.

'I have a copy of the diary that George kept while he was on Gallipoli,' she said. 'I wrote it out long-hand, because it was written in indelible pencil and is so faint it can't be photo-copied. I'll fax it to you. The original is at the Australian War Memorial for safekeeping.' I could hardly believe my good fortune.

Eileen said she would have a look around and see if she had anything else of George's that might be of use to me. I asked if I could call back the following day.

'Hmmm,' she pondered. 'Tomorrow is Wednesday. I have to go to Mt Gambier on Thursday, I have an outing with the girls on Friday . . . yes, tomorrow should be all right.'

'You're keeping pretty busy,' I said.

'Well, I'm getting on and I might have only a few more years to live, so I believe in using the time I have,' she replied. 'Last Saturday, I had a strong desire to go horse-riding, so I did.'

I was a bit flabbergasted. 'Horse-riding at 95—that's got to be some sort of record,' I ventured.

'Not a bit of it,' Eileen shot back. 'I went with Mrs Sharrock, and she's 104. They were quiet horses, of course. I didn't go galloping or anything. I'll send you a photo.'

And she did. She looked as if she had never had a day out of the saddle. The Moore side of the family, I decided, was bullet proof. At that point, I hardly knew the half of it.

George's diary, copied in Eileen's perfect copper-plate, came zipping to my fax machine. Although a letter I found later in his official papers held by the Australian National Archives states that he arrived at Anzac on 25 April 1915, he did not begin jotting notes into his diary until 23 days later. Perhaps he was a little busy.

The first entry is 18 May 1915. 'Very hot day on the beach with shrapnel,' it begins. 'Dooley shot and taken to hospital. Carting 100-pounders for 6-inch howitzer. Dragged 6-inch howitzer into position. Fat Darrow killed with shrapnel bullet.'

And so George's diary found a special place in my backpack.

The first time I shouldered a backpack was a very long time ago—so long ago it was called a rucksack. At 19, while others snapped up in a lottery called conscription went off to Vietnam, I escaped, hitch-hiking the length of the Australian east coast. The feeling it left, that selfish buoyancy, has never fled. Do men ever properly advance within their dreams beyond the age of nineteen?

We skittered through streets building with commuter traffic, my daughter and I, she jockeying her little Suzuki, tyres hissing through the skim of last night's rain, and me a bit smug watching the sun glancing off the windscreens of vehicles taking their charges off to factories and offices. I looked, too, at the sun lighting the face of my child. She was 21. My great-uncle George was 21 as he sailed towards Anzac Cove. It seemed impossible to equate the two.

We loitered around the airport, awkward at the parting. Jessica had a lecture waiting at university, and through the window I could see my ride—a jumbo with a flying kangaroo on the tail.

My daughter stuffed a few sheets of folded paper into my hand. 'I wrote something for you. Don't read it now—wait until you're on the plane,' she said, and hurried away, taking care not to look back.

The plane lifted into the day, Sydney unfolding below with the harbour performing its never-ending magic. I first saw Sydney during that long-ago hitch-hiking adventure. I walked off a big night one early morning, down from the naughty brawling strip of Kings Cross, past the warships moored at Woolloomooloo, up to the glittering city, loitered beneath the

Moreton Bay figs of Hyde Park and trekked on to Circular Quay to catch a ferry across the harbour to Manly. I felt like an explorer seeing a land of gold for the first time.

I unfolded my daughter's offering.

'Dear Papa Bear,' it began, a little girl again. The letter said many things that will remain locked away in my heart. 'All my life I have associated travelling and the craft of writing closely with the essence of my dad,' she wrote. I recalled bringing home mementos for my children from each of the countries I had visited over the years. Mickey Mouse ears from Disneyland for Melanie, beefeaters from London, dolls carved by miners from Dresden, giraffes and elephants and tribal dolls from Kenya and Rwanda and Zaire and Zimbabwe and South Africa, models of the Eiffel Tower and berets from Paris, *matrushkas* from Russia, hideous wood carvings from the Solomon Islands and Bougainville, Thai dancing dolls from Bangkok and, from Cambodia, where toys had disappeared under Pol Pot, old silver shells containing coins from the French colonial era. Almost all of these trinkets are gone now, destroyed by a fire that wrecked our home years ago. Only the memories remain, which is enough.

Jessica herself had travelled around Europe, and she offered me some advice in her letter about the business of backpacking.

'Always sleep on the the top bunk (bedwetters!),' she warned. 'If the place looks flea infested, it is. If someone looks like they want to knock your bag off, they will!! Jeans will not dry on the heater overnight, no matter how hard you try, and you will have chafing the next day.' My child had become my parent.

A couple of years ago, Jessica and I motored together across Ireland in search of the Donegal village of Rathmullan, from which my mother's side of the family had emigrated during the Potato Famine of the 1840s. Perhaps she was remembering this when she finished her letter with what she called 'An Irish

(Jessie) blessing': 'May your backpack be light; May the Sun dry your muddy shoes; May the fleas be scarce; And may you write of the land of those brave men called Anzacs'.

I folded away the letter and stared out the window. Below, Australia streamed slowly away, grassy plains transmogrifying into waves of red sandhills. I slept, dreamless, waking occasionally, my bum feeling as if I had been sitting on concrete and the man sitting next to me, a New Zealander involved in the mysterious business of information technology, remained engrossed in a novel he had downloaded on to his palm computer. He had downloaded all his business papers and a stack of novels, checked the share-prices and written his emails on the thing, he told me. Best travelling companion he'd ever had. Perhaps I should have brought such a contraption with me after all.

Dusk was gathering as we fell towards Singapore, ships and fishing boats filling the sea. A bank of monsoonal storm clouds reared up into the evening, and when I left the plane and climbed the stairs of Changi Airport to its rooftop garden, it felt like walking into a sauna. I knew then that I was away.

Transferring to a Turkish Airlines plane, bound for Istanbul, I found myself surrounded by a party of greying Australians, off to Gallipoli too, on one of the scores of guided tours that have risen on the new tide of nostalgia for everything Anzac.

I was seated next to a couple from Newcastle, New South Wales: Cathy and John Mathieson. There are not too many degrees of separation among Australians, and I discovered soon that their daughter, Sharon, was a journalist. She worked, they told me, for the news agency Australian Associated Press.

When they learned I was a journalist too, we were all noisily astonished to discover that Sharon's office was in the very same corridor as mine in the press gallery of Parliament House, Canberra. We worked within 50 metres of each other. Pretty soon, the Mathiesons and I became friends of the sky, swapping guidebooks.

Cathy and John had a son too, a pilot in the Royal Australian Air Force. Perhaps he was sharing the heavens not far from us as we sailed towards Turkey. He was part of Australia's newest war: the battle against terrorism. The Mathiesons told me their son was assigned to fly a Boeing 707 out of Kyrgystan which was operating as an airborne tanker, refuelling fighter jets on their raids into Afghanistan against the Taliban and the terrorist camps of al Qaeda. Their protestations that they did not worry much—that he was well-trained and that he was not in the sector of danger—came too quickly. They had persuaded themselves of this so often—many times, I imagine, during sleepless nights—that it sounded like a mantra for their own reassurance. I caught John glancing out the window often, but I could not ask him whether he was searching for the shape of a Boeing 707 in the distance. I thought of my own family, safe in the safest corner of the Earth.

And I thought of parents staring out windows during other wars.

We slept, and woke to the sight of high, snow-covered mountains below. We were over Turkey. Was that giant Mount Ararat rearing beneath the belly of the plane? The flight steward was unsure, but we decided it was and the Mathiesons produced a video camera to record it. It was their first trip to Turkey, and they were as excited as anyone going to a new place. Noah's Ark is supposed by some to lie on the slopes of Ararat, and it wasn't so long ago that an Australian was taken hostage by Kurdish rebels as he fossicked around, intent on proving the Bible story. He was released eventually. Mount Ararat slumbers on and the ark lies undisturbed within the myth that is its proper owner.

We landed in a cold dawn and, if we hadn't caught sight of the Sea of Marmara as we wheeled across it, we could have been anywhere. Istanbul's airport is a disappointment to those expecting to alight in one of the world's most ancient and exotic cities. Industrial parks and great blocks of chunky apartments line the field, and the terminal is just another grey concrete building.

The Mathiesons gathered with their Made Easy Tours group and finally I was alone.

I set off in search of the visa counter. Australians have to pay US$20 before they can get through the Customs gate into Turkey, and it has to be in American currency. The Turks have endured galloping inflation for so long that they trust only the greenback.

Outside, a dark-haired young man held up a sign with my name on it. Some backpacker I turned out to be. My first day on the road and I had a hotel booked and a driver waiting to take me there.

He did not talk much, this young man. 'I am from the agency,' he said, and I took this to mean a travel agency linked up with the hotel to which I was bound, and which I had found on the Internet. 'Sorry, no English,' he said.

It was okay with me. Istanbul is probably my favourite city, though I had been there only once before. We rocketed down the freeway as towers of concrete apartments began giving way to signs that this was an old, old place. The ruins of thick ancient walls began appearing by the road and soon we were bumping through a gate in a wall that has stood since Istanbul was Constantinople. It had stood, indeed, since Constantinople was the capital of the Byzantine world: East Rome, greater than Rome itself, before the Ottomans came and built their own stupendous Islamic capital 550 years ago.

We crept through the narrow cobbled streets of Sultanahmet, hardly a soul stirring at this early hour. It is a city within a city, a crumbling reminder of Eastern magnificence, where the ghosts of the ancients are not yet quite crowded out by the tramp of modern tourism.

The hotel turned out to be a faded wooden Ottoman House a few metres wide and six storeys high. The receptionist, another young man who was yawning, could do nothing for me until a woman—also 'from the agency'—bustled in and relieved me of US$50. I had the vague feeling I was being ripped off. Still, a taxi ride from the airport would have cost US$10 or so.

My room turned out to be a cramped space three storeys up the stairs, with a view of a concrete wall. The bathroom could have done with some plumbing work and a scrubbing. There seemed to be no water in the dunny until I turned a faucet and received a jet of cold water up the behind.

Breakfast was in the basement as the touted 'rooftop terrace' was closed by the cold weather. It couldn't have been colder on the open roof than in the basement, where a crone tending the buffet watched as I loaded up a plate with my complimentary breakfast: black and green olives, a boiled egg, a tomato, strawberry jam. There was, happily, a large pile of bread. The coffee—Nescafé—was hot. It was the traditional breakfast of Istanbul hotels and I began to feel well-disposed, despite an atmosphere that told me I was the only guest in the establishment.

So what? I was alone with the whole city to explore. And I had travelled across half the world to get there.

The Anzacs of 1915 had tried and failed to get to Constantinople. I was, then, completing their journey before I travelled on to the thin spit of land that had stopped them: Gallipoli.

2

ISTANBUL

I wondered what might have happened if great-uncle George and his mates had managed to get to Constantinople. I rather suspect a jewelled dagger or two might have made it back to Heywood. A bit of looting would hardly be out of place—it was an artform in the ancient city.

The early morning streets of Sultanahmet seemed perfect for the task I had set for myself, which was to travel alone to soak up the sights and the sounds and store them all in my notebooks. The first mistake on any journey, of course, is to make plans.

I strolled a few hundred metres up to the Blue Mosque, blowing frost in front of me. Everything in Sultanahmet—which is to say almost all the obvious attractions of Istanbul—is within a short stroll, and you can't miss the Blue Mosque. Its great dome sits at the highest point of Sultanahmet. Istanbul was built on seven hills, and each hilltop has been given over to a mosque.

A big tour bus inched along the street, pulling up outside a hotel near the mosque, which floats easy as a hovering spaceship on its hill. The hotel was painted blue and rejoiced in the name of the Blue Hotel. Blue Mosque, Blue Hotel. Get it? Except the mosque isn't blue, at least not on the outside. It gets its name from the riot of blue Iznic tiles which covers the interior of its dome. The bus disgorged a chatter of old Australians, part of the Made Easy tour. Some of them waved, but the Mathiesons weren't among them. They were staying at another hotel. I kept walking.

Even at that cold hour an urchin approached, unfurling a string of postcards and declaring them very cheap. It took five minutes to get rid of him, and I felt all the while guilty at my stinginess. He danced and skipped along, demanding to know whether I needed a guide. 'Can get anything for you, special today,' he chanted. I needed nothing, I said. I had no money. It was a lie. He dropped away only when he spied an elderly couple trudging towards us.

I wandered through the gardens that separate the Blue Mosque from the world's most confused religious building, the pink-ochre Sancta Sophia, also known as the Aya Sophya and the Haghia Sofia, the Church of Holy Wisdom. For 1000 years after it was built in 537AD by the Emperor Justinian, it was the greatest church of Christianity, and the largest enclosed space on Earth.

Then the Ottoman Sultan Mehmet the Conqueror blasted his way through the walls of Byzantium in 1453, and had the building converted to the world's greatest mosque. Intricate and stunning Byzantine mosaics were plastered over, and minarets were added. Even the earthquakes that regularly shake Istanbul could not bring down the Sancta Sophia, though the building began leaning until a famed Ottoman architect, Sinan, built giant buttresses to save it from sliding towards the sea.

Since the 1930s, after Turkey became a secular republic, the ancient building has been neither church nor mosque: it simply stands there as a monument, overrun by tourists, and the plaster has gradually been scraped away to reveal the astonishing millennia-old mosaics.

I stood in the garden between the domes of the Sancta Sophia and the Blue Mosque, feeling the tug of history. Beneath my feet, chariots had hurtled around what was the Hippodrome, urged on by their fans seated in the amphitheatre's stands, buried 2 metres deep now by the dust of ages. Right here, in five days in 532AD, a very grumpy Emperor Justinian, urged on by his even grumpier Empress Theodora, put down rioters by ordering troops to slaughter 30 000 of them. The rioters had burned down the original Sancta Sophia. Fortified by their blood, Justinian, a fine Christian, decided it should be rebuilt in stone to glorify his reign.

Cold, weary and suddenly lonely amid all the gory antiquity of my surroundings, I wandered back to the hotel for a jacket.

The place was in mild uproar. 'Where have you been?' the receptionist demanded. 'Your guide has called. He is coming in ten minutes.'

My guide? Back in Australia, I had talked with the Turkish Ambassador, Tansu Okandan, about my planned journey. You must have a guide, he had said, magnanimously. I had tried to explain that I wanted to travel detached. A trained guide himself, he wouldn't hear of it. Irrationally, I felt mildly irked to hear that a guide had been dispatched on my first day. Still, this generous gift would mean company, and it would be only a day.

Ömür Tufan arrived wearing a black beanie, a scarf swaddling the lower half of his face, and a heavy overcoat topping a roll-neck pullover. Only his eyes were visible. He bustled into the hot, cramped foyer and immediately began apologising about the exceptionally cold winter. Soon I would learn that he always dressed for the cold, even when the sun came out.

Ömür was no off-the-shelf guide. He was a curator at Istanbul's most remarkable museum, the Topkapi Palace. He specialised in the stupendous collection of Eastern ceramics amassed by the Ottoman sultans, and spent much of his time fossicking around in damp cellars and musky rooms. The chill of his work had seeped into his bones.

When he unwound himself from his scarf, Ömür revealed himself to be a young man, dark and intense and concerned that I should be at ease. He and the receptionist, who sat perched upon the arm of a chair, insisted we drink tea, known as *çay*. It came in small curvaceous glasses. I would soon discover that this ceremony was one of the more charming traits of Turkish social behaviour: every meeting must begin with the drinking of tea or coffee. A visitor is genuinely an honoured guest in Turkey.

'You must excuse me. I am learning English and it is not so good,' Ömür said. 'We have program for today. First to Topkapi Palace.'

It was the start of a whirl that would last a week. My reservations about accepting a guide, and intentions of limiting his assistance to a single day, began to melt within hours of meeting this young man.

Our thimbles of tea finished, Ömür wrapped himself in his scarf, pulled down his beanie, and we set off for the palace, its outer gate just around the corner from the Sancta Sophia. Trinket shops sat along the wall of the church. One boasted a sign declaring: 'Sorry, we are open'. Right alongside was another stall with its own peculiar sign: 'Sorry, we are not closed'.

Ömür had no reason for concern about his English. Indeed, in the next few days, I would come to learn he possessed several languages, including Japanese.

The Turkish people, he declared when we passed one of his colleagues and they exchanged greetings in Japanese, were originally from the eastern edge of Mongolia in Central Asia. It was easier for a Turk to learn Eastern languages like Japanese than to become fluent in English, because their grammar was constructed in similar ways.

We entered the reinforced metal gate of the Topkapi Palace's outer wall and sauntered through a vast courtyard towards the inner world of the Ottoman Empire.

Ömür grew relaxed. He was in his domain. The Topkapi, he explained, was built as an enclosed city for the Sultan and his court. Once, more than 5000 people lived within its walls. There was a farm, complete with animals and orchards and crops to feed the chosen inhabitants.

The immense palace within a city, no more than a tourist attraction now, sits upon the finest real estate in Istanbul. It inhabits a high-set promontory wrapped by defensive waters— the Bosphorus, the Golden Horn and the Sea of Marmara.

Its harem alone held up to 1000 women guarded by a small army of black and white eunuchs—the only men, other than the Sultan and his young brothers, who were ever allowed to clap eyes on the women. The eunuchs held privileged, often powerful positions, but it was an unhappy road that led them there. I had wondered often about how all the eunuchs had been created and was less than thrilled, once I learned, that I had sought answers. Most were purchased from slave traders, and the black eunuchs from Africa in particular suffered fearfully on the route from masculinity to emasculation. As children, they usually had both their testicles and their penises hacked from their bodies. Hot oil was applied to the wound and they were then immersed in a dung heap for the healing to begin. Many, pretty obviously, did not survive. Those who did then had a wooden or metal tube inserted into the urethra to allow them to urinate. Others had only their penises severed, or their testicles removed or twisted into uselessness. Such practices were not allowed under Islamic law (though it allowed eunuchs to be used in the harem), so the slave traders had to carry out the vile operations before making the transaction with the Ottoman slave buyers.

The women of the harem—wives, concubines, servants and entertainers, most of them stolen or presented as gifts from conquered lands—also had to behave. If they displeased the Sultan—or worse, his mother, the Begum, who held the real power—they would find themselves bundled into a sack and drowned in the Bosphorus or the Golden Horn, a strip of water below the palace into which, legend has it, the old Byzantine emperors would toss so many gold coins for the pleasure of the Gods that it fairly glittered.

The Sultan lived within the harem, but many of these spoiled gentlemen endured the paranoia that they would be murdered by jealous brothers. A lavatory within the harem still has a gilded cage around it, built by a Sultan who was afraid that he could be caught by a knife-wielding assassin, literally with his pants down. The Sultan couldn't simply stagger around the place grabbing every girl who took his fancy, either—his feared and revered mother vetted the women she thought might be good enough for her son. And then he had to contend with his first wife, his second, his third and his fourth.

All of which placed a bit of a pall over the absurd extravagance still on display around the Topkapi: rooms of jewelled daggers, headpieces set with rubies as big as a fist, intricately carved gold and silver contraptions studded with precious stones, a diamond-encrusted suit of chainmail, bejewelled turbans, thrones of gold and an 86-carat diamond supposed to have been found in a Constantinople rubbish dump more than 300 years ago.

I wondered what might have happened if Great-uncle George and his mates had managed to get to Constantinople. I rather suspect a jewelled dagger or two might have made it back to Heywood. A bit of looting would hardly have been out of place—it was an artform in the ancient city. When the Ottoman army broke through the walls of Byzantium, soldiers were given three days to loot everything they could get their hands on. Everything remaining went to the Sultan. It was a good deal for everyone except those who had been conquered, because there were so many treasures that the soldiers simply couldn't stagger off with a thousandth of it. In turn, the Ottomans happily looted the distant countries they conquered in pursuit of empire. The wonderfully named Selim the Grim grabbed no less than Arabia, Egypt and Syria during just eight years in the sixteenth century, and his troops carried back to Constantinople riches that beggar the imagination.

Call me a cynic, but on close inspection of some of the jewels in the Treasury I got the impression that some of the stones were coloured glass. Ömür protested that I was quite mistaken, but there must have been serious temptation, as the Ottoman Empire began reeling beneath impossible debt early last century, for officials to have quietly flogged off the originals.

If the past hovered uncertainly, the present managed to intrude. Ömür was explaining how the Sultan would sit on a golden throne outside one of the ceremonial gates, reviewing his subjects, when four Turkish fighter jets screamed out of the sky. It felt as if a chainsaw had ripped through our skulls.

'So sorry,' said Ömür. 'Why?' I inquired. 'Maybe you think another war has come,' he said. 'These are strange times.' Iraq shares a border with Turkey, and there was much talk of George W. Bush requiring Turkey's air bases for a new assault on Saddam Hussein. September 11 and its aftermath hung heavily in Turkey, a secular nation whose population is more than 90 per cent Islamic. Apart from the obvious religious and geographically strategic considerations, September 11 had carved deeply into Turkey's tourist industry too, which is why it was possible to wander the Topkapi Palace without having to endure long queues. Ömür recalled that, the day after September 11, mobile telephones began ringing throughout the palace—virtually all Japanese tourists received calls from their travel agencies informing them that if they did not leave Turkey immediately, their travel insurance would be void.

'In one day, every Japanese left Istanbul,' Ömür said. 'Turkey was considered unsafe because of Iraq. So silly.'

Ömür was unusually well informed on the subject. He flies to Japan almost every month to give a lecture on Japanese ceramic art, and his girlfriend is Japanese.

He took me to the kitchens of Topkapi to explain. They were his realm, because part of the kitchen wing—as big as the stables of an army—had been converted to a museum of ceramics. The Sultans were crazy for Chinese porcelain. It is possible that they carried this love all the way from the steppes of central Asia, from whence the Turks had migrated, conquering everything in their path. Pick a country with a 'stan' in it, and the Turks had been through—Afghanistan, Kyrgystan, Turkmenistan and all the rest.

Various Sultans managed to build a Chinese ceramics collection that remains the world's largest outside China, mainly by purchasing everything that came down the Silk Road. From time to time, though, the supply would dry up—the Chinese, bothered by war, would stop exporting.

Japanese craftsmen recognised these periods as golden opportunities, and began to manufacture ceramic bowls of similar quality to the Chinese. The Japanese traded with the Dutch, then among the world's greatest seafarers and themselves traders of some renown. The Sultan, sitting around in Constantinople with none of the latest Chinese ceramic designs to take his mind off his troubles in the harem, was only too happy to talk Turkey with the Dutch.

The Sultan got exquisite collections of Japanese ceramics to be used in the kitchens along with those from China, the Dutch got gold and, a few hundred years later, Ömür my Istanbul guide got his chance to become one of the world's experts on Japanese ceramic art.

The Dutch got something else, too. The tulip is a flower native to Turkey. It was revered and became the royal flower, its shape engraved into thousands of the Sultans' most precious belongings. It was, indeed, the symbol of the Ottoman Sultanate. I had noticed during the morning that tulips were beginning to flower in the Sultanahmet garden between the Blue Mosque and the Sancta Sophia, and they were sprouting in the parks of the Topkapi Palace.

During one of the haggling sessions over ceramics, it seems a gift was made of tulips by a Sultan in thanks for Dutch willingness to fill the void left by the empty treasure routes of the Silk Road. Thus the Dutch began the business of growing tulips, and that's how they, not the Turks, are now most linked to a flower that grows in gardens in almost every country of the world.

I felt ashamed of my early-morning pique at the arrival of Ömür. He was beginning already to become more than a guide as he shepherded me around, opening my eyes to things I would never have known about. I suggested lunch, and he said there was a place he must take me to. On the way, we visited the Sancta Sophia, and he led me around its cavernous interior, pointing out the ancient Christian mosaics, marble slabs on which Byzantine emperors were crowned, a spot on the first floor, far from the ceremonial areas, where empresses—and later Ottoman Sultans' wives—were allowed to sit. The whole place was designed to mirror the heavens, and the dome—an architectural miracle for its time—floats almost as high as heaven itself, although its mosaics have been replaced by Koranic scriptures. For years now, soaring builders' platforms have dominated the interior in an apparently endless restoration effort undertaken by UNESCO.

Across tram tracks and up one of the main streets of Sultanahmet, Ömür steered me into a packed restaurant and up the stairs to a table near a window. It was so hot that even Ömür shed his coat and beanie. This, he told me, was the most famous of the old restaurants in Istanbul. Faded photos on the wall showed that presidents, Turkish film stars and even the great Ataturk himself, hero of Gallipoli and first president of the Republic of Turkey, had dined here since the 1920s. And in most of the pictures was the wizened little owner, to whom I was introduced with great ceremony. 'Aussie,' he said. 'Turks and Aussies—we love each other. You come back, bring friends. All Aussies are friends here.'

In fact, I was the only foreigner in the whole crowded place. It was called the Tarihi Sultanahmet Kofteçisi, and its kitchen was supposed to have invented a particular style of the Turkish dish known as *kofte*. Naturally, I ordered *kofte*, which turned out to be elongated meatballs. It was delicious, but then so is almost all Turkish food, which is often a great deal more elaborate than meatballs. We finished with a dessert named *irmik helvasi*—pine nuts in sweet bread.

Ömür was curious about just what I was doing in Turkey. I explained I was travelling to Gallipoli to write a book, and that Istanbul was simply a stopover. He looked disappointed. 'There is much to see,' he said. 'I can have program each day, long as you like.'

It was to prove a promise. Each day after that I would think of leaving Istanbul, and each day Ömür would be on my doorstep with a new 'program'. He would show me every mosque worth seeing, every museum he could think of, every bazaar and bridge and street that a visitor might wish to visit.

During the afternoon of that first day, Ömür led me out of Sultanahmet down a long hill through the Bazaar Quarter and across the Golden Horn on the Galata Bridge to a district known as Beyoglu. I could have stood on the bridge for hours, watching scores of fishermen dangling their multi-hooked lines into the waters of the Golden Horn and hauling in 20 sardines at a time.

Beyoglu proved another world from the ancient surrounds of Sultanahmet. The surging crowds were more neatly dressed and there was a purpose to their movement. Business was happening, and buildings lacked the age of the promontory across the water. We struggled uphill and caught a light rail car that took us under-ground further uphill, where we emerged in Taksim—the modern centre of Istanbul. Women click-clacking down the street appeared to be dressed by Dior, the men by Armani. Embassies stood in large grounds behind impressive gates. The great game of the nineteenth and twentieth centuries—spying—had its roots around here. So had the end of the Ottoman Empire. Passages led off the main drag—Istiklal Caddesi—and we drifted through one of them, known as the Ciçek Pasagi (Flower Passage). Inside, smart little cafés lined the walls and we continued around until we found a place with tables outside. This area was the Nevizade, the night haunt for rich city dwellers, intellectuals and bohemians. Gay men dressed in drag minced by, and Ömür appeared uncomfortable. 'What do people in your country think about people like this?' he inquired, and I gathered he was worried I might be concerned. Sydney, I told him, was one of the gay capitals of the world, and no one much raised an eyebrow anymore. Ömür seemed relieved.

In the early part of last century, Nevizade was the favoured meeting place of the Young Turks. Ataturk had spent long nights there, drinking coffee and stoking himself with the aniseed-flavoured liquor known to Turks as *raki*. Ömür and I were sitting where the end of the Ottoman Empire was plotted.

We drank a couple of beers and decided to order dinner. The café owner implored us to come in out of the cold wind of the passage, and brought trays of food from which we could choose numerous morsels—dips of all types, prawns and fish, *kofte*, pickled vegetables and yoghurt, accompanied by slabs of *pide* bread.

Glasses of *raki* were brought and I made an ass of myself by refusing to add water to the clear liquid—a process that turns the firewater milky white and softens it. Songs, I believe, may have been sung.

Some time later we hailed a taxi and I returned to my hotel, determined to find new accommodation in the morning.

Yet I could not sleep. The strange effect of jet lag took me back into the street, and I walked downhill a bit to a road every Australasian backpacker finds almost by instinct. It is a street of youth hostels and bars and the last time I had been there it had been wall-to-wall with familiar accents and bonhomie. Most famously, it contains the Orient Hostel, storey upon storey of dormitories.

This early in April, though, the street was almost deserted. Loud music spilled from a bar across the way from the Orient, but when I pushed open the door, a single barman stared at an empty room. I ordered a beer, deciding it would be a lone nightcap.

The door burst open and a young man fairly leapt in. His long, tangled blond hair and open-faced grin told me where he came from before he opened his mouth. 'Mate,' he said, sticking out his hand. 'The name's Davin Phillips, I'm from Perth and I can't bloody believe I'm here.'

His mood was infectious. Even the barman began grinning. Davin, it seemed, had woken up in London, decided he had to go to Gallipoli to attend the Anzac service and had jumped on a plane for Istanbul during the morning. Beyond that, he didn't have much of an idea. His budget stretched to about £50, and he wasn't quite sure where Gallipoli was. We seemed to be the first independent travellers from Australia to have arrived in this part of Istanbul pre-Anzac.

I bought him a beer. 'Mate,' he said, 'this is the best town. I met an old Turkish veteran today and he showed me around. He fought with the Australians. Bought him lunch and everything. He was great.'

The story of a Turkish veteran fighting with Australians was puzzling. He couldn't have been in Gallipoli, though Davin seemed to think he had been. It would emerge later that this old man was a veteran of the Korean War during the 1950s, where the Turks had indeed fought with the coalition that included Australians. It didn't matter to Davin. He was in Istanbul and he was going to Gallipoli and he'd met a Turkish fighting man. All in an afternoon.

'Where are you staying?' I asked.

'Oh, mate, that's the best part,' he said. 'I've met these Turkish blokes who are setting up a new restaurant and bar and I'm going to help out. They're going to let me sleep on the floor.'

It sounded a bit worrying. Sultanahmet feels benign, I told Davin, but there are traps for new players. Over the past couple of years stories have emerged among travellers about scamsters who prey on backpackers. Young men who hang about the park near the Blue Mosque often approach visitors fresh off the plane, offering friendship and guiding services. They point out automatic teller machines, declare they know of cheap hostels and lull their marks into a sense of security. Then comes an offer of a soft drink, or a biscuit. And that's about all the victim remembers until he or she wakes up in an alley, wallet, money, passport and backpack missing. The scam, according to hostel operators and police, involves the use of knock-out drugs like Xanax or

Rohypnol. A soft drink or a piece of food is laced with a heavy dose, and then it's good night and a rotten morning after.

The ruse had become so common around Sultanahmet that most hostels had posted warnings advising guests to avoid strangers at night and under no circumstance to accept food or drink from strangers on the street.

Davin looked a bit concerned about the story, but assured me the fellows establishing the new restaurant and bar weren't like that.

'How are you getting to Gallipoli?' I asked. Davin seemed surprised, and said he thought it wasn't far away. When I told him it was about six hours by bus, and that accommodation would be tight, he announced he'd find a way, no worries. He was good, optimistic company, and we swapped email addresses.

I could have saved my breath warning him about the Istanbul night. Within a week, he would become a minor celebrity among Australian and Kiwi backpackers. His faith in the Turkish entrepeneurs, and theirs in him, was well-founded. The restaurant and bar opened, and Davin stood out the front, cheerfully persuading travellers to pack themselves inside for a beer and a meal. He had worked nightclubs in Perth, he told me. I don't believe the word 'setback' was in his lexicon.

I was ready for sleep and we said good night. I trooped back to my hotel and discovered that the door was locked. There was a night bell, but it brought no response. The night was cold and the street was empty. It took ten minutes of knocking and ringing before the receptionist appeared and unbolted the door. He had been asleep, he said. Half your luck, I replied. My first day in Istanbul was done.

3

EYUP

Even here we could not escape the present. Lines of police stood around, and preparations were being made for a mass demonstration in support of Palestinians and against Israel and the United States. It was Friday, and demonstrations like this had become a feature at mosques all across Istanbul every Friday.

A wailing blew me out of a dream. It rose and fell and rose, doubling in intensity. I clawed around for a light switch and knocked a lamp off the bedside table before finding a curtain to pull aside from the window.

My wristwatch announced it was 5.17 a.m. The wailing went on, and this night's short sleep was over.

In every Islamic city in the world, the first sound of every day is a *muezzin* calling the faithful to prayer at dawn. Once, the *muezzin* climbed to the top of a thin tower, the minaret, that graces every mosque and set to his song using the power of his Allah-given vocal chords.

No longer. Technology has given the prayer-caller a more powerful tool in the business of soul-seeking. The *muezzin* has no reason now to climb the dizzying steps of his minaret. He sits at its foot and bellows into a microphone. Loudspeakers bolted to the top of the tower amplify his voice a thousand times, and no member of the faithful has the excuse of failing to hear the cry.

The call to prayer—repeated five times in Arabic every day between dawn and dusk—is a beautiful thing, particularly heard from a distance, and the best *muezzin*s are highly trained vocalists.

But my hotel was hardly 200 metres from the Blue Mosque, and its loudspeakers are possibly the most powerful in the Islamic world.

I crawled into the shower recess, turned on the water and the attachment holding the hose to the wall fell off. I dressed, threw the pack on my shoulders and took to the street.

In the dull light of the early morning, I felt a bit of a dill. Where would I go?

Right across the road was a hotel I had failed to see the previous day. The Side [pronounced See-day] Hotel and Pension. It was a place I had planned to visit. It had good write-ups in the travel guides and on the Internet, and a couple of people had recommended it. Yet I had taken someone else's advice and the business with the shower had been the result.

A young man at reception was happy to assist. He had a room vacant, it was on the ground floor and, with a little bargaining, we settled on a daily rate of US$35. The room was perfectly clean and had a double bed with a white cotton spread, a TV on the wall and a bathroom with a sturdy-looking shower set-up. In the foyer was a small lounge where guests could help themselves to tea or coffee and watch CNN on TV. I climbed the stairs and found a breakfast room and rooftop garden sporting a view across Sultanahmet to the Sea of Marmara, where ships sailed. Right next door was the roof garden of Istanbul's most expensive hotel, the Four Seasons. I could wave to people who were paying hundreds of dollars a night. The Four Seasons is a high-rent conversion of what was the most unpleasant accommodation in Istanbul: the city's prison, portrayed grimly in the movie *Midnight Express*.

Ömür was waiting down the street. He had a surprise. Two, actually. He handed me a leaflet he had found in the window of a travel company. 'Red Poppy Tours' it read. 'Anzac Day 2002. BOOK NOW.'

Ömür looked glum. 'Maybe someone has been first,' he said. I failed to understand what he was talking about.

'Look,' he said. 'Book now. Is okay?' I still had no idea what was chewing at him.

'Book now. Anzac Day 2002.' Eventually, I followed his meaning. He knew I was in Turkey to write a book about the journey to Gallipoli and Anzac Day, and he was concerned that some other writer had beaten me to it. 'Book now'. It took long minutes to explain that the poster was imploring travellers hoping to attend Anzac Day to make a tour reservation straight away. The English language was a serious puzzle if there were two quite different meanings to a word like 'book'.

Ömür was relieved, and I was touched at his concern.

His second surprise waited at the end of a long taxi ride. Ömür had decided that I should be given the opportunity of seeing how Turkey's sweetest food was cooked. We were off to a factory specialising in Turkish Delight and *baklava*. The factory, owned by a family-run company called Gulluoglu, was the newest, highest-tech outfit in Istanbul, featuring stainless steel at every turn. Managers and scientists spoke at great length about the processes involved in this multi-million-dollar venture, and I was invited to taste some of the 37 flavours of Turkish Delight and fifteen kinds of baklava, and to watch artisans in white dust-jackets rolling layers of starch to the consistency of tissue paper and boiling up vats of sherbert. Ömür, ever the enthusiast, took video footage. The purpose of the visit escaped me, but it was kind of fun. Turkish Delight is, well, a delight. And then one of the managers began enthusing about worldwide franchises. Yes, like McDonalds. The *baklava* would be snap-frozen to −40°C in Istanbul, flown to America, London, Greece, Dubai and, ummm, Sydney, where it would be cooked in situ. Would this work in Sydney? Oh, absolutely, I said. Never let a chance go by.

Later, I wondered what Ömür had been up to, taking me to a shining food factory. I came to the conclusion he had worried that I was seeing too much that was old and broken down and wearing the dust of centuries, and wanted me to know that Istanbul had stainless steel and machines that worked without a hitch. Besides, the new *baklava* factory was part of a recent restoration and parkland development on the shore of the Golden Horn, Istanbul's most revered natural feature, which had become blighted with rusting and rotting factories and disused warehouses on its shores.

We were at cross-purposes. I was there for a history, complete with warts, that astounds a person born in Australia. But ancient Istanbul was all too familiar to Ömür, whose work was the past and who, like most young, well-educated Turks, hopes for a better future.

We said farewell to the factory and, munching on sticky *baklava*, took a taxi straight back into that past. We wound around the higher reaches of the Golden Horn, climbed a steep hill and alighted at the summit. There was a café and a terrace with one of the few uninterrupted views in all Istanbul of the length of the Golden Horn. We sat and ordered soft drinks, and the sun came out. This was Pierre Loti's café, and all around, travellers jabbered in French. Loti was a French novelist who fell in love with Turkey in the nineteenth century, and also fell for a married Turkish woman. He not only lived to tell the tale, but wrote a flowery novel about it called *Aziyade*. His writing style and photos suggest he was an unbearable dandy, sporting a moustache with the ends twisted and tweaked up in the fashion of the self-satisfied bohemian of a certain period. However, the Turks thought he was the bee's knees, not least because he wrote impassioned pleas for greater understanding of the Turkish people at a time when the Russians and Europeans were using terms like 'the unspeakable Turk' and referring to the Ottoman Empire as 'the sick man of Europe'.

Certainly Loti had chosen a fine spot for his favoured café.

Right next door was a graveyard from the Ottoman period, and we found a path that sloped steeply down the hill, wending among carved tombstones set in thick vegetation.

At the bottom lay the village of Eyup, one of the holiest places in the Islamic world. Its principal feature is the white marble Eyup Mosque and in its grounds is the tomb of Eyup Ensari, who was the standard bearer for the Prophet Mohammed. Eyup was killed when Arabs laid siege to Constantinople around 1300 years ago. The fact that his body lies there means Muslims from throughout the world make pilgrimages to Eyup, and it is also the reason that the rich from Istanbul's Ottoman period wanted to be buried on the hill nearby.

Even here we could not escape the present. Lines of police stood around, and preparations were being made for a mass demonstration in support of Palestinians and against Israel and the United States. It was Friday, and demonstrations like this had become a feature at mosques all across Istanbul every Friday. There was little anger in evidence—men washed their feet in ablutions fountains outside the mosque and the faithful filed past Eyup's tomb, holding out their hands to receive his blessing and then washing the blessings over their faces. Women in veils and full-length black robes sat and chattered, and grey-bearded men walked back and forth discussing soccer.

We found an eating place nearby, and Ömür the guide was amused to discover it was named The Guides Restaurant. We ate lamb as the leaders of the demonstration outside the mosque began revving up their loud hailers.

The police began to look bored and the demonstration seemed to be a bit of a fizzer, so we caught a bus and strap-hung our way back to the city and across to the more modern European side of the Golden Horn to visit the last of the Sultans' great follies—the Dolmabahçe Palace. It was built by Sultan Abdul Mecit in 1856. The Sultan, who had taken to wearing trousers rather than Ottoman robes, felt that the Topkapi Palace was too 'yesterday'. He wanted the approval of European aristocracy, but he didn't have the money. So he borrowed it from European banks, hastening the already steep decline of the fortunes of the Ottoman Empire. The cost was astronomical, and you need to take no more than one look at the absurd opulence of the Dolmabahçe, perched on the edge of the Bosphorus, to figure it would break any bank. It was an attempt to outdo the Palace of Versailles, with the addition of a vast harem, but even Versailles didn't have a staircase built of Baccarat crystal and brass. A chandelier weighing several tonnes, transported piece by piece from England, hangs above a ceremonial hall that could seat more than 2000.

Ataturk, who eschewed the extravagance of the Ottomans, couldn't resist setting up office there after the last of the Sultans had gone. Perhaps he thought it was fair trade for his months of discomfort on the battlefields of Gallipoli. He died in a bedroom in the Dolmabahçe on 10 November 1938, and every clock in the entire palace is stopped at the moment he expired: 9.05 a.m.

Ömür had slipped away to chat with fellow curators, and I trailed along with a tour group until the whole place became too much.

Afterwards, Ömür and I sat at a tea house in the grounds of the palace, and I tried to explain to him my reasons for travelling to Gallipoli. It was difficult to find the words that might enlighten him, but Ömür brightened visibly when I mentioned I had my great-uncle's diary with me. The young archaeologist could grasp an artifact, and he wanted the history to go with it.

I had no idea whether my story would make sense to him, but I told it anyway.

It was not possible now to know what might have been in George Moore's mind when he signed up in faraway Australia in 1915, I said. Maybe he was intent on fighting for King and country and empire. Perhaps his heart was kindled by the idea that Australia, a nation just thirteen-and-a-half years old, should take its place in the great and tumultuous affairs of the world. And perhaps he was moved to go along with his mates because they had dared each other to leave the bush behind.

My own, unprovable, theory is that he was riding towards the sea because there was a horizon beyond it—one that held the promise of adventure outside anything his existence on a windswept sheep and cattle station could offer him.

Disappearing across the horizon was in his bones: George's grandfather—my great-great grandfather, James Moore—ran away from home in England when he was twelve years old in the early part of the nineteenth century. Family folklore is foggy and divided on precisely what happened to him for the remainder of his boyhood. What is known is that he became a whaler in the South Seas and eventually he washed up on a Victorian beach some time in the early 1830s just outside what would become known as Portland.

The whaling fleet was run by a tough old Tasmanian seadog by the name of William Dutton. Dutton's whaling station on a beach on Portland Bay was the first permanent white settlement in Victoria, unknown to the authorities for years, so James Moore's adventuring made him a Victorian pioneer.

Major Thomas Mitchell, who thought he was exploring territory entirely unknown to Europeans in 1834, did not believe his Aboriginal tracker who claimed he had seen boot marks on the beach ahead. When he came upon men running the whaling station, he named the place The Convincing Ground because the meeting was the only thing that could have convinced him.

James Moore eventually tired of whaling in Portland and moved inland a little where he took up farming.

There is continuity in my family—my own parents now live on the stretch of beach still called Dutton Way, a few kilometres from the Convincing Ground, and old whale ribs lie scattered in their garden. My brother and I, as children, discovered a whale-oil melting pot lying in the scrub above the sand during a long-ago beach holiday.

Whatever it was that drove young George Moore to follow the ghost of his grandfather back to the sea three-quarters of a century later, his decision took him to a place he could scarcely have conceived.

A little over two months after he left his parents' home, he stepped aboard His Majesty's Australian Transport A9 *Shropshire* at Port Melbourne.

Shortly after, the ship became part of an Australian and New Zealand armada that steamed off to war out of the old whaling port of Albany in King George Sound, Western Australia. It was 1 November 1914.

Armada is not too bold a word for the convoy: there were 28 Australian and ten New Zealand transports, protected by four big warships—the Australian cruisers *Melbourne* and *Sydney*, the *Minotaur* from Britain and (here's one for the strange tides of history, considering what happened less than three decades later) the *Ibuki* from our ally Japan.

George and his mates thought they were going to England to ready themselves to fight the Germans. Instead, they were deposited in Egypt.

The day before they set sail from King George Sound, an event that was to have a profound effect on their young lives had occurred: Turkey had declared itself on the side of Germany in the war against Britain. And so, through the clashing and grinding of the gears of nations half a world away from Australia, George Moore would find himself within a few months at a place he and his mates would have been hard-pressed to find in an atlas.

Ömür listened closely to the story, nodding and tossing an occasional question about the meaning of some of the words I used. If the tale was beyond him, at least he was a good listener. I was, I realised, beyond caring much.

It was a long time since the *muezzin* had heralded the dawn. I wanted to get back to the Side Hotel, check out the workings of the shower and lay my head on a pillow.

Tomorrow, Ömür had promised a boat trip on the Bosphorus.

4

A SMALL VOYAGE ON THE BOSPHORUS

'I do not know much about him. He was just a man from my village. He went away with all the other men to fight with Ataturk, and he did not come back. No one knew what happened to him. The government and the army did not write letters to families in those times. There were no records. No diaries. Where he died, no one knows. It was sad.'

It was supposed to be a languid day of sightseeing. It turned out to be a journey to a place of the heart that eludes most who travel towards Gallipoli.

We were steaming, my Turkish friend Ömür and I, on the Bosphorus, the thin, crowded strait that joins the Black Sea in the north with the Sea of Marmara in the south, and which divides Europe from Asia, cutting Istanbul in two.

The big old rusty ferry we had boarded that foggy Saturday morning was staggering north, weaving from the Istanbul suburbs of Europe to the city's Asian suburbs and villages, depositing and picking up groups of carefree Turks and tourists out on what is surely one of the world's great weekend jaunts—and certainly one of the cheapest.

It cost 1.5 million Turkish lira, less than two Australian

dollars, to travel from the core of Istanbul to the most distant fishing village on the Asian shore, a little place called Anadolu Kavagi, close to the mouth of the Black Sea. We had battled our way through the crowds at the ferry terminal at Eminou—down the hill from Sultanahmet and near the fishermen-infested Galata Bridge—and bought tickets.

It is a journey of around 30 kilometres, and the return trip costs the same pittance, though tour companies offer similar trips aboard private vessels for vastly greater sums. Only those who do not know about the public ferry service would waste their money on the alternatives.

A little knowledge of the Turkish *ferrybot* system would, as it turned out, serve me well when I finally reached the Gallipoli Peninsula.

But this day, our simple plan was to sail north, disembark at Anadolu Kavagi, indulge in a leisurely lunch at one of the cluster of rudimentary fish cafés there and return on the mid-afternoon boat.

On its outward journey the ferry rolled past the grand palaces of the Ottoman period—the Dolmabahçe, the Çirağan (now one of Europe's most luxurious hotels) and, on the Asian side, the Beylerbeyi, with twin ornate bathing pavilions: one for men, the other for the women of the harem.

I stood on the stern among a crowd of camera-toting Koreans, Americans, Germans, Swedes and locals, watching the bulk of old Constantinople disappearing in the haze, the outline of the Sancta Sophya and the minarets of the Blue Mosque and the crumbling walls of Byzantium speaking of times when this was the centre of the world. Soon the shores became lined with gorgeous wooden villas known as *yalis*, once inhabited by the courts and the favoured families of the sultans during hot summer months and now the playthings of the rich.

Ancient men in tiny fishing boats bobbed like corks in our wake and in the whirlpools that spun behind container ships.

We sailed beneath soaring steel bridges, and between the Fortress of Europe and the Fortress of Asia, stone bulwarks straddling the strait. The forts were built in the fourteenth and fifteenth centuries by Ottoman invaders as they laid siege to the stronghold of Constantinople before they took it from the Byzantines.

Dizzied by the weight of history staring back from the shores, and the deep holes in my knowledge of it, I bought a glass of çay and sat with Ömür, listening for a while as a Turkish tour guide tried to unravel the mysteries all around for a party of politely bewildered Korean package tourists. The Turk spoke in English, and another guide translated it all rapid-fire into Korean for the benefit of his charges. It was exhausting.

Later, Ömür and I got back to wrestling with the reasons why an Australian would travel across the world to visit a place called Gallipoli. I told him again of my great-uncle, and all the thousands of other young men from Australia and New Zealand who had splashed ashore in 1915 and soaked the place in their sweat and blood for next to no benefit. I talked of the hole it had begun to carve into the heart of my country, a ditch that had turned into a chasm that is still to be filled, all these decades on, after tens of thousands more of those boys—one of them my mother's father—had been sent to the fields of northern France and Belgium, many of them never to come back. It must, I mused, have been a similar appalling experience for the Turkish people, although one leavened by the fact that they had successfully defended their country.

Ömür listened in his courtly, patient manner, nodding.

'You know,' he said. 'My grandfather's father went to the Çanakkale War. He never came back. It was a great sorrow inside my family.'

Ömür had, pretty obviously, understood my story yesterday about George.

'I do not know much about my grandfather's father,' he continued. 'He was just a man from my village. He went away with all the other men to fight with Ataturk, and he did not come back. No one knew what happened to him. The government and the army did not write letters to families in those times. There were no records. There was no diary. Where he died, no one knows. It was sad.'

Little by little, Ömür struggled to tell his story. He had been born in a village where his father's family had lived as peasant farmers for many generations, a little place called Danigment in the Balikesir district, only 80 kilometres from Çanakkale, the city the British Navy had all but destroyed in its botched attempt to storm the Dardanelles in March 1915. Right across the strait from Çanakkale is what we call the Gallipoli Peninsula. The Turks rarely talk of Gallipoli, which is, anyway, nothing but the English version of the name Gellibolu—a pleasant fishing village that sits at the northern end of the Dardanelles and which had little to do with the war. To them, the whole campaign is simply the Çanakkale War.

When Çanakkale, and a month later the Gallipoli Peninsula, came under attack, the villages all around emptied as men of all ages hurried to join the defence of their land.

Both Ömür's great-grandfathers—'my grandfather's father and my grandmother's father' as he put it—marched away. The silence from the distant front must have been deafening to the families left behind as the months dragged by—as deafening as the anxious silence in farms and townships and cities across Australia and New Zealand at the same time.

'Only my grandmother's father came home,' Ömür said. 'But some years later he went away again, to the Greek War, and this

time he did not come back either.' In short, one of Ömür's great-
grandfathers lies beneath the earth at Gallipoli, and the other was
swallowed by the land in no place that will ever be identified.

The 'Greek War' was the War of Independence fought on
many fronts by the Turks after World War I when the victorious
powers of Europe decided to carve up Turkey among themselves.
The Turks were to be left about half of nothing, but they fought
back and won what essentially is the land they now call their own.
The man who led this remarkable defence was Mustafa Kemal,
who would later call himself Ataturk, 'the father of the Turks', and
would go on to create modern Turkey out of the rotted corpse of
the Ottoman Empire. He was the very man, in fact, who had led
his troops against the Anzacs.

Ömür and I sat looking out at the European shore of the
Bosphorus—wooded hillsides almost bare of houses now. Ömür,
having listened to my narrative of an Australian family, was
doing me the honour of relating his own family's story.

'You see, there were many wars around that time. The
Çanakkale War was of importance mostly to the people around
that area,' Ömür said. 'The Çanakkale War. That was the one
that brought sadness to my family first. I have regret that I do
not know more from my family.'

It's okay, I said. I didn't know much about George Moore and
his family before I decided to travel to Gallipoli. I had to ask
around and undertake all sorts of research.

'I will ask my mother more of this story,' said Ömür.

And then he began humming. It was a beautiful, rhythmic
sound. Soon words that meant nothing to me came fluttering
through, fragile as a sparrow.

'What is that?' I asked.

'It is a folk song from that time,' Ömür said. 'It is called
"*Çanakkale Margi*"—the "Çanakkale March".'

It was a disturbing, lovely thing to hear this song in Turkish, and I was astonished altogether when I looked at Ömür and saw his eyes were pricked with tears. A few Turkish passengers nearby turned to listen and suddenly they were humming along, too, their shoulders squared.

'Could we translate this song into English?' I asked. Ömür looked doubtful, but agreed to try.

We spent the remainder of the ferry ride tussling with it. Eventually, my notebook revealed a song:

> In Çanakkale
> There is a mirrored bazaar
> My mother, I am going to meet my enemy
> Oh, my youth!
> In Çanakkale, there is a tall cypress
> Some of us are engaged, some are married
> Oh! My youth
> In Çanakkale
> I have been shot
> I have been put in my grave, still alive
> Oh, my youth!
> In Çanakkale
> There is a broken water jar
> Mothers and fathers have lost hope
> Oh! my youth.

It was a strange song to a western ear, but no stranger, certainly, than another song of longing for home from the other side of the trenches, 'The Road to Gundagai'.

Ömür could offer no convincing explanation of the reference to a mirrored bazaar, and no one else to whom I have spoken since has been able to do so with any certainty, either. Perhaps, said Ömür, it was simply a flight of poetic fancy that fitted the rhyme and the rhythm—a mirror, after all, is a brittle thing, easily smashed; and in Turkey, like everywhere else, there is the superstition that a broken mirror brings bad luck. Perhaps, too, there really was a bazaar in Çanakkale featuring mirrors, things of beauty set within intricately carved silver. Messages were sometimes written backwards in Arabic script as a form of code among Ottoman scholars, and could be deciphered only by reading them in a mirror. But if there was a mirrored bazaar, it no longer exists. The city of Çanakkale was all but destroyed, with whole sections burnt to the ground during the British naval barrage of March 1915.

As to the mention of 'a tall cypress': it is the practice of Turkish people to plant a cypress that grows thin as a pencil at the foot of the grave of a family member. The cypress is a symbol of death, and not only in Turkey. Across the world, in Australia, country graveyards moan to the sound of wind through old groves of cypress pines.

Ömür had let me into a section of the Turkish heart that remains a secret to many of us who too blithely make the march to Çanakkale and on to Gallipoli. It is a secret of great simplicity: wars leave widows and memories and sad songs, whatever one's nationality.

When we reached the ferry terminal at Anadolu Kavagi and had found ourselves a quiet little restaurant within the village, I made another request of Ömür. Would he, I asked, teach me to sing the 'Çanakkale March' in Turkish? And so, in this tiny village beneath a ruined hilltop Byzantine fort of the fourteenth century, as a cigarette-smoking chef whipped up a meal of fried mullet, squid, mussels, salad and a mountain of bread, I took another step on the road to the Turkish soul.

Within a few days, I would learn that all I had to do to win friends among strangers would be to sing the first haunting words of that old song. In a restaurant or a bar, I could simply utter 'Çanakkale iginde, Aynali garzi . . .' and people all around would stand and finish the song for me. Soon we would be drinking *raki* together.

I would also learn that the soccer-mad Turks had even woven Çanakkale into the vernacular of the game that seems almost as important to them as a war. A Turkish artist and musician told me late one night that when the Turkish defence is so strong that an opposing soccer team simply can't break through, diehard fans cry out victoriously 'Çanakkale, no pass!'

Ömür and I dawdled over our food, and I drank a couple of bottles of Efes beer. It felt good to be away from the restless crowds of Istanbul. We were as far north of Istanbul as it was possible to travel on this route. Beyond was all military land designed to defend Istanbul from an attack from the Black Sea. Turkey had been blessed, said Ömür wryly, with interesting neighbours: Russia, Georgia, Iran, Iraq, Syria, Greece and Bulgaria.

Still, enmity seemed far away this day. Children played on fishing boats moored next to the ferry terminal, and forest climbed a hillside above.

Returning down the Bosphorus, Ömür decided to instruct me in an important slice of Istanbul's history: the invasion of Byzantium by the Ottoman Sultan Mehmet the Conqueror. It was 1453, and the Ottoman Empire had been encircling Byzantium for years.

Perhaps it was the drowsiness of a warm afternoon, a large meal and a couple of beers, but I mistook the central point of Ömür's story. The Ottoman invaders, he told me, had gathered out of sight on the far side of Taksim Hill, across the waters of the Golden Horn from the walled peninsula that was Byzantium's Constantinople. The Ottomans had, he said—or I thought he said—gathered with their 'sheeps'. 'Sheep?' I asked. 'Not cows?'

'No, sheeps, not cows,' nodded Ömür. I had a vision of the invaders cleverly disguised as shepherds.

'They waited for night, and brought their sheeps over the hill. They had built a wooden road.'

I was getting confused, but I listened hard. 'They had horrible oil on the sheeps, and they pushed them into the water,' Ömür continued.

I imagined he was talking about the lanolin that is found in wool. But good Lord above, the Ottomans pushed their sheep into the water? Did they expect the flock would float on lanolin?

'Yes, there were many, many sheeps. In the morning, the Byzantium emperor and his people were very surprised to see the Ottomans on the Golden Horn,' said Ömür, nodding vigorously at my questions.

Surprised? I envisaged the Ottoman troops with Mehmet the Conqueror standing on the drowned bodies of hundreds of thousands of sheep creating a woollen bridge across the Golden Horn.

'They brought very big cannon and knocked down walls of Constantinople,' said Ömür. The story was getting out of hand. Yet Ömür was a leading archaelogist, a man who knew his history. What would I know?

We went through the tale a few times, and Ömür pulled out a pen and drew rough diagrams. The Golden Horn was the only undefended frontage to Constantinople—the Byzantines had stretched a massive chain across its mouth, where it entered the Bosphorus, ensuring no sea craft could enter its waters. The wide waters of the Horn, then, provided a natural defence.

But here was the Ottoman army, pouring across the Horn on—what?—a gangplank of sheep! It was preposterous.

The story would worry me for days. Could I really be ignorant of such a monstrous historical occurrence?

A week later, Ömür introduced me to his English teacher, a young man named Ibrahim Ozan who spoke with an upper-crust British accent. We sat in the courtyard of a university tea room and I managed to wangle the discussion around to the subject of 1453. Ibrahim was vastly amused when I asked him about the business of the sheeps. Ömür appeared ready to crawl under the table as Ibrahim set me straight.

'No, not sheeps,' he chortled. 'You have misheard. Ships. The Ottoman conquerors brought ships up behind Taksim and built a wooden road over the hill and down to the Golden Horn. They could not get into the Golden Horn from the Bosphorus because of the chain. So they decided to go overland. They poured olive oil on the wooden road so it would be slippery and used bullocks and men to drag the ships over the hill and down to the water during the night. Mehmet had a huge cannon which he used to pound the walls of Byzantium. That's how the Ottomans conquered Constantinople. Brilliant, don't you think?'

It was beyond brilliant, and I apologised to Ömür for having embarrassed him by mistaking his words. A whole story had become an absurdity because I had heard the word 'ships' as 'sheeps', and 'olive oil' as 'horrible oil'.

But the clarification—something that would become a running joke between us—had unlocked another thought. What Mehmet had done so elaborately was almost precisely the strategy that, 460 years later, the British had tried with disastrous results at Gallipoli.

If you were to transpose a map of Istanbul over that of Gallipoli, you could see the picture. The British, having failed to breach the Dardanelles, decided to get to that crucial strip of water overland. The hills of the narrow Gallipoli Peninsula, over which the Anzacs were supposed to clamber, could have been the hill that was Istanbul's Taksim. And the Dardanelles could have been the Golden Horn.

Was it possible that the brilliant young Turkish military man Mustafa Kemal—a man educated at an Ottoman military academy—could have reached back into history and foreseen that the British would try Mehmet the Conqueror's very strategy, minus the wooden road?

I have no idea, of course, and I am not aware of any document that suggests it. The Turks had been aware the British would make a land assault, but they did not know precisely where.

The fact remains that when Kemal realised an invasion was underway on Gallipoli, he recognised instinctively that the most dangerously undefended spot was the impossible height above what would become known as Anzac Cove. If the British—in the guise, as it turned out, of the Anzacs—reached the high ground above Anzac Cove, then Turkey was lost.

And so it was that he ignored his duty to head off to the southern part of the peninsula, swung on to his horse and galloped to the high ground, where he rallied the last of the Turkish defenders to stand against the Anzacs until reinforcements arrived. Those cruel hills were the last place anyone would imagine an invading force would try, and they had been the least fortified. But then, so had it been at Taksim and Byzantium had fallen. It seemed to me, having heard Ibrahim so easily clarifying Ömür's story, that Kemal had taken his psychic orders across the centuries from Mehmet. I still believe it.

Ömür and I might have found a language gulf obscuring this story, but Ibrahim checked our cobbled-together translation of the 'Çannakale March', and declared it to be perfect.

We went to dinner and, at every break in conversation, Ibrahim spluttered, 'Sheeps, sheeps! You think we are barbarians?'

No indeed, I thought. You Turks knew a lot before my nation had even been thought of.

5

CAPPADOCIA: THE ORIGINAL DIGGERS

'The Anzacs were the Diggers, right? Wrong, actually.'

I was dragging my bones up the deserted main street of the village of Ortahisar, Cappadocia, when a fearsome honking and whistling caused me to leap half a metre in the air. I scrambled to the footpath, afraid I was about to be squashed by a truck fitted with a super-charged horn.

Spinning around, I discovered two old men trying to hide their grins behind their white whiskers. They were mounted on donkeys, and judging from the fact that one had a shovel tied to his animal's withers and the other had a bag of fertiliser balanced in front of him, they were heading to the fields for a day's farming. The donkeys were roaring at each other. The farmers of Cappadocia don't bother neutering their donkeys, with the result that if two jack asses pass each other on the road, they bellow testosterone-charged challenges. When my heart returned to a manageable beat, I laughed until I could hardly stand.

It was the perfect clash of eras. Here I was returning from an excursion to find the local Internet café (it was closed), and a couple of farmers from the pre-industrial age had stripped me of my modern, western, Netscaped dignity.

I staggered back to the hotel to share the misadventure with Serkan, the barman, who was just arriving for work. Serkan was a serious young man, and the joke was lost to him as he steamed up a coffee. So two donkeys made a noise. There are too many donkeys in Cappadocia, he said. Serkan thought it was time farmers began using tractors.

He was a serious fellow, Serkan. And he was tired.

'I have three jobs,' he told me.

'I have taken a loan to purchase a mini-bus to take children to school. I start each day at 6.30 in the morning, when I drive around and take all the children to school.

'I also own a tea garden in the town. Most days I work there, but sometimes, like today, my father and mother must tend it so I can come here to the hotel. But they are old, and it is hard on them.' (I had visited the 'tea garden'—it was a smoky little room where the men of the village gathered to drink tea and to gossip.)

'Then in the afternoon I take my mini-bus out again and bring the children home from school.

'After that I come here to the hotel to work the bar. I leave when there are no more customers. This morning, I left at 3.00 a.m. I do not get enough sleep.'

Serkan was 26 years old. He was, he said, making just enough money to keep abreast of the loans he had taken in order to grab himself a future.

'In Turkey, you must work and study hard if you are to make something,' he said, his eyes drooping.

'Study?' I asked.

'Yes, I am studying, but I do not have time or money to go to university. I study from books.'

He brought out a dog-eared copy of a book entitled *English for Turks*.

'I am teaching myself to speak English. But I am stuck. Here.' He flicked through the pages. 'Here. Could you please explain the idea of the past participle in a sentence constructed in the present tense?'

I floundered. The book was written by a pedant. The nearest I could come was to construct a sentence: 'I have got a cup of coffee.' The sentence was present tense, the word 'got' was the past participle.

Serkan was triumphant. 'Yes,' he said. 'But how do you define this word "got"? It is the past participle of get, but it is the most difficult English word.' He had me, and both he and I knew it.

I remembered Ömür back in Istanbul saying precisely the same thing. 'My English tutor says if you can get the word get, you can truly understand English,' he had mused one day. 'You can get on a bus, you can get a sandwich, you can get lost, you can get going. You can get someone to do something, you can get around, you can get down and you can get by. It has too many meanings. Can you get get?'

So here was I trying to understand a foreign land and I was being forced to learn something about a part of my own language that I had never considered.

I gave up, leaving a rather too satisfied Serkan to the dishes he had left the previous night, and was rescued by my tour guide arriving an hour late for my promised trip to an underground city.

I was in Cappadocia because I had seen enough of Istanbul. My Turkish Airlines ticket offered me a return trip to anywhere in Turkey, return from Istanbul.

That was easy. If you are in Turkey, you must see Cappadocia, Self-justification is simple. So, it turned out, is self-delusion.

Cappadocia is way out in central Anatolia, the Asia Minor that makes up most of Turkey. I was supposed to be travelling to Gallipoli, which is nowhere near it.

But Cappadocia is the home of the underground people. For perhaps 10 000 years—and certainly 3000, which seems an absurd disparity, but which is hardly more than a blink of an eye when we are talking pre-history—people have been burrowing into the soft volcanic soil of the great valleys of Cappadocia, building homes and cool places to store their fruit and vegetables and taking refuge in underground cities and caves of worship. It is a birthplace of civilisation, and it is one of the wonders of the world. I had seen pictures. I had also seen the movie *Star Wars*, part of which was filmed in this bizarre landscape.

So why was I going there? Simple, I told myself and anyone who would listen. My destination was Gallipoli, but first I wanted to see the original home of the original Diggers.

It was thin, but it worked for me. The Anzacs were the Diggers, right? Wrong, actually. I discovered this only after I returned to Australia and began studying the history of the Anzacs properly.

The word 'Digger' is so powerful to Australians that it still causes angry exchanges about who owns it. In August 2001, Athletics Australia declared it had adopted the name 'the Aussie Diggers' as its moniker for the World Athletic Championships in Edmonton, Canada. The idea was to market and profit from the sale of merchandising the name, which would be incorporated into a logo. It brought half the nation down upon it, with the then Minister for Veterans' Affairs, Bruce Scott, and the national president of the RSL, Major-General (Retired) Peter Phillips, joining journalists, radio talkback callers and anyone else with access to a public forum fairly fuming about the plan. It caused so much outrage that the strategy was dropped, complete with public apologies.

Yet Australians use the word with abandon. 'G'day Digger,' we say to each other.

The first Australian Diggers were goldminers during the goldrush of the mid-1840s. They dug the earth seeking rare fortune. In Ballarat, they took up arms and fought the colony's soldiers and police because officialdom demanded they buy licences for the privilege of pursuing what for most of them were dry dreams.

The battle of the Eureka Stockade, where perhaps 22 miners and five soldiers were killed in a hillside skirmish that lasted a quarter of an hour, deposited within the Australian heart a legend of ordinary folk standing against ruthless authority, and gave us the finest flag we'll never have, the Southern Cross of Eureka. The flag was appropriated in the 1970s by a union, the Builders Labourers' Federation, which managed to disgrace itself through thuggery and corruption, effectively placing the flag off limits for any group that might want to revive it.

The miners might have been the original Aussie Diggers, but after World War I, the legend grew that the poor buggers who went to Gallipoli and were forced to dig themselves into the hillsides for survival were the new owners of the name. They lived in dug-outs, scuttled along trenches clawed out of the earth, and tunnelled towards the enemy in order to lay explosives to destroy the Turks tunnelling from the other side. Of course they were Diggers.

Not true. There is not a single reference from Gallipoli suggesting the soldiers called themselves Diggers.

This comes as a bit of a shock, particularly to those like me who had allowed themselves to believe the legend of the Digger had been born on the very night of the landing at Anzac. In this version of events, the word had its battlefield genesis in a message penned by General Sir Ian Hamilton, the general officer commanding the Mediterranean Expeditionary Force. As the bodies piled up and confusion reigned above Anzac Cove and along the peninsula, Hamilton was forced to consider whether to withdraw his Gallipoli landforce. As the evening of that first day wore on, he received word that an Australian submarine, the *AE2* which had sailed all the way from Melbourne, had made its way through the Narrows of the Dardanelles and was harassing enemy shipping in the Sea of Marmara. It was a near-miraculous voyage—one of the great stories of the Dardanelles campaign, which is re-told splendidly by my colleague at *The Bulletin*, Fred Brenchley, and his wife Elizabeth in their book *Stoker's Submarine*. *AE2*'s exploits gave heart to Hamilton, who decided that it boded well for his campaign.

He dictated a message to the troops ashore, which concluded 'now you only have to dig, dig, dig until you are safe'. Legend has it that, from that moment, the Anzacs became known as Diggers, unlikely as it may seem that the Australians and New Zealanders would allow an ineffectual English general to dub them with what would become one of the most affectionate and proud terms in the Antipodean nomenclature. It would be a neatly tied tale if it were not for the fact that neither the Anzacs in their diaries nor those chronicling their deeds at Gallipoli for newspapers and magazines or for history, actually used the word.

It was only when Australian troops arrived on the Western Front of Northern France that the Digger from the goldrush was revived. The *Australian National Dictionary* devotes almost a page to the subject, and finds the first wartime reference to Diggers appearing in 1916 in France.

The dictionary quotes *The Bulletin*'s Red Page of 8 June 1922:

> Digger is a title coveted and often stolen. It originally meant the infrantryman or artilleryman who was always 'digging in' or rebuild-ing his parapet after enemy fire . . . It did not mean a staff-officer or

any of the AIF serving in Palestine or Egypt. It meant the man in the front line in France, and no one else . . . There were no 'diggers' at Gallipoli where we dug most—the word had not come then!

My friend, the historian Dr Michael McKernan, suggests the first use came from the poor bastards thrown into the first battle in which Australians took part on the Western Front, at Fromelles, south of Armantierres. It was 19 July 1916. Thousands of men from the 5th Division were required to attack the Germans in a salient—a bulge into the Germans' lines. Such an attack was tantamount to suicide. The salient meant the Australians would be exposed to machine gun fire from the high ground, which was hardly discernible on those flat fields.

I went there years ago with McKernan and a group of World War I veterans, and recall being appalled at the exposed nature of the place. A small cemetery sits within a copse of trees nearby. It is known as VC Corner—not, as commonly thought, because it contains the bodies of men who won the Victoria Cross, but because the troops of 1916 declared that anyone who marched the dreaded road past it ought to be awarded a VC. Between six o'clock on the evening of 19 July and eight o'clock the following morning, the Australians suffered more than 5000 casualties, with another 400 or so taken prisoner. That fourteen hours was worse than anything that had happened to the Anzacs on Gallipoli. With machine-gun bullets filling the air, the Australians, with survival on their minds, had no choice but to lie flat on the ground and try to dig in with their bare hands and their entrenching tools. They were Diggers all right. Some of their bodies lay out there on the ripped soggy field for the remainder of the war, because it was too dangerous to venture there again. The first recorded use of the term 'Digger' came just 23 days later, in the diary of C.A. Hemsley (12 August 1916) who wrote: 'The officer in charge of the parade was addressing the men, and at some kindly expressed sentiment some wag interjected with "Hear hear, old Digger".'

So I was a blockhead. No Diggers at Gallipoli, but I was still going to the diggings of Cappadocia.

I had nipped in to the travel agent next door to the Side Hotel in Istanbul and had handed over US$250 for a three-day tour: a couple of nights at a hotel in a cave in a town called Urgup, transfers from the airport at somewhere called Kaiserai and a guide with car to show me the sights. It didn't quite turn out that way—my hotel wasn't in a cave, and it wasn't in Urgup, either. It was an above-ground establishment called the Burcu Kaya Hotel in the village of Ortahisar. The mistake was all in my favour.

Ortahisar is a village that is a bit off the track of the hordes of tourists who tramp the by-ways of Cappadocia. The houses of the village appeared to grow straight out of the ground. Each was, in fact, *of* the ground—steps led into underground caves and cellars beneath each dwelling. All around, trapdoors opened into caves in hillsides where fruit and vegetables lay in natural coolstores. The village had its own castle—a massive outcrop of rock riddled with tunnels and a Turkish flag fluttering at the top. The hotel was almost empty when I arrived, save for the most captivating staff, including Serkan, and it had an open fire.

Cappadocia is an immense area, bounded by volcanoes that over millions of years spewed layers of a sediment called tuft across the great valleys. Wind, rain and rivers did their work, creating a landscape like no other. 'Fairy chimneys', great phallic upthrusts of tuft, each with a hard granite cap, sprout like mushrooms, and almost every one of them contains a warren of tunnels and cave homes dug by the people of cascading civilisations. Hittites, Phrygians, Cimmerians, Medes, Persians, Romans, Byzantines, Sassanids, Arabs, the Seljuks and the Ottomans all had their day in Cappadocia. The word is Persian, meaning 'Land of Well-Bred Horses', though nowadays most of the horses appear to be scrawny things.

Great-uncle George would have appreciated a place dedicated to well-bred horses. He was a man who had always loved horses. Like the rest of my father's side of the family, he could ride like the clappers. His sister, my grandmother, was the last woman anyone could remember who not only rode side-saddle, but rode side-saddle over jumps at country shows.

At such shows, George was famous for riding his horses flat out at jumps and clearing them all. My father, the best horseman and bushman I will ever know, spoke well of George's skill on horseback, which is saying much. When I was six years old, my Dad—a man born on a farm just across the paddocks from George's boyhood home—took me droving cattle. I have imprinted on my mind a picture of him lying flat on his horse, flying full gallop into a thick forest after the mob had broken and scattered in the bush. Hours later he was back, sitting calm in the saddle with his hat pulled low, whirling his stockwhip and trailing the mob, every beast accounted for. If he said George could ride, then George could ride.

George had been in love with racehorses since he was a boy, though he never laid a bet in his life. The beauty of a horse was the thing that spoke to him: its lines and its bearing. He was in the habit of clipping pictures of favourite racehorses and pasting them to the wall of the family home, which stood in a valley of a big sheep and cattle station called *Oak Bank*, just outside Heywood, where his parents raised ten children. George's sign-up papers listed him as 'station hand, *Oak Bank*'.

When he went away to war, his mother refused to allow even one of those fading photographs to be removed. To do so, she believed, would be to bring bad luck. George might not come home if the pictures of his horses were not waiting for him. She loved her boys. Years after the war, when one of them went away shearing and died of pneumonia brought on by heat stress because the boss, it is said, wouldn't give him enough water to sustain him during hot shifts in the shed, she never properly recovered. Couldn't even listen to the gramophone records that had brought music to the house for all the years her children were growing up.

But George had seen too much suffering himself in the war. He was no wimp—I have his war records, which show him being confined to quarters while training in Egypt for arriving drunk on parade, for refusing orders and for frequenting the wrong end of Cairo.

The suffering that bothered his soul was that of the horses, ter- rified in their limbers as he drove them and their ammunition wagons under fire on to the battlefields of the Western Front, where he went after Gallipoli. He never quite recovered from watching horses screaming with their guts shot out or their backs broken by artillery shells. Like everyone else in his job, he had to shoot his lovely big-boned horses as they were drowning in the mud of the Somme and at Passchendaele, their eyes wide with terror and their nostrils flared for the want of another breath of life. When he came home and when he was among his mates, drinking quantities of brandy that would put two other men under a table but which never robbed him of the power to tell a story, he talked occasionally of these things. The result was that he could never bear the thought of causing suffering to a living thing.

Both my father and George's nephew, Claude Moore, have told me that George upset the neighbours because if he was walking through the bush and found a snake curled in his path, he would walk quietly around it, talking to it, soothing it. At the time, it was considered a responsibility to kill any snake that had the misfortune to show itself. But George was done with killing.

'He couldn't even kill an ant,' his nephew Claude told me. 'He'd just let an ant trail crawl across a table.'

At Red Cliffs, a settlement on the Murray River where he went to grow grapes after the war, old mates would arrive at his vineyard, pestering George to take them fishing.

George considered such outings to be nothing more than picnics on the riverbank, and would explode when his friends insisted on producing fishing tackle. 'The problem with you blokes,' he once hollered, 'is that every time you want to go fishing, you want to catch a poor bloody fish!'

The war, then, had given him something of the attitude of the rough-hewn holy man who reveres all life. Perhaps in another time he could have found sanctuary in a place like Cappadocia.

Cliffs lining deep river valleys were hollowed out to become secret homes for ancient monks and hermitic mystics, their subterranean bedrooms joined by tunnels, and more tunnels led to hollowed-out churches, their walls covered in religious paintings.

The two most spectacular remnants of the past are the cave churches of the Goreme Valley, and underground cities that were rediscovered only in 1964.

I have an in-built aversion to guided tours, but Cappadocia proved to be a place where they are necessary. I had been told it was possible to hire a motorcycle and scoot around, but April was considered too cool for such an excursion. Anyway, it would be difficult to find your way between all the far-flung sites, and a guide is needed to explain the strange history.

A van driven by an old man who appeared about to fall asleep conveyed me the 50 kilometres from Kaiserai airport to the Cappadocian township of Urgup. A volcano reared into the sky, covered in snow, and the land lay flat and dusty for much of the journey.

A gentleman from Red River Tours met me in his small shopfront in Urgup and transferred me to his own car, a brand new Ford. Business was slow, and I would have a personal tour. We drove through valleys that were as alien to my eyes as if we had made a detour to Mars. Fairy chimneys sprouted everywhere. Occasionally, we stopped at particularly bizarre outcrops at the foot of which hopeful locals had established little trinket markets to tempt tourists. Often, a camel drowsed in the dust, and a hawker would implore me to take a photo for a dollar. Camels have been in Cappadocia since the Silk Road wended its way from the East. Every 40 kilometres along this road were *caravanserai*—stupendous stone 'travellers' palaces' built by the Seljuk Empire during the thirteenth century. They were places of safety and hospitality. A camel train could travel 40 kilometres from dawn to dusk, and bandits roamed the countryside. The Seljuks, a Turkik Islamic tribe who built the pre-Ottoman empire, knew the Silk Road traders needed shelter at night. Their *caravanserai* were each big enough to provide sanctuary for as many camel trains that might arrive, and they offered three days' and nights' accommodation at no charge. Saddlers were on hand to stitch ripped packs, food was provided for camels and their drivers, and a mosque was available to the faithful. It was probably the finest example of hospitality to distant travellers in history, but there was a pay-off. The Seljuks got the first chance to trade for precious ceramics, spices, silk garments, jewels and carpets. Fine examples of *caravanserai*, visited only by tourists now, still stand on the Silk Road—in reality, a maze of traders' roads. And camels left behind by the travellers remain in Cappadocia, offering nothing more than a buck a photo.

Among those who found sanctuary in Cappadocia were early Christians fleeing Roman legions. St Paul is said to have made the trek, but it was St Basil of Kaiserai who had the biggest impact. His followers scooped stunning churches out of the earth, particularly in an amphitheatre-like formation of outcrops above the village of Goreme, known as the Goreme Open-Air Museum, a World Heritage site. Enter a little doorway or climb stone steps to a tunnel and you find yourself in a cave decorated with frescoes protected by gloom for a thousand years or so. Church after church is ferreted away beneath the earth. Some of the frescoes have been badly damaged because, years ago, locals lost all value for these strange leftovers of Christianity. Farmers sealed some of the churches, carving small openings to allow pigeons—in fact, doves, but the Cappadocians call them pigeons—to enter and roost. At the end of each year, the churches would be reopened, and the mass of pigeon droppings would be removed to be used as fertiliser. The birds pecked at the frescoes, made from a mixture of natural dyes and eggs, destroying many ancient works of art. Still, there are so many underground churches that the neglect of ages has been unable to demolish the sheer gobsmacking wonder of the place. My guide relished my astonishment. 'I always leave this to the last stop of the day,' he said. 'It is the cream on the cake.'

He knew about the cream on the cake, this fellow. As we roved the valleys of his territory, he made a couple of stops that were not on my itinerary. The first was at an underground pottery in the town of Avanos. It seemed fine enough, watching artists throwing pots and painting intricate patterns. The owner produced a cup of *raki* and invited me to indulge in his hospitality. A cup of *raki* at 11.00 a.m. tends to go straight to the head, which was the purpose, because I was then guided through a tunnel to a vast showroom of splendid ceramics. It took all my concentration and nerve to turn down the opportunity of purchasing a delicate set of Turkish coffee cups for a mere US$1000, with the *raki*-provider pushing hard. He would take any credit card, and would ship any purchase to anywhere in the world, Federal Express. I emerged embarrassed and angry. The guide simply shrugged when I told him not to try a scam like that again—I was here to see, not to buy things that would line his pocket with a fat commission.

A few hours later, he drove into the courtyard of a carpet factory with the cute name of Carpedocia. No, I said. I don't want to buy carpets. It's okay, he said, it's a special Tourist Commission business to show traditional carpet-weaving skills. You don't need to buy anything. And so I learned about dyes and spinning and kilims and the difference between wool carpets and silk and wool combinations and the back-breaking esoterica of weaving . . . and shortly found myself in a large showroom with a smooth salesman offering a drink and the opportunity to part with a few more thousands of dollars. 'Your wife,' he said, 'will never forgive you if you ignore the opportunity to purchase one of these unique items.' Two young men sweated as they threw rug after rug beneath my nose.

I demanded to be driven back to the hotel.

Cooling down with a beer, I watched a bustle of elderly German tourists arrive. They were tired and some were grumpy, but they were being shepherded patiently by a young man who sorted out room keys and arranged for bags to be portered. He sat next to me at the bar and ordered a beer.

His name was Korçan, and he spoke English with an Irish accent. 'I met this girl on a tour and she was from Dublin and we stayed together for a long time,' he explained. 'She was great. We had a real thing going. But she dumped me.' He was morose for all of a minute. Korçan seemed incapable of sustained melancholy.

'So you're an Aussie. Going to Gallipoli, I bet,' he said. 'I meet so many Aussies and Kiwis, and they're all going to Gallipoli. It's a great thing.'

It was, I agreed.

'You know why you go there, don't you,' he said. It was a statement, not a question. 'That's where your people learned that they were different from the English. You found your soul there, so you have to keep coming back to pay your respects. Your country started there, and so did our country. You know about Ataturk? If he hadn't fought your grandfathers at Gallipoli, he wouldn't have become the man to save Turkey and make it a new independent country.

'That's why we like each other so much, the Aussies and the Turks. We made our own futures in the same place. Cheers, mate.'

Korçan had to take his German party to dinner. He returned shaking his head. Some of the dinner party had become angry at having to pay for wine, and felt the prices were too steep.

'These people, they're rich, they think they can come to Turkey and get everything cheap,' he fumed. 'Europeans think they can rip off the Turks and that's a good day's work. Where else can they go to see things like this? There is more history in a few kilometres in Turkey than almost anywhere else. You want to see Greece, go to Greece. If you want to see real Hellenic culture, you must come to Turkey. Cappadocia—you'll never see anything like Cappadocia anywhere else, and they want to argue about a few lira for the wine.'

Korçan's mood passed as quickly as it came. Serkhan had lit a fire, and Korçan and I pulled up chairs designed as camel saddles and called for drinks. He was proud to be a guide, showing people his country. It was, he said, an honourable profession. Guiding even had a patron saint, known as The Shepherd, who had established the system decades ago in Thrace, the European side of Turkey.

But it didn't pay well enough for Korçan. He had ambition. The problem was that he still had to undertake compulsory military training, like every other man in Turkey. It would take two years out of his life, and that wasn't part of his plan. He wanted to get to New York, maybe lever himself into a car dealership with some friends who were already there and make enough money to return to Turkey and buy his way out of the military contract. For US$5000, he said, he could reduce the time in uniform to a couple of months, part-time.

Korçan wanted to know about opportunities in Australia. He felt the Australian immigration system was stacked against young men like him. He had made inquiries. Still, he'd like to visit because he liked Australians. They were, he said, open people who enjoyed travelling and laughing. Like him.

We toasted each other with a few *rakis*, and Korçan declared he would be disappointed if I suggested in my book that Gallipoli was just another battle to the Turks in thousands of years of battles. It wasn't just another anything, he said—it was the start of Turkey's modern history.

The next day, I returned to ancient history. In the company of a Japanese couple who kept to themselves and a gregarious couple from Canada, Bill and Molly, I went back underground. This time, it was the underground city of Derinkuyu, which made the churches of Goreme seem little more than surface scrapings.

No one knows how many underground cities exist across Cappadocia, though 36 have been found. Some archaelogists believe there could be more than 200, which means a whole lot of digging was going on a couple of thousand years ago. These really are cities, each capable of sheltering several thousand people.

They were built not as permanent metropolises, but as defensive warrens. Villagers normally lived in homes above-ground, but virtually every residence had a secret entrance to an underground city. Each time a new army came marching across the plains and valleys, sentries at the top of rock 'castles' gave the warning, and the entire population would vanish. Goats, donkey, horses and cattle were led down tunnels to stables carved deep in the earth. Enough food was stored in the cool caverns to last months.

At Derinkuyu, our guide took us down and down. He showed us how the villagers rolled carved rocks, the size and shape of a solid wagon wheel, across the entrance tunnel to keep invaders out. And if an enemy tried to breach the wheel, he would find himself scalded by boiling oil that could be poured from a tunnel above.

A dodgy-looking wiring system fed electric light bulbs, and I kicked myself for leaving behind my torch. A power black-out—not uncommon in rural Turkey—would leave us in a pickle, and I felt a wave of claustrophobia. 'Do we stay down here long?' I asked the guide. He grinned. 'You have phobia? It's okay, not long.' It was not true, but soon I was lost in amazement at the place. There was a schoolroom with a long rock table and rock benches. Around a corner was a winery, its vat sunk deep into the earth. A church, empty and echoing, was nearby. Passages ran in every direction, and hallways plunged down. The city was eight floors deep, and the creators of this subterranean world had thought creatively. An air shaft served other purposes: at the bottom, it was a well for fresh water, and inhabitants could use the shaft to communicate over all eight floors by simply calling out. If invaders were to find its camouflaged entrance at ground level, they couldn't do much about it: the shaft's vertical walls were smooth, and to fall would mean to drown in the well far below. The Anzacs' tunnels and dug-outs were never this sophisticated.

Emerging from the underground city felt like arriving on a new planet. Across the street, old village women were stoking up the oven of a communal bakery, sending black smoke belching into the air. Each brought her own fuel for the fire—dried grass and dung—and jars of dough. One of the women, giggling from behind her veil, dragged a disk of flat bread fresh from the oven and offered it to us. We ripped it apart and feasted on it.

Rain fell, and farmers plodded by on their donkeys. The

Cappadocian landscape, snowed under in winter and blasted by the sun in summer, looks as if it couldn't grow a pea, but its weathered volcanic soil is high in nutrients, and it grows everything from apricots and grapes to enough potatoes to feed the nation.

A little later, we found the Ilhara Gorge, and I forgot everything about the tough landscape. The gorge, a deep river valley, was a Garden of Eden. Parts of the high walls of the gorge had collapsed, revealing dozens of churches and monks' rooms that had been carved secretly into the rock. On the valley floor, we walked within a green forest beside a tumbling river. We hopped from moss-covered rock to moss-covered log, time collapsing. We walked for perhaps an hour and a half, Molly calling to Bill to look at this plant or that, to take a photo here and to pose there. Cherries, wild pistachio and blossom trees lined the path. The rain gave way to sunshine. Enchanting, Molly kept saying. Occasionally, an ancient woman staggered by, burdened by a load of firewood that would have a horse folding at the knees.

Eventually, we came to an open-air restaurant by the river and filled ourselves with spicy lentil soup and *kofte* and rice, and the owner heated the remainder of our bread from the communal kitchen. Cappadocia, we decided, needed a week or two.

Later that night, a busload of young Australian and New Zealand backpackers rolled noisily into the hotel at Ortahisar. We said a few g'days, and they told me they were swinging south and along the Aegean coast before heading to Gallipoli. I wasn't in the mood to join their revelry and, anyway, they had an evening planned at a Turkish bath and a show featuring whirling dervishes. Neither attraction beckoned, and Korçan and I trooped off down to the village's Internet café. I wanted to tell my family of the strange place in which I had found myself.

Next morning, I wandered around the village, nodding to old men, taking tea in Serkhan's smoky tea garden and watching a couple of young daredevils climbing the rocky castle. It is a natural rock outcrop, soaring 80 metres above the landscape, and is riddled with tunnels and rooms. I thought of the sentries of 2000 years ago standing at the top, watching for another plundering army to march across the plains. There was a small terrace café at the castle's base, and I chose a table and began writing up my diary. Nearby, a minaret rose above the village mosque and, at 1.00 p.m., a *muezzin* began his wail. Almost immediately, his voice was joined by another a kilometre or two across the valley. And then another, reedy in the distance. Battling *muezzin*s.

High above, a motorised hang-glider soared, taking another tourist across the ancient world. Come summer, the sky would fill with coloured balloons, giving travellers a great view for more than US$200 a trip.

But this part of the journey was finishing for me. I found an open-air café in the village square and ordered a Turkish pizza, salad and beer, all for a couple of bucks.

A stray cat mewed around my feet and my mobile phone trilled.

A familiar voice came down the line.

'Mate, it's Tom. I'm here,' it said. It was Tom Malone, a young radio journalist who had worked in the Canberra press gallery before he shouldered his tape recorder and lit out for London.

'You're where?' I said.

'Istanbul. I'm here. Where are you? Let's have a beer.'

I told him I was in Cappadocia, and he sounded crestfallen. 'It's okay, I'm flying back tonight,' I said. 'Where are you staying?'

6

TOM JOINS THE TRAIL

'Is special pudding,' he whispered in my ear. 'Is called sex pudding. After this, you go three, four times in one night.'

Tom Malone is a leprechaun. His face is the map of Ireland, he is built low to the ground and he is about the most amicable bloke in the world. Back in the Canberra press gallery, he had been a radio journalist with Sydney's 2UE network and no one believed he was just 21 years of age—his voice had a resonance to it that suggested it had taken decades to mature. He was forever trundling around behind politicians, thrusting a microphone in their faces and getting surprisingly direct answers, as if he had been doing it for years. Prime Minister John Howard instantly chose him as his favourite reporter, and none of the other journalists resented it. They forgave him everything, even when a prime ministerial press conference was held up until Tom arrived. He is a sweet-natured fellow who tries very hard to be serious, sings Gilbert and Sullivan songs after a few beers and who always seemed, in the ego-driven, back-stabbing world of Canberra politics, forever surprised at the idea that anyone would deliberately mislead anyone.

I found him in a restaurant around the corner from Istanbul's youth-hostel strip, regaling two young women with a story about flying into the city that morning from London and instantly meeting a couple of Americans who had offered him a free taxi ride direct to the hostel where he had found a bed. He seemed astonished at this act of generosity, but it seemed perfectly understandable. People warmed to Tom within seconds of meeting him, but he was unaware of it. He was one of those rare souls born beneath a rainbow.

'Mate,' he cried, knocking over a chair and leaving his companions smiling. 'I told you we'd catch up.'

He had, too. Tom had quit Canberra months before, flying off to London to discover the wide world. Before he left, he declared he would visit Gallipoli for Anzac Day, and we'd agreed to hook up.

'Rightyo,' he said. 'How are we getting to Gallipoli?' He had made no reservations—didn't even know how he would travel from Istanbul. After wandering alone, I didn't feel quite ready to transform into a travel agent. I had just flown back from Cappadocia and checked into a cheap hotel. I was weary and reluctant to take responsibility for anyone else.

In fact, I had used the Internet months previously to arrange for myself a bus from Istanbul to Çanakkale, the largest town near the Gallipoli battlefields, and to pay several hundred dollars to secure through the Anzac period a bed at Çanakkale's Anzac House hostel and a hotel nearby. I informed Tom of these arrangements.

'Terrific,' he said. 'What's the phone number of Anzac House and who should I talk to there?' He produced his phone and began dialling. Soon he was talking to Serif, the communications and accommodation manager at Anzac House, introducing himself as an Australian radio journalist travelling with me.

'No worries,' he said when he was finished. 'I'm on the bus with you and they reckon they'll find me a bed. Let's get a beer.'

It seemed he had charmed himself an invitation to Anzac House without a single word being uttered about the vulgar matter of money.

My solitary journey was over. I was travelling with Tom. It was okay with me—I can take only so much of my own company.

Since I had been away in Cappadocia, the hostel strip of Sultanahmet had built a new night-time population. Tables and bench seating had been dragged into the street, bars had flung open their doors and Australian and Kiwi kids in sneakers, cargo pants, t-shirts and fleece jackets were roaming and lounging about, buying bags of pistachios from hawkers pushing barrows. Waiters ran jugs of beer to the tables and loud music spilled from doorways.

I greeted a block of a man called Murat who worked as a spruiker, bouncer and barman at one of the establishments. The last time I had seen him, less than a week previously, he had sat alone in the street outside an empty bar and had told me his story. It wasn't a very complicated tale. He spent much of the year as a deckhand on merchant ships, plying the world's sea-lanes. But come each April, he said, he would 'jump ship' and work the bars of Sultanahmet. He liked to be around when the Australians came through on their way to the Anzac Day ceremonies, he said. The Australians were full of life and friendly. His months aboard ships were lonely, I surmised, and the sudden awakening of the streets of Sultanahmet in April were a holiday for him, even if he was working. Here, he was somebody: strangers engaged him in conversation, assuming he was a local, and they would introduce him to new arrivals, giving others the impression they were old hands who knew their way around. Everyone was happy with the arrangement, especially Murat. A travellers' street is a series of harmlessly fabricated identities, and Murat knew the score better than almost anyone.

He shook hands and I introduced him to Tom. 'You see,' said Murat, nodding towards the crowd, 'I told you this place would change in a few days. They are coming now, the Australians. You are not alone any more.'

Tom and I continued along the street, seeking quieter surroundings to swap travel tales. We found an almost-deserted wine bar in a basement, even though we had walked only a block from the cluster of hostels. Most young Australians and New Zealanders obey a flocking instinct when they are away from home. They gather where the action is, and they usually *are* the action. The wine bar's owner had erected a blackboard outside, advertising hearty home-cooked meals, but he could have hoisted a neon sign a hundred metres tall and he still wouldn't attract the crowd from down the street. The action, which is to say the opportunity for boys to meet girls, was at the other end of the road and that was that. The wine bar had a slightly rakish, bohemian atmosphere. The only other customer wore a week-old stubble and a black beret, and turned out to be an artist with a studio upstairs. His paintings of Istanbul streetscapes and skylines hung on the walls. Trifles, he told us when we got talking to him; mere commercial frippery for tourists to keep him in brandy and the creditors at bay. His real works were for connoisseurs, he confided.

Soon, a small Frenchman minced through the door and engaged the Turkish artist in an animated conversation in French. The Frenchman, it seemed, had heard there was an artist of some talent in residence. He wanted to see the artist's paintings—the real ones, not the things on the wall. The barman, who also owned the place and who appeared to be in the habit of tasting frequently the beverages he was having trouble selling, bustled about and produced a slide projector. We were treated to an impromptu exhibition of works captured on photographic slides beamed on to the wall. They appeared to be an unusual blending of styles—Impressionist and Japanese, if I was not mistaken. The Frenchman cocked his head, lifted an eyebrow, flapped one hand, put his other hand on the artist's knee and tut-tutted. The artist became impatient and demanded, in English, 'Do you wish to buy, or not?' The Frenchman pursed his lips and inquired, also in English, if he could see the actual paintings. This seemed out of the question—the artist, it transpired, didn't have any canvases on hand, but if the gentleman wished to place an order for any of the pictures photographed, he could dash out a precise replica, overnight if required. The Frenchman giggled and flapped his hand and said that perhaps he would think about it and return at another time. He ordered a drink, crossed his legs and attempted to engage us all in chit-chat, swapping from English to French and back again, sighing at the beauty of Istanbul and lamenting the difficulty of the life of an art collector. It was, however, a conversation going nowhere—the artist had lapsed into a sulk and the bar owner was huffily packing up the slide projector. Tom and I were having a splendid evening. We felt as if we had walked into a theatre and were sitting onstage with the actors.

Eventually, the little man flounced out. The mood lifted almost immediately and the artist burst into laughter. 'Ha,' he said, 'He knows nothing about art. He is—what do you say—a girl-boy. Maybe he was looking for an Australian to collect!'

Tom and I had somehow been accepted as members of the little bar's natural constituency. The Frenchman's strange antics had united us in disdain. The little man had deliberately raised the artist's hopes and then dashed them, said the barman's wife, appearing from the kitchen. It was mean, and a waste of the artist's time. The Frenchman had bought just one drink and had not offered to buy for anyone else. The barman/owner was unimpressed. Tom and I offered drinks all round, to unanimous approval of the tiny gathering. The barman set aside the glass from which he was drinking and poured himself a fresh one. The artist dragged a guitar from behind the bar and began playing a tune resembling a tango. I asked him if he knew the 'Çanakkale March'. He, the bar owner, the bar owner's wife and a couple of locals who had wandered in stood and sang the old folk song as if the thing had been written about their own fathers. Tom and I were required to reciprocate with 'Waltzing Matilda' and 'Advance Australia Fair', although I couldn't remember the second verse of my own country's national anthem. At some stage, a drunk from the street fell down the stairs and demanded that we drink a glass of *raki* with him, because it was his birthday. We sang 'Happy Birthday' and he decided we were his brothers. The artist took him by his collar and threw him back up the stairs and out into the street.

'So, Tom,' I said. 'Welcome to Istanbul. What do you think so far?'

'Bizarre,' said Tom, and we went our separate ways, promising to meet in the morning.

We were both a little shaky when we found each other the following day, but Tom was intent on sightseeing. We had only 24 hours before we were to leave the city for the Gallipoli Peninsula. I figured Tom needed a quiet, shady place near cool water, and led him past the Sancta Sophya to Istanbul's most extraordinary feature: the underground Cistern Basilica.

The Byzantines, like the Romans, understood that no civilisation could flourish without a reliable supply of fresh drinking water. Constantinople had no suitable water on its peninsula, but there was plenty 18 kilometres away in the hills and the cool depths of the Belgrade Forest. The solution was purely Roman: channels and aqueducts. A massive aqueduct was completed in

378AD by the Emperor Valens to the heart of the city. Only about 900 metres of the structure still stands. Ömür had taken me to see it one day, and the sight of it took my breath away. Its intricate stonework, constructed without cement or lime 1624 years previously, soared 60 metres above the landscape, supported by doubled-tiered archways that had been subsumed by modern Istanbul—a six-lane highway called Ataturk Bulvari ran through the arches.

The aqueduct system brought water to a number of substantial reservoirs within Constantinople. The reservoirs were essential—enemies outside the city could stop the flow of water to the aqueducts, or even poison it, but the reservoirs were so large that they would sustain Constantinople's population for months. Many of these water storages have disappeared, and one of them has been converted into a sunken soccer stadium.

But the greatest of all of them remains below ground right in the heart of Sultanahmet—the Cistern Basilica. It was built by the Emperor Justinian I in the sixth century and was used during the Byzantine period to provide water for the Grand Palace of the emperors. During the Ottoman period, it watered the sultans' Topkapi Palace and its residents.

When the Ottomans first arrived in Constantinople, they did not know the cistern existed, and they did not discover it for 100 years, even though it is just across the street from the Sancta Sophya. A curious archaelogist is said to have made the discovery after he investigated stories of local inhabitants lowering buckets through holes in the floor of their cellars and drawing water. What he found was a stupendous underground palace. Its cavernous interior is supported by 336 columns on marble bases, topped by Corinthian and Doric capitals. Mysteriously, two large Medusa heads—believed to have been pillaged from a pre-Byzantine pagan site—support two of the columns.

The cistern is no longer used for Istanbul's water system. The water level has been reduced to little more than a metre, and white fish swim among the columns. Visitors drift around walkways above the water, eery music echoes around the great vault and coloured lights add a weird quality to this weirdest of ancient creations.

Tom was struck dumb by the place, and when he emerged, he seemed to be in another world.

It was time, I felt, to jolt him awake. We set off to the Covered Bazaar, known to the locals as Kapali Carsi or Grand Bazaar. There's not a modern shopping mall on the Earth that can hold a candle to the Covered Bazaar, built in the fifteenth century. Beneath a single roof, it has somewhere between 3000 and 4300 shops (depending on who has done the counting), more than 60 streets and passageways, a mosque, a Turkish bath, a school, a tomb and about a thousand of Turkey's most in-your-face carpet salesmen. You can choose to be affronted or amused by the salesmen standing outside their little shops, and I advised Tom to be amused because you could die of old age before any of the them would give a toss that anyone had taken offence at their tactics. Anyway, plenty of them are genuine comics. The first time I tried to negotiate my way through the labyrinth, a moustachioed gentleman selling leather jackets leapt in my path and roared: 'Up the mighty Tigers!' Within minutes he was slipping a leather jacket over my shoulders ('very cheap, mister') and explaining that he had picked me as Australian the moment he clapped eyes on me. 'I lived in Melbourne for eight years,' he said. 'Bridge Road, Richmond. Best bloody footy team in the world, Richmond. Up the mighty Tigers.' I very nearly bought the leather jacket, but I was a Collingwood man. A friend claimed he had found a carpet salesman who, whenever he saw an Australian, roared the only ocker phrase he knew: 'Jeez mate, some bastard's stolen me fuckin' ute.' Sadly, I was never able to find this inventive fellow. It would have been worth buying one of his carpets just to see the performance.

The bazaar was teeming with shoppers, browsers and gawkers as Tom and I battled our way through its passages, and most of the salesmen were too busy with other victims to bother us much. We threaded our way through streets sparkling with jewellery, a lane dedicated to the trade in gold, another for copperware and another for handpainted ceramics. Passages were populated by sellers of fabrics, there was a section for swords and other weapons, and rows of specialists in meerschaum pipes. Tom made a bad mistake—he stopped to inspect a rack of fake brand-name shirts, and a salesman pounced. Shirts of every colour and size were dangled before Tom's eyes, and Tom said he couldn't afford the pitiful price of any of them. The salesman looked pained, and dropped the price by 25 per cent. Tom held up his hands, indicating he wasn't interested, and the salesman looked delighted, complimenting Tom on his hard bargaining skills and dropping the price another 10 per cent. Tom began walking away and the salesman yelped, ran after him and offered to trim even more off the price. If this kept up, I thought, Tom would find himself being paid to take away the whole rack of shirts. Finally, even the salesman knew Tom was a lost cause, and he returned to his store, throwing his arms in the air in a gesture of despair.

I had been keeping what I imagined was careful note of all the changes of direction we had taken through the endless market streets. Naturally, we were hopelessly lost. The gate we had entered should have been behind us, and there should have been an exit straight ahead. There seemed neither. Claustrophobia began creeping into my heart. Happily, a couple of Tourist Police appeared and we begged for directions. The Tourist Police, who are to be found in all the major tourist areas of Istanbul, are that rarest of uniformed species: they are invariably helpful. These two spoke excellent English and led us to the nearest gateway to the outer world. We were pathetically grateful.

We picked our way through crowds of shoppers, everything from veils to sensible shoes spilling off trays on the sidewalk, down a cobbled street towards the Golden Horn, and entered the Spice Market, breathing in its scents. Tom was entranced—here, without doubt, was the exotic east.

I led him out and up to the Galata Bridge, and we snapped pictures of each other standing among grizzled sardine fishermen, our hair ruffled by a cool breeze blowing from Europe to Asia. We were, I told Tom, in no-man's land, with the two great continents of the old world on each side of us. Tom was as excited as a kid on a school trip to an adventure park. I knew how he felt—I had hardly trodden a step in Turkey without it sending a tingle through my being.

I had arranged to meet Ömür for the afternoon, so left Tom to explore Istanbul at his own pace. Ömür was waiting impatiently in his office at the Topkapi Palace. He had organised one of his programs—lunch at the Sultanahmet Grand Saray (Palace) Hotel, a visit to the Museum of Turk and Islamic Arts to help me understand the historical and cultural importance of carpets through the Turkic people's epic migration from the steppes of Central Asia, afternoon tea at The Pudding Shop (the one-time gathering place of hippies on the the road from London to Kathmandu and Australia) and dinner with Ömür's English teacher. It all seemed too much, but Ömür was insistent. It would be our last day together, and it was important to him. We were no longer simply guide and the guided—we had formed a friendship. As a Turk, hospitality was an essential part of Ömür's soul. I had come to understand that even the most humble Turk considers it a duty and an honour to offer rest, conversation and sustenance to the traveller. In turn, the traveller bestows honour on the host by accepting these gifts. Even the most aggressive carpet salesman is likely to offer a chair and a glass of apple tea to a customer before the hard bargaining begins.

I remembered my childhood on the farm and the ritual of tea and scones performed by my mother the moment a visitor walked through the door. There was an easy, unquestioning grace to it. My parents were in the habit of picking up hitch-hikers and bringing them home for a meal and a yarn before sending them on their way with carefully wrapped sandwiches. Once, they brought home a pair of travellers who had lost their luggage. They left a day later carrying two of our sleeping bags and, months afterwards, the bags were returned by courier with notes of thanks.

The urgency of consumerism and economic hard-ball has whittled away at these softer, courteous edges of much of western behaviour, even in Australia, but the Turks seem unable to imagine life without instinctive acts of generosity. It is as if the memory of the *caravanserai* of the Silk Road or the shared comfort of a carpet on the floor of a lonely *yurt* on the steppes is built into their bones. Still, no one should get too dewy-eyed. No people with a history like the Turks are one-dimensional. The Kurdish people remain a significantly repressed community in Turkey; Armenians remember massacres at the hands of the Turks; hundreds of thousands of Greeks lost their homes and their land in forced deportations during Greek–Turk population swaps soon after Turkey became a republic; an international force, including Australian police, has had to keep an uneasy peace for decades across an ugly divide on Cyprus; and tensions simmer along a number of Turkey's borders. A riled Turk is a formidable foe, as the Anzacs, the British, the French and the rest discovered to their cost in 1915.

Still, my last ramble with Ömür was hardly the time for sorting out the quandaries of ethnic and international relations in a country in which I was a brief visitor, and where I was being treated like a prince to boot.

Ömür had a friend who was the general manager of one of the lovelier hotels, the Sultanahmet Saray. It was built of pink stone on the ruins of the ancient Byzantium Grand Palace, offering a view of ships steaming through a mist on the Sea of Marmara. A melancholy hoot of foghorns floated up from the water. We ate in a large restaurant devoid of customers, and the manager lamented the loss of trade following the September 11 attacks on New York and Washington. Americans and Japanese had stopped travelling. His beautiful hotel, built for affluent tourists, was almost empty because Turkey, a secular nation since 1923, was perceived to be Islamic. The vast majority of Turks are Muslims, but most of them are more relaxed and tolerant of westerners than many westerners are of Muslims these days. Far from taking offence at western culture, many Turks feel most offended because their nation, mired in the evil economic twins, stagnation and inflation, was being denied access to the European Union. I drank wine for lunch at the insistence of Ömür and his friend, who sipped cola.

The hotel manager took me on a tour of his establishment. Every room had a Turkish bath, where guests could sit on a marble slab, slosh water over themselves with a copper pitcher and disappear into a cloud of steam. In a world terrified by Islamic demons, the steam rooms, exotic pleasures from an old Islamic empire, were idle.

The Sultanahmet Saray was a luxurious world away from my new lodgings. On my return from Cappadocia, I had checked in to the humble Star Holiday Hotel, right on the main drag of Sultanahmet, a few doors from the famous old restaurant where

I had eaten my first Turkish meal with Ömür all those days ago. The Star was utterly without character (it was a narrow yellow-brick block that would not look out of place in any Australian suburb developed in the 1960s), but it was cheap—US$15 a night for a single room with shower.

I wasn't going to be able to return to the hotel for a while, though. Ömür was steering me to our next date with food.

'You have seen the movie *Midnight Express?*' he asked. I had indeed—it was the film that gave Turkey a fearsome reputation among foreign travellers. It dealt with a young American, Billy Hayes, who fell afoul of the Turkish authorities during the hippy era when he was arrested for trying to smuggle several kilos of hashish out of the country. He was a bit of a dill, in my opinion, but he hardly deserved the treatment he got in Istanbul's gaol, assuming the movie's depiction of events was even halfway accurate. He was beaten, degraded, thrown into solitary confinement, had his prison sentence increased from a few years to life, and eventually lapsed into insanity, traipsing aimlessly around a pillar in the prison's dungeon. His final dash for freedom, during which he impales the head of a sadistic guard on a coathook while resisting the guard's sexual advances, remains one of the more confronting moments in modern film history. The medieval gaol no longer exists. It seems a delicious mockery of its brutal past that it has been converted into Istanbul's most upscale hotel, the Four Seasons, beloved of wealthy American tourists.

I had no idea why Ömür was inquiring about my knowledge of *Midnight Express*. I still had no clue when he led me into a restaurant specialising in Turkish desserts. The owner, a small man of advancing years and dancing eyes, came bustling towards us. He shook Ömür's hand and slapped his back and led us to a table. There seemed to be no one in all Istanbul who didn't know Ömür.

'Welcome to The Pudding Shop,' said the little man. 'Is famous everywhere, yes? Oh, we have had many Australians, many, many.' He chuckled and gave an order to a waiter he introduced as his son. The waiter, who looked about 40, brought a grubby old hard-bound journal to the table and flipped it open. Rows of names, addresses and comments were scrawled on the pages. It was a guest book, and the dates on the page I studied were all in 1969. 'Far out', someone called Jim from Boston, USA, had written. 'Man, the Pudding Shop is the best', another entry read. People from London, New York, San Francisco, Melbourne, Rome, Sydney, Paris, Brisbane, Memphis, Perth—all over the place—had immortalised themselves in the book. Many of the entries were all but illegible, and a few had mysterious little cartoons and pictures of flowers in the comments column. I didn't recognise any famous names.

The old man produced press clippings. They all referred to The Pudding Shop and its heyday in the 1960s and 1970s. A faded picture showed a garden and kids of indeterminate gender—they wore beads and hair at least to their shoulders. A couple played guitar, but most of them simply gazed at the camera, stoned. The clippings described The Pudding Shop (some referred to it as The Pudding Shoppe) as the first stop in Asia for hippies en route from London to Kathmandu and beyond. It was, of course, the last stop in Asia for those travelling the opposite way, and plenty of them were Australians taking the overland trail to swinging London.

'They all came here, yes,' chuckled the old man. The Pudding Shop was the place to leave messages for friends, to buy and sell clapped-out Kombi vans and, it seemed, to find dealers in the finest Turkish hashish. That, according to one of the newspaper clippings, was where *Midnight Express* came into the picture. After Billy Hayes got busted trying to board a plane to America, there is a scene in the film where he leads police and a US under-cover drug cop to a café, promising to point out the dealer from whom he had purchased his stash of hash. Then he makes a break for it, running out the back of the café before being recaptured.

'Yes, yes, that was here,' said the owner of The Pudding Shop proudly. 'Very famous happening.'

The name of the café, its owner, the clippings and the guest book are all that remain in evidence of those vanished times. The overland route has long fallen out of favour. The idea of piling aboard a rickety bus or a kombi van for the trip through countries like Afghanistan, Iran and Iraq lost a lot of romance when massed armies, warlords and assorted maniacs began shooting at each other and anyone else who got in their way. Kalashnikovs, tanks, rockets, artillery pieces, warheads loaded with chemical weapons and anti-personnel landmines were never going to mix easily with the middle-class kids who hung out at The Pudding Shop.

Anyway, most of the hippies eventually grew bored and old and the Australians and New Zealanders among them became the parents of young travellers who come to Turkey these days determined not to leave until they have visited Anzac Cove.

The Pudding Shop no longer has a garden. It is just another café behind a street window catering to tourists. Happily, it still specialises in Turkish milk puddings of all flavours.

The owner brought me a pudding bursting with fruit and berries. 'Is special pudding,' he whispered in my ear. 'Is called sex pudding. After this, you go three, four times in one night.' He formed a fist and pumped his arm, winking.

'Maybe for a Turk,' I said. 'An Australian—oh, maybe twelve, thirteen times.'

The old man roared. 'For you, this pudding is free. No charge.'

Ömür appeared confused. He asked the owner to translate the exchange into Turkish. The old man interpreted at the top of his voice, guffawing. Ömür blushed and looked at the table.

The evening was advancing, and we had one more engagement. Ömür wanted me to meet his English teacher, Ibrahim Ozan, and we walked through lengthening shadows to a university tea-house. This was the occasion when I asked Ibrahim, a young man with piercing green eyes, to clarify the story of the 'sheeps' that were used in the 1453 Ottoman assault on the walls of Byzantium. Poor Ömür: his embarrassment at my failure to comprehend his English, and the revelation of the depth of my misunderstanding, all in the presence of his language teacher, was excruciating. He had blushed at The Pudding Shop, but now he turned scarlet. His honour was rescued only when Ibrahim checked Ömür's English translation of the 'Çanakkale March', and judged it to be perfect.

It was curious to watch the interplay between Ömür and Ibrahim in the tea garden. They were about the same age— Ibrahim may have been even younger than Ömür—and were obviously close friends. But Ömür deferred to Ibrahim, apparently because Ibrahim had such a mastery of languages. Yet Ömür was an internationally famous archaeologist whose opinion on Japanese ceramics was sought regularly by Japanese scholars, and he gave lectures in Japanese.

I remembered Ömür telling me he had spent his childhood in a rural village, the child of a peasant-farming family. I could only imagine the social and financial struggle involved in levering himself to his position at the Topkapi Palace. The power of his intellect must have been the single quality that carried him through. Yet here he was, beating himself up because his command of English wasn't strong, and feeling embarrassed in front of a teacher and friend no older than himself. Was there no end to the pressure young Turks placed upon themselves in the cause of achievement?

I realised suddenly that Ömür had been battling deep frustration as we had wandered the streets of Istanbul. He had been cast in the role of guide, yet he had been unable properly to articulate his vast knowledge of the history and the significance of all the places he had shown me. We had never been able to share a conversation involving truly complex ideas. I had been unable to fulfil his hunger for knowledge of Australia and Australians, either. I remembered a day when he had inquired about the relationship between white Australians and Aborigines. An expression of despair had came across his face as I launched into a discourse on the subject. He could not follow me, and I hunted for words that might convey some meaning to him. It was not an issue that could be plumbed adequately without a shared vernacular that had a depth to it, so the discussion trailed away.

In the tea garden, I felt a sorrow that we would have no opportunity to take our new friendship to a more absorbing level. His was surely an intellect that could provide a key to an ancient culture struggling with modernity, with which my own nation's identity was entwined because of happenstance 87 years ago.

Regardless, as Ömür and Ibrahim chatted away over their glasses of tea, I reflected that I was glad that I had met Ömür. He had introduced me to an Istanbul I would not have known. We had walked through night-time backstreets way off the tourist path, surrounded by families who had moved to the city from remote communities in the east and who dragged chairs and tables into the street to commune with their neighbours because they could not abandon their village traditions. We had stood within the great echoing mosque of Sultan Suleyman the Great, and Ömür had taken great pains to explain how the architect, Sinan, had spent weeks and months sitting in the centre of his unfinished masterpiece, smoking a water pipe and blowing the smoke into the air. While Suleyman raved that the building must be completed or Sinan would be executed, Sinan—who appeared to have lost his mind—smoked serenely. Eventually he revealed that he had been perfecting the ventilation system. When the mosque opened, oily smoke from thousands of candles and lamps used to illuminate the heavenly tiled dome and walls wafted magically to a special venting room, rather than staining a single tile. The carbon that collected in the venting room became the most valued ink ever used for sacred calligraphy, and Sinan was once more hailed a genius.

Ömür and Ibrahim decided we must have a farewell dinner. We walked together across the gardens of Sultanahmet and down a hill by the single exposed crumbling curved wall of the Hippodrome's amphitheatre, arriving at a two-storey restaurant called *Doy-Doy*. The name explained everything anyone needed to know about the restaurant: it meant 'fill up, fill up'. It was, said Ibrahim, cheap and served satisfying food. It was popular with students, office workers and families, and budget travellers had known about it for years. We took a table on the second floor, ordered Turkish pizzas, salad and Coke, and Ömür unwound enough to tell Ibrahim about the business with the 'sex pudding'. They laughed merrily at the idea of an Australian managing to upstage the owner of The Pudding Shop, who they said considered himself an authority on all matters carnal. Ibrahim kept snorting with glee at the memory of me confusing sheeps with ships, and Ömür eventually saw the comic side to it too. It was a relaxed, happy way to end my Istanbul sojourn. We swapped email addresses, slapped each other on the back and set off in different directions along the street. When I reached a corner I looked back, and Ömür was standing beneath a street light, waving.

I dropped in on Tom at the Orient Hostel and we arranged to meet at my hotel at 6.00 a.m., when the bus to Gallipoli would pick us up.

The young receptionist at the Star Holiday Hotel was tapping at a computer when I walked in. He was, he said, having trouble with his English studies. Could I help? Well, why not—trouble with English was going around. His name was Ramil Abdulhalikov and he was undertaking a postgraduate course in journalism and public relations. I was a journalist, I told him. 'I dream of being a journalist,' he said wearily.

Like so many other ambitious young people in Turkey, he was doing life tough. He worked twelve hours a day at the hotel, and earned US$145 a month—less than guests in some of the better rooms paid to stay a week in this budget-priced lodging. It was not really enough to live on, Ramil said, but he had to complete his studies before he could hope for a better job.

He handed me the paper that was giving him grief. I could understand why. He was required to rewrite in simple, easily grasped English an extraordinarily complex story concerning financial markets and the media. He had completed much of the task, but some of the terminology was a mystery to him. What was a company float, he asked? What was a vested interest? What did the term 'mushrooming' mean? I did my best, and he grasped the gist quickly. There was one more thing: a passage relating to the need for a workable system to guarantee transparency within financial news agencies to prevent insider trading. He needed to explain the concept in a few concise lines.

I wondered how I might handle such an assignment if I was learning Turkish, and felt weak at the prospect. Ramil looked exhausted. There was an obvious brilliance about him, and I thought about Ömür, frustrated as hell at his inability to explain or understand elaborate concepts in English.

I took Ramil's assignment to a table, completed it and asked him to read it and explain what it meant. I felt like a schoolmaster. He had no difficulty. He had simply been too tired to do the paper himself. Kids like him, born a bit over a century ago, died by the tens of thousands defending their land from people like my great-uncle. Now Turkey, economically mangled, excluded by the European Union and required to barter its territory as a military platform for US strategy in the Middle East in order to ensure American financial aid, needs kids like Ramil to build a new future.

'Good night,' I said. 'I'm leaving early tomorrow.'

Ramil hardly heard me. He was busily packing his papers away. Twelve hours a day, a postgraduate course and hardly enough money to feed himself. Istanbul. Exotic one day, a tough slog the next.

7

TO THE DARDANELLES

The legend is that the architect given the job of designing a new fort at the spot in 1462 by the Ottoman Sultan Mehmet the Conqueror fell in love with a local village girl. He was so bowled over that he designed the world's first and only fort to be shaped as a heart—one that his loved girl could see wherever she walked.

A grey dawn's mist hung over the empty streets of old Sultanahmet when Tom and I struggled down the stairs with our packs and found the Hassle Free Tours mini-bus to Gallipoli waiting outside the hotel.

Our fellow passengers were all New Zealanders: a young couple named AJ and Sasha, and a fellow named Steve and his wife, whose name somehow never entered my notebook, though she was the liveliest member of the party. Perhaps she talked so excitedly about her adventures in Istanbul and the doings of a Maori ancestor at Gallipoli that I never quite got the chance to scribble her name down.

As the bus plunged through the interminable outer suburbs of Istanbul, skirting the hazy northern shore of the Sea of Marmara, Steve's wife kept us entertained with her description of a visit to a *hamam*—a Turkish bath. With hand gestures and graphic sounds of whooshing, she took us through the process of being covered in suds and slapped around by the *hamam*'s masseuse, who had scrubbed her skin to a pink glow with an exfoliating mitten, and of having buckets of water sloshed over her body and more slapping. 'Oh, it was wonderful,' she giggled and sighed.

Steve, the more circumspect of the pair, listened through it all before informing us he too had visited a *hamam* the previous evening. He seemed to be in shock at the memory.

'I think I stumbled into Istanbul's gay bath house,' he said, his eyes wide. 'The bloke in charge asked me how I liked my men. Can you imagine? After lying around on a hot slab, all these customers began disappearing into these booths and you could see them doing their thing.'

Steve looked as if his nerves were shot. His wife hooted with amusement. None of us could bring ourselves to ask Steve just what 'thing' his fellow bath-house clients had been doing in the booths.

It would be a long trip—almost six hours—and we slipped easily into conversation about our favourite places in Istanbul. We had, it seemed, visited many of the same sights and markets and food halls. Soon, though, I began worrying about the state of the bus's rear axle. There was a rumbling. We swivelled to investigate, and discovered Tom stretched out on the back seat, his mouth wide open and a sound halfway between strangulation and a truck with its exhaust muffler torn off thundering from his throat. 'Jeez,' said AJ, impressed.

The mist lifted, and the Sea of Marmara shimmered silver on our left. AJ rummaged in his bag and produced a packet of biscuits.

'Let me be the Kiwi who offered an Aussie a Negro in Turkey,' he said. The packet of chocolate biscuits bore the label 'Negroes' in large letters.

'This would have to be the last country on Earth where you're allowed to sell anything called Negroes,' AJ remarked. Indeed, I thought. Should go down a treat if George W. Bush launched an attack on Iraq and stationed thousands of his US troops and Air Force crews in Turkey. (Something that, as it turned out, didn't eventuate as a new Turkish government turned Bush down, at an immense cost to the country.)

A couple of hours into the trip, we pulled up at a service station equipped with a large modern cafeteria. Only two years previously I had been to this very place, but there had been nothing but a petrol pump or two and a broken-down hut where you could purchase chocolate bars, soft drinks and stale potato crisps. Now, banks of cooks manning stainless steel hotplates awaited our orders. We chose cheese toast and tea and felt lonely, surrounded by scores of empty tables and chairs. Next door, the toilets could have accommodated the passengers of a couple of large tourist coaches. The growing crowds of Gallipoli-bound travellers had created the opportunity for local entrepeneurs to cash in. Even the cost of entering the toilets was 200 000 lira.

Happily, we were way ahead of the surge of travellers who would come down the road for Anzac Day.

The first time I visited Gallipoli was in the year 2000. I was part of the media mob travelling with the prime minister of Australia, John Howard.

It was a trip where money was no object, but time was limited, as these things tend to be. We flew into Istanbul where a party of embassy officials waited to shepherd us into a waiting coach. The coach floated through the city's demented traffic, a police escort clearing the way, to a hotel sitting at the very edge of the Bosphorus. The hotel was one of the most expensive in Turkey or anywhere else—the Çirağan Palace. It was a real palace from the Ottoman empire, with a few modern touches: a vast swimming pool at the edge of the sea, which gave one the impression of actually swimming in the Bosphorus without the inconvenience of mixing with passing tankers and swallowing polluted water; a pad for the hotel's helicopter; and a lounge where guests nibbled cucumber sandwiches and tea cakes and looked across the water to Asia.

My room at this extravagant establishment was large enough for a country dance, which was just as well, for I was invaded by friends who were backpacking to Gallipoli. I had stowed away a bottle of duty-free Bundaberg rum for just such a turn of events. A photographer named Michael Bowers, who was to take the pictures that would accompany my newspaper articles, had packed another. The following morning, the room looked as if a country dance might actually have occurred. I recall awakening to discover plates of half-eaten room-service food that must have arrived and been consumed some time after the first bottle had been opened and the first strains of the previously-and-since unknown song 'Prosperous on the Bosphorus' had been sung.

The morning light revealed John Howard undertaking, along the sea front, the final stages of his daily power waddle. Bowers and I had difficulty facing the scene, or the monstrous breakfast laid out in the dining room, and promptly decided to hire a car and set out for Gallipoli ahead of the prime minister and our fellow travellers, who were to fly to the Turkish capital, Ankara, before flying to Anzac the following day.

With the car came a driver. His name, to our delight, was Mustafa Shat. That, at least, was how it was pronounced. I was moved to recall a letter allegedly written by a British diplomat who had endured the misfortune of being posted to Moscow in the glum days of World War II. 'My dear Reggie,' he wrote to Lord Pembroke, obviously a chum, back in the British Foreign Office in London.

In these dark days man tends to look for little shafts of light that spill from Heaven. My days are probably darker than yours, and I need, my God I do, all the light I can get. But I am a decent fellow, and I do not want to be mean and selfish about what little brightness is shed upon me from time to time. So I propose to share with you a tiny flash that has illuminated my sombre life and tell you that God has given me a new Turkish colleague whose card tells me that he is called Mustapha Kunt. We all feel like that, Reggie, now and then, especially when Spring is upon us, but few of us would care to put it on our cards. It takes a Turk to do that, *signed, Sir Archibald Clerk Kerr.*

I have never researched the authenticity of this gem, for fear I would discover it is a myth. It is one of those things that, if not true, ought to be. Mustafa Shat turned out to be a tolerant fellow, enduring without complaint Bowers using his name to direct lavatory stops on the journey. It was, of course, the rum speaking, and afterwards we felt so ashamed we shouted Mustafa a night's accommodation on a tourist ship moored in the Dardanelles. We renamed this floating gin palace 'The Shit' because the toilets in the cabins would not flush. Lavatory humour clearly overtook our better judgement on the trip— something that tends to infect westerners right through the Middle East, thanks to the strangeness of the dunny systems— though there was little that was comic about crawling out of a bunk in the middle of the night, tramping down the gangplank and trotting through the streets to find a hotel that had working toilets.

Still, the ship's shortcomings provided some entertainment. Bowers and I shared a tiny cabin, and the bulkhead dividing us from the neighbouring cabin appeared to be paper thin. Our neighbour was a young woman from the New Zealand military and, late in the night, she had company. 'Yis, yis,' her voice, employing the peculiarly strangled vowels of the Kiwi, came floating through the wall. 'Yis, oh yis, oh yis, yis, ohhhh, yis.' Bowers couldn't stand it.

'For Christ's sake, mate,' he roared, 'Will you stop asking her bloody questions!' The silence that followed was immense.

The road between Istanbul and the Gallipoli Peninsula had not changed much between that trip and this. Often, there were concrete blockhouses lining the roadside, apparently unfinished. Steel shafts prodded the sky above flat roofs, as if waiting for more concrete to form an extra storey. On that first trip Mustafa explained that the Turkish government did not levy building taxes until a building was complete. Thus householders would build a house to accommodate the family's needs, but leave formwork on the roof, as if further building was contemplated. How long before the taxman came knocking, suspicious that a rort was being perpetrated, I wondered? Mustafa shrugged. 'Forever,' he said. I went back to sleep, content that there was such an understanding tax department in the world. Mustafa, of course, may have been pulling my leg. We were paying him US$400, so he could afford to be jolly.

Now, two years later and travelling on a US$12 bus fare, way south of our morning tea break, the villages and townships began petering out and we barrelled into rolling farm country. Shepherds stood patiently with little flocks of sheep and goats, and in valleys the land had been planted with canola and barley and rice.

Finally, we swung around a bend in the road and, below us, the long finger of the Gallipoli Peninsula poked into the Aegean Sea. We drove across the high reach of the peninsula, exhilarated as children, to the fishing village of Gellibolu which gives the peninsula its name, and cruised along the western shore of the Dardanelles. Almost within touching distance, it seemed, ships steamed back and forth on what looked little more than a wide river. Tom and I speculated about what the crew might have felt aboard the Australian submarine *AE2* that managed to break through the Dardanelles in April 1915, forced to surface often to get a bearing or to vent the foul air within or to drag free of a sandbank, all the while swept by searchlights from forts along the banks of the strait and pursued by Turkish and German seacraft. Whatever they felt at the time, it could hardly have been worse than a little later in the war when the crew was captured and sent off to prisoner-of-war camps across Turkey.

Finally, we bumped into the town of Eceabat. 'This looks a bit of a rough joint,' said AJ. It did, and it's hardly surprising. Eceabat, called Maidos during World War I, sits at the edge of The Narrows in the Dardanelles, and was shot all to pieces by the big guns of British warships in the failed attempt by the British Navy to break through the Dardanelles in March 1915.

The township is not much more than a ferry port now. Its streets are cobbled and crooked, and the shops and houses are whitewashed in an easy-going sort of way, though the term 'white-wash' is not altogether accurate. There is a tumble-down feeling to the place, which we would soon come to find endearing.

We stopped at a long open square next to the ferry terminal. A couple of boys kicked a soccer ball around, but the town seemed all but deserted. Across the 1200 metres of water known as The Narrows stood the larger town of Çanakkale, in Asia. A cold wind blew and we wandered to the seafront street to warm ourselves with coffee, a few café owners imploring us to enter their empty establishments for 'the best kebap'. 'Kebap, kebap, kebap,' they cried, and we felt mean ignoring them. AJ and Steve sat hunched at a table on the footpath and declared the quest for the world's worst coffee was over.

Tom and I waved farewell to the New Zealanders, who were booked on a Hassle Free bus tour of the Anzac battlefields up in the hills above Eceabat. Steve's wife was bursting with excitement at the prospect.

We were in no such hurry and boarded a ferry, half as big as a cruise liner and weighed down with trucks and buses and cars, and crossed the Dardanelles to Çanakkale, accompanied by the driver who had brought us from Istanbul. He was tired, and explained that he had driven to Istanbul overnight to pick us up—a twelve-hour round trip.

Tom was wide-eyed to be crossing the Dardanelles for the first time.

Just about every warrior civilisation of Europe and Asia has spilled blood into and around this strip of water.

In 481BC, the Persian king Xerxes I, intent on spreading his empire's control to Greece and beyond, is supposed to have become so enraged that a storm had wrecked his engineers' efforts to string a bridge across the Narrows at Çanakkale that he flogged the waters with a horse whip, and branded the sea with hot irons.

The storm ceased abruptly (as storms around these parts tend to do), but Xerxes' fury was still not quite spent. He ordered that the unfortunate engineers whose bridge-building efforts had come adrift be put to death. His next team of engineers took vastly greater pains to get things right. Along with his massive land army Xerxes had 1000 ships sailing the Aegean, and the engineers lashed 300 of them side by side across the Narrows. Then they duplicated the effort to form another bridge downstream for Xerxes' herds of horses. Thick ropes were used to lash the boats together and then pulled taut by windlasses anchored to each shore. Finally, stone, timber and soil was used to lay roadways across the bridges of boats. It took Xerxes' vast army seven days to march across the bridge.

A century and a half later, in 334BC, Alexander the Great, on his way to capturing everything as far away as India, pinched

Xerxes' idea and constructed his own bridge of boats so his army could cross in the opposite direction.

You need only look at the massive forts at the entrance to the Dardanelles, at either side of the Narrows and at various other points along this ribbon of water to know the battles that have taken place here. For a thousand years the Byzantines, and then the Ottomans for another 600, knew precisely what the passage meant: it held the key to Constantinople, the world's most fabulous city. If you could get through the Dardanelles, you could challenge Constantinople and have a shot at passing through the next strait, the Bosphorus, into the Black Sea and to the belly of Russia.

The forts had two purposes. Their guns, capable of hurling large stone balls a kilometre or so across the water, could lay waste to unwelcome invaders. Their presence also made it plain that even welcome seafarers must pay steep tolls before proceeding or face the consequences.

There is one fort, however, that was built to inspire the opposite of dread and, floodlit in the evening, it retains the power to bewitch. Aboard the ferry, our eyes were drawn to Kilitbahir, the name of the fort which means 'lock (or key) of the sea'.

Sheltering beneath the escarpment on the western shore of The Narrows, Kilitbahir is built in the shape of a heart. It is even built on the angle of its slope so its walls can be discerned as a heart from any vantage point.

The legend is that the architect given the job of designing a new fort at the spot in 1462 by the Ottoman Sultan Mehmet the Conqueror fell in love with a local village girl. He was so bowled over that he designed the world's first and only fort to be shaped as a heart—one that his loved girl could see wherever she walked. It is not known whether the lovelorn architect ever won the girl's own heart, or even whether the legend has a grain of truth. Still, why else would a stone fort, its only practical purpose to strike fear into the breast of a would-be invader, end up built as a Medieval Valentine? And what did Mehmet the Conqueror think of it? Perhaps the old Sultan, whose kind enjoyed the idea of a harem of a few hundred women, understood perfectly.

What we call Gallipoli is known to the locals simply as part of the Province of Çanakkale, a place vast both in physical size and in the sweep of history. Çanakkale town, with 67 000 souls, is the capital of the province of 400 000. Read Homer's *Iliad*, immortalising the Battle of Troy, and you are reading of Çanakkale. The ruins of Troy—nine quite separate cities built on top of each other from 3000BC to 500AD—are barely a half-hour drive to the south of the city.

And yet, with all this endless history, the war of 1915 is as important to the Turkish people as any of the battles of myth. When we talk of the Gallipoli campaign, the Turks speak of the Çanakkale War. And when they do that, they are not speaking about just another war. Their eyes tell you that instantly.

Tom and I lifted our own eyes from the stone heart of Kilitbahir and found, emblazoned in huge letters on the hillside, the first words of a Turkish poem by the patriot Necmettin Halil Onan, entitled 'To a Traveller': '*Dur yolcu!*' it commanded. 'Stop traveller!' Translated, the poem requires that the traveller halt and realise: 'Unbeknown to you this soil on which you tread/ Is where an epoch lies/ Bend down and lend your ear, for this silent mound/ Is the place where the heart of a nation sighs'.

The last verse of the poem, which does not appear on the hill, cuts right to the chase: 'Think! The consecrated blood and flesh and bone/ That make up this mound is where a whole nation/ After a harsh and pitiless war; alone tasted the juice of freedom with elation'.

Sweeping our gaze north and east, across the waters from this compelling hillside, we found, hovering above Çanakkale, another hill bearing words written by a giant. '18 Mart 1915' is all it says. It needs nothing more because, as far as the people of Çanakkale and all Turkey are concerned, the Çanakkale War was won on 18 March 1915.

By the time the British and Anzac landing came around on 25 April, the game was all but up for the British forces, despite the fact that half a million lives—and half of those Turkish—were still to be lost or wrecked a few kilometres across the Peninsula from the narrows of the Dardanelles, in the gullies and along the ridges of Anzac, at Cape Helles and Krithia and on the shores of Suvla Bay.

The people of Çanakkale, whose very beings are immersed in the knowledge that their ancestors had spent forever beating back challenges from the sea, recognise something that many of the rest of us have forgotten: that what turned into the bogged-down trench war known as the Gallipoli campaign was always supposed to have been a naval assault.

In 1915, Britain's First Lord of the Admiralty, Winston Churchill, was possibly inflamed by the historical knowledge that, in 1807, British Admiral John Darkworth had broken through the Dardanelles. Indeed Darkworth had, but his was a pyrrhic victory. Trying to upstage the Russians in the Franco-Russian War, in which the Ottoman Empire had become an ally of France through a series of diplomatic insanities, Darkworth and his small fleet of British ships battled their way up the Dardanelles on 13 February 1807.

He declared for himself a British victory, but was astounded to discover that, when he reached Constantinople, the Sultan of the time simply refused to surrender. Darkworth, running low on ammunition for his ships' guns, had no choice but to turn around and battle his way back through the Dardanelles the day after having breached them. Churchill perhaps should have noted that this futile little adventure cost Britain several ships and 600 men when the Ottomans let rip with their cannons from their fortifications along the shores of the Dardanelles, cutting the retreat to ribbons.

Churchill chose to ignore that inconvenient caveat.

If one British Admiral could break through the strait, then the First Lord of the Admiralty of the greatest seafaring nation on earth, now complete with massive iron ships armed with big guns, could surely demand that the effort be repeated, and successfully.

Britain had to do something to undo the mess it had created when it all but forced the Ottoman Empire to side with Germany in World War I. The once-great empire had been reduced in size to the place we now call Turkey, and the Sultan and what remained of his power had been sidelined by a group of young nationalists, revolutionaries and deal-makers known as the Young Turks. In a world going mad around them, in charge of a decayed and bankrupt so-called empire, the Young Turks desperately needed an ally.

They played footsies with Germany, and made a secret pact to join their Axis. But Britain still had a card in the game. Britain was building, in its River Clyde shipyards, two battleships for Turkey. The ships had already been paid for. Ordinary people throughout the Ottoman Empire had subscribed, often with the last of their meagre funds. Family treasures had been turned into gold for the British.

At the last minute, Churchill decided Britain needed the battleships more than the Turks, who he thought anyway needed a lesson for playing up to the Germans. The ships were simply confiscated, and no compensation was offered.

It was destined to end in tears. The Germans sailed two of their own battleships through the Dardanelles, declared they now belonged to Turkey, and that game was over. Turkey was firmly in the German camp.

Britain, bogged down in a medieval war with modern weapons in the trenches of northern France—the Western Front—hatched a plan to create a backdoor for a possible Eastern Front.

Russia was allied to Britain, and was already battling with Turkish forces in Anatolia, the vast eastern lands of Turkey. If Britain could force Turkey to its knees and out of German hands, then Russia—ice-locked to its north—could be kept supplied with ammunition through the warm waters of the Mediterranean, the Dardanelles, the Bosphorus and the Black Sea. Russia could then properly drive an Eastern Front, and Germany would be caught in a pincer movement.

All that would be needed was for Britain's Navy to force its way through the Dardanelles, threaten Constantinople with its guns and Turkey would accede. That was the theory, all of which went to hell on a stick when Çanakkale's hold on the Dardanelles proved unpassable.

The guns on the Dardanelles' forts proved tougher than the British planners had envisaged and then, on 18 March 1915, mines laid secretly the night before by a small ship out of Çanakkale laid waste to Churchill's ambitions.

British and French warships ended arse-up in the gutter of the Dardanelles, with the loss of hundreds of lives.

The British went away to dab tar on their wounds and to dream up another plan. It was this: to land a great force of foot soldiers on the Gallipoli Peninsula, which would storm across that narrow strip of land back to the Dardanelles, capture the forts and make sure the Turks could lay no more mines. Then the Navy could sail through and complete its original intention of forcing the surrender of Constantinople.

The land force would include British, French, Senegalese and

Indian troops. Oh, and, by the by, there was already a large contingent of Australians and New Zealanders under training in Egypt, where they had been since November 1914, waiting to discover what role they would be given on the Western Front.

While all this was being hastily and poorly planned, the Turks figured out the British would be back, and began massing their own troops all over the Gallipoli Peninsula.

And so, a bit over a month after the first instalment of the Çanakkale War had been lost by the British, another, much greater tragedy was about to occur, this time on land.

As the oars dipped and the men who would be called Anzacs hunkered down in their boats in the pre-dawn of 25 April 1915, preparing to take their little slice of the Gallipoli Peninsula, other men from farms and villages all around Çanakkale province and beyond were waiting to defend their own country.

'Ooh, my youth,' they would sing later. 'Mothers and fathers have lost hope.' In any language, it would prove to be a truth of that place.

But in the end, the invasion force—what was left of it— would sail away, having captured less than 2 per cent of the Gallipoli Peninsula.

The Australians and New Zealanders, if they won anything, captured their right to begin to think of themselves as people of their own nations, separate from Britain.

The Turks won for themselves a new leader, his own legend born there, to create their own new nation, which they would not surrender. 'Çanakkale, no pass.' Indeed.

Our 20-minute ferry ride across the Dardanelles ended, and our friend the Hassle Free bus driver pointed the way to our home for the next week: Anzac House. It was a short step from the ferry terminal in Çanakkale, beyond a clock tower. To the left, little fishing boats, yachts and large cruisers lay moored in a marina, and seafront cafés sat empty.

Anzac House had a few chairs and tables lining a wall in the foyer, a couple of computers for Internet access and, down the back past a small servery, two men were installing a big television screen.

The receptionist allotted me a room on the second floor with no window and a bathroom up the corridor, while Tom found himself in a small dormitory.

Finally, I was a backpacker.

8

ANZAC HOUSE

There seemed little place for memories of an old war during the upheavals of the 1960s and 1970s as the nation's most affluent and self-indulgent population bulge—the baby boomers, my own generation—tried to re-make society and the world in their own image.

One look at Hanifi Araz lumbering down the Anzac House stairway told us who was boss around here. He had a tiny mobile phone pressed to an ear above a bull-neck and he wore the air of intense assurance you might find on a prize fighter or a big-time real estate developer.

He shook my hand, still speaking rapid-fire into the telephone. He waved me to a chair and with another flick of his wrist ordered one of his staff to bring tea and cake.

'Sorry,' he said, snapping his phone shut. 'I have too many things going on. Welcome to Anzac House.' He patted a giant white dog that plomped itself at his feet. 'Anatolian sheep dog,' he said. 'The best.' It looked capable of taking the head off a ram in a single bite.

Hanifi is owner, general manager and ideas man of the Anzac House empire, which is to say he is among the most powerful men in the Çanakkale–Eceabat–Gallipoli tourism industry. He was in his mid-twenties when he recognised that his destiny and his fortune lay with the burgeoning number of Australians and New Zealanders travelling to the Dardanelles for Anzac Day.

'Anzac tourism was born after the *Gallipoli* movie was made,' he said, referring to the 1981 film directed by Peter Weir and starring Mel Gibson, Mark Lee, Bill Kerr, Ron Graham, Harold Hopkins, Charles Yunupingu, Heath Harris and Gerda Nicolson.

'Before that, only a few people from Australia and New Zealand came here. But during the 1980s, the numbers began growing.

'In 1989, I told my father I was going into this industry. He had this building, so we put up the name Anzac House and made a small hotel with 37 beds in 20 rooms. It was very old and not very good, but it was a start.'

Hanifi's timing was perfect, even if the idea that Anzac could be seen as an industry jars somewhat.

The film *Gallipoli* might have begun to inflame a new nationalism associated with Gallipoli among Australian travellers, but it was ABC-TV's *Four Corners* program *The Fatal Shore* in 1988 that accelerated the tramp of feet back to Anzac Cove.

The program was made by reporter Chris Masters. The producer was Harvey Broadbent, who speaks Turkish and still visits Gallipoli regularly. *The Fatal Shore* was the most popular video produced in Australia in the late 1980s, and its release came during the Australian Bicentenary, when the quest for what it meant to be Australian grabbed the emotions of millions. Half the nation seemed to be searching for a First Fleet ancestor, or at least a convict. The other half searched for an Anzac in the family.

Masters took the viewer through the history of the Gallipoli campaign, interviewed shaky veterans—all gone now—and stood among a scattering of young backpackers at Lone Pine, evoking a distant part of the Australian heart as few reporters could, and puzzling why so many Australians had so recently rediscovered Gallipoli. He reported that 12 000 Australians a year were visiting Gallipoli. That was then. Today, more than 15 000 turn up for Anzac Day alone, and any day of the year there are scores—often hundreds—more, picking through the cemeteries of the peninsula.

Back in 1988, history teachers in high schools across Australia grabbed Masters' documentary with both hands. Here was an opportunity to fill an hour in a school day with a compelling narrative of Australian history in a medium—videotape—that schoolkids were prepared to absorb. The result was that a new generation of youngsters was granted some knowledge of a past that spoke to them in a way many of their parents never had.

Gallipoli and its Anzac legend had been marginalised as those parents, young themselves in the 1960s and 1970s, grappled with the divisions and confusions accompanying the Vietnam War, the Whitlam era and its dismissal, the rise of feminism, the subtleties of multiculturalism, the explosion of consumerism and the vacuous search for meaning in postmodernism.

There seemed little place for memories of an old war during the upheavals of the 1960s and 1970s as the nation's most affluent and self-indulgent population bulge—the baby boomers, my own generation—tried to re-make society and the world in their own image. Young Australian and New Zealand travellers in Turkey in the late 1960s and through the 1970s were more intent on trading Kombi vans and blissing out at Istanbul's Pudding Shop than spending time at Anzac Cove.

But something insidious was at work in the Australian heart during that period. While the anti-Vietnam movement of the late 1960s and early 1970s defined a large part of a generation's view of war, another slice of that same generation was in uniform, fighting in the rubber plantations, the jungles and the paddy fields of Vietnam itself.

More than 500 Australians died in Vietnam, but their deaths were not often universally mourned and honoured in the manner accorded Australia's war dead through all previous conflicts. Young Diggers, many of them conscripted into the armed forces, found themselves reviled by protestors on the streets when they returned from Vietnam. This treatment was so shocking and alien to the Digger culture that it caused deep and lasting trauma in the lives of many Vietnam veterans. Late in the war, it became routine for soldiers returning to both Australia and New Zealand to fly home dressed in civilian clothes in order to avoid becoming the target of protesters. Men in uniform were spat upon.

Anti-Vietnam War attitudes were undoubtedly valid. The United States-led action to prop up South Vietnam's corrupt regime rested on a platform of lies and a daft Domino Theory that saw communism swamping all Southeast Asia if South Vietnam fell to the red tide. The Domino theorists chose to ignore a simpler truth—Vietnam was involved in a post-colonial civil war. Australia simply blundered blindly along in America's wake. The political establishment also chose to turn its back on the Australian tradition of fielding all-volunteer military forces and began conscripting 20-year-old men. They were judged old enough to lose their lives at war, but too young to vote (the voting age at the time was 21).

Dissent was inevitable. However, large sections of the anti-war movement's views mutated into vitriolic anti-Digger sentiment. An unpopular war had turned reverence for the Anzac spirit on its head. In World War I, able-bodied men who failed to sign up and sail away often found themselves handed a white feather by women on the streets. The feather denoted cowardice. Half a century later, at the height of the anti-Vietnam period, able-bodied men who signed up and sailed away returned to be taunted as 'baby killers'.

A measure of the depth of the divisions in Australian society was that the Vietnam Diggers—who after all were nothing more than instruments of their nation's government policies—were not given a welcome home march when the last of them were withdrawn from the conflict in 1972. No ticker-tape, no bunting, no cheering crowds. The veterans and the nurses who had patched them up were expected to creep politely away, and many of them did, taking their bitterness and their confusion with them and storing it within their hearts. It was a shameful stain on Australia's soul, one which claimed more lives through suicide, alcoholism and torn families.

It was not until 3 October 1987—fifteen years after the end of Australia's role in the Vietnam War—that veterans were given their first official welcome home parade. Around 25 000 veterans marched through the streets of Sydney, many of them weeping openly. Hundreds of thousands of civilians turned out to cheer them. It amounted to a lancing of a boil that had been infected for too long.

I suspect the parade prompted within many adult Australians a deep, private and perhaps guilt-stricken reassessment of personal attitudes to veterans in general. With Vietnam-era soldiers finally welcomed home, the awkward arguments and the embarrassing exclusion of a generation of soldiers from the national story were no longer relevant. It was possible to take a fresh look at the role of soldiering in the Australian narrative. This re-examination revealed one stark fact that had received relatively scant attention: the oldest soldiers, the Anzacs, were dying out. In a country short on historically defining moments, the physical links to Australia's most enduring legend were fading away, day by day. Soon enough, there would be no one left to relate first-hand the stories of Gallipoli. The realisation gave birth to what would become a massive reawakening of enthusiasm for Anzac Day and all it represented, particularly among the young.

The irony is inescapable. Belated recognition for one group of Australian veterans who had been all but invisible for years helped set the scene for a renewed fascination with ancient veterans who were disappearing forever.

Into this environment was released Masters' documentary, with its message that Gallipoli was an accessible and spiritually engaging destination for those wishing to commune with the spirit of Anzac.

Two years later, while *The Fatal Shore* was still being absorbed by the baby boomers' kids, Prime Minister Bob Hawke spent $10 million taking 58 Anzac veterans to Gallipoli for the 75th Anzac Day in 1990. The old men flew in a chartered jumbo jet with a medical team—the youngest, after all, was 91 and the oldest 103. Opposition Leader John Hewson and other political leaders—including those of New Zealand and Britain—attended, and Australian warships stood off the cove. The event gained enormous media coverage, commemorative stamps were issued, *Gallipoli* the movie was revived and newspapers, radio and TV carried special features about the meaning of Anzac. Back home, there were more marchers in Anzac Day parades, and vastly more onlookers lining the streets, than had been seen for years.

Anzac, and the distant site that gave birth to the word—no longer simply an acronym—was back.

In Çanakkale, Hanifi divined the gathering tramp of feet and decided he needed to expand. There was only one travel agency dealing with Australian and New Zealand visitors and it offered little more than a short bus tour of the battlefields. Hanifi decided to establish his own travel agency, linked to Anzac House. He recognised early that most of the new visitors were young, had limited budgets and were accustomed to staying in hostel-style accommodation. He renovated his hotel to include dormitories, banged out walls to build new bathrooms and installed a system that guaranteed hot water 24 hours a day—a revolution in 1990.

His travel agency needed a catchy name. When Hanifi heard young Australians using the term 'hassle' to denote problems, he dubbed his new business Hassle Free Tours. He wanted to promote the idea that his tours took the problems out of the Gallipoli experience. And he figured that anyone who would travel halfway across the world to visit Gallipoli needed more time than a night and a day to attend the Anzac Day ceremonies. So he designed four-day guided tours, including buses travelling to and from Istanbul, where travel agents push his products. By 1995 he had linked his empire to the Internet, and the Anzac House Website evolved into the most impressive in the business.

While all this was happening, others set up in competition. The best-known set up right across the water in Eceabat: TJ's Tours. TJ is a likeable young man named Ilhami Gezici. He has spent much of his life on the Gallipoli Peninsula, where he says his great-grandfather died in the fighting in 1915—for the Turkish side. In 1996, he fell in love with and married an Australian taking one of his tours, Bernina Aitchison, of Corowa on the Murray River. Bernina believes her own great-grandfather fought at Gallipoli, although a complicated family history makes confirmation difficult. And so the world turns. TJ and Bernina have their own hostel at Eceabat, and a TJ's tour includes soulful moments of silence on Anzac Cove, a rendition via ghetto blaster of Eric Bogle's 'And the Band Played Waltzing

Matilda' followed by 'The Last Post'. TJ has moved into cyber-space too, and his Website offers a service guaranteed to find the gravesite of any Commonwealth soldier buried on the peninsula. He will also arrange a photo or a charcoal engraving of a head-stone for visitors who discover later that they have a relative beneath the ground at Gallipoli.

Hanifi didn't blink when I mentioned I had met TJ. He didn't comment either. Competition in the Anzac trade, clearly, was fierce. Indeed, both Anzac House and TJ's Tours and Hostel offer similar package tours and their prices tell a story about Gallipoli.

Any day of the year, a traveller wishing to stay in one of their hostels, or most of the other budget establishments around the area, can get a bed for somewhere between US$5 and US$9— any day, that is, but the four days over the Anzac Day peak, from 23–27 April. During that period, the house-full signs go up, and accommodation is limited to those travellers who have booked a full tour package, which includes transport to and from Istanbul, some meals, tours of the Gallipoli battlefields, transport to and from the Anzac Day ceremonies on the peninsula and a tour to the ancient ruins of Troy. These packages require advance payment by bank draft or credit card in British pounds. Anzac House prices start at £189 and TJ's at £159. These are signifi-cant figures for an Australian, who is required to fork over almost $3 for every British pound. But if you want a roof over your head around Anzac Day and a bus ride to the Peninsula on the impossibly crowded night before the dawn service, this is the sort of money you need to start thinking about.

The fact that the tour prices are quoted in British pounds tells another side of the story. The large majority of young trav-ellers during the Anzac period do not fly in from Australia or New Zealand. They come from London, where a couple of hundred thousand of them live and work these days. It has become a rite of passage similar to the 1960s when young Antipodeans thirsty for an experience beyond Sydney or Auckland turned Earl's Court into Kangaroo Valley. One leaves school or university, saves enough money to fly to London (and perhaps visit Southeast Asia or Africa on the way), gets a job in a bar or as a nanny, takes a flat with a few mates and begins saving British pounds. Armed with one of the strongest currencies in the world, the doors of Western and Eastern Europe, the Greek Isles, the Middle East and northern Africa are wide open, and each is only a short flight away compared with the journey from the Southern Hemisphere. Turkey, with its weak currency, is a bargain for anyone with a money-belt containing British pounds or Euros. Magazines set up specifically for young Australians and New Zealanders in London, such as *TNT* or *LAM*, fairly bulge with offers of cheap flights and lightning tours to Gallipoli, and bus or truck tours across the continent and around Turkey with a stop-over for Anzac.

An alternative is to fly independently to Istanbul and to find a travel agent offering one of dozens of quickie tours costing between £40 and £50 that provide a rushed bus trip from Istanbul on 24 April, a night in the open on the peninsula and a late bus trip back to Istanbul after the Anzac Day ceremonies. It's an exhausting journey that offers little opportunity to gain a real appreciation of the battlefields, but thousands who have only limited time visit Gallipoli this way simply to attend the ceremonies.

The truly independent find their own way to the peninsula and rely on pot luck at the numerous hostels and hotels at Çanakkale or Eceabat, or pitch a tent wherever there is a piece of open ground.

Those who require a higher level of comfort and a less frantic itinerary need to visit a travel agent in Australia or New

The Blue Mosque floats easily on its hill, resting on the foundations of long-gone civilisations at the peak of Sultanahmet, Istanbul.

A shaft of sunlight illuminates one of the hundreds of passages in the Covered Bazaar—also known as the Grand Bazaar—in Istanbul. This is the lair of the most in-your-face merchants in the world.

Cappadocia, home of the underground people. Chapels, temples, tunnels, cells, homes and entire underground cities are burrowed into the Earth over a vast area. The passage of time has exposed the secrets of many of these natural citadels dotted across the bewitching landscape.

From the heights of the Anzac between Walker's Ridge (right) and The Sphinx (left) Turkish snipers had a clear view down to North Beach and the little point of Ari Burnu—where the first Anzac soldiers came ashore on 25 April, 1915—and across the azure Aegean Sea.

Anzac Cove, a sacred place to Australians and New Zealanders, is nothing more than a small sweep of beach beneath the fierce slopes of the Gallipoli Peninsula. The foundations of Watson's Pier can still be seen (bottom centre).

The Anzac Commemorative Site sits above North Beach, a few hundred metres north of Anzac Cove, where thousands gather each year for the dawn service.

The Turkish Memorial, where the entire Turkish 57th Regiment died on 25 April, 1915, defending the heights of Chunuk Bair. The memorial is both a graveyard and a mosque.

A single Judas Tree in glorious bloom spreads its branches over the graves in Shrapnel Valley.

The Statue of Respect of the Turkish Soldier honours an extraordinary moment of bravery and compassion on the first day of fighting at Anzac. During the heat of battle on the slopes beneath Chunuk Bair, an unarmed Turkish soldier walked from his trench, lifted a wounded British soldier and carried him to the safety of the Anzac trenches. The story was documented by Lieutenant, later Governor-General, Richard Casey.

The air, during the relentless months of fighting at Anzac, was often alive with bullets. At the Kabatepe Museum, these astonishing relics sit behind glass.

A lonesome pine, buffeted by wind, stands above the gravestones of the Lone Pine Cemetery, where thousands of men died fighting for a piece of land no bigger than a football field.

On Anzac Day, thousands of Australians cram together, protecting the graves of the Lone Pine Cemetery, for a memorial service where the mood swings between that of a high-spirited big day out and the awestruck goosebumps of a ritual you might expect in a cathedral.

The gang from the Boomerang Bar sets off for the Anzac dawn service aboard a gypsy cart. Earlier in the night, the Boomerang Bar truck had blown up, stranding the little group of pilgrims.

Gregg pets a feathered friend outside the Boomerang Bar, Eceabat.

When the first soldiers landed on 25 April, they were confronted by a natural outcrop, which reared above the beach. Fresh from training on the Plain of Giza outside Cairo, they instantly christened it The Sphinx.

The Sphinx gradually emerges, a ghostly silhouette above a sea of young faces at the dawn beachside service.

Zealand, many months ahead of Anzac Day, to arrange a tour that suits. There are dozens of tours designed for every taste and age group, most of which also offer a swing around the more popular areas of Turkey. Some of the best are associated with the Australian War Memorial, ex-service organisations such as the RSL and war historians such as Dr Michael McKernan. Most good travel agencies can provide details, and some of the more useful Websites are detailed at the back of this book.

With competition growing, Hanifi has no intention of sitting still. His dreams are expansive, and a touch alarming to the authorities responsible for maintaining the integrity of the Gallipoli Peninsula Peace Park. Part of his vision, he told me, was already underway: he had bought fourteen horses and planned to conduct riding tours from a village on the peninsula called Buyukanafarta to the heights of the Anzac battlefields—a distance of about 8 kilometres. Hanifi was also investigating sea-kayaking tours around the peninsula.

If this sounded like Anzac was in danger of becoming a theme park, it was merely the start. Hanifi had ruffled feathers locally by taking over a decrepit building on the seafront across the strait at Eceabat, and was pouring money into it. For years it had been known simply as The Vegemite Bar, and attracted a rowdy crowd of Antipodean wanderers. But Hanifi saw its position right on the water as an opportunity to introduce a little class. In the weeks before I arrived, he had renamed it the Maydos Vegemite Bar and Restaurant, brought in builders and decorators and was busily drawing up plans to install motel-style units on the roof. God knows what the Kraft company thought of the use of its copyrighted Vegemite brand on a Turkish restaurant and bar. Those travelling on Hassle Free Tours would be served lunch there before venturing to the battlefields, said Hanifi, entirely unconcerned. Anyway, he had more immediate matters to engage him about the use of the Vegemite Bar—an aggrieved local, who had apparently operated the Vegemite Bar previously, was threatening Hanifi with legal action, claiming among other things that he had no right to rebuild the old place. Hanifi appeared to be accustomed to ignoring such minor aggravations—he told me he envisaged a wharf out the front, a private boat to ferry passengers back and forth across the Dardanelles and perhaps even a large craft to sail guests all the way to Anzac Cove and North Beach for the Anzac Day ceremonies. 'Land them on the beach, just like the soldiers,' he said.

I was, I suspect, displaying disbelief at the audacity of Hanifi's commercial plans. He switched to a new vision of promoting closer cultural ties between Australians, New Zealanders and Çanakkale.

'We need a real festival here,' he said. 'A peace festival, celebrating peace between the Turks and the Anzacs. Ninety per cent of Australians and New Zealanders who visit Turkey come for Gallipoli, and we need to make this a greater cultural connection. I don't want only to sell beer and food and beds. So I think, what can we do? We could have music groups from our countries performing together; there could be plays, art, a conference, sporting groups. Çanakkale's young boys could learn to play Rugby, maybe.'

In fact, the Çanakkale university had set out to create cultural exchanges, complete with a conference on the Anzac and Turkish perspectives on the Gallipoli campaign. Hanifi thought this was all very fine, but the academics had started planning only three months before. He, on the other hand, had been in the business for more than ten years. 'We have to use the knowledge people like me have gathered,' he said. Modesty is not a quality readily attached to Hanifi.

While we had been chatting, a handful of young Australians and Kiwis had wandered in to Anzac House, and a busload of Hassle Free tourists had taken to the chairs in the back, awaiting the next showing of the *Gallipoli* movie and *The Fatal Shore* documentary.

Most of the hostels in Çanakkale and Eceabat pay daily obeisance to these two videos in recognition of their contribution to the growth in travel to Gallipoli Peninsula. Some of their posters proclaim, with mild inaccuracy: '*Gallipoli* with Mel; *The Deadly Shore*, every night'.

Fourteen years after he made the documentary, Chris Masters still gets occasional phone calls from total strangers who have arrived at Çanakkale. 'Chris, Chris,' they say, voices shaking with emotion. 'I'm in Gallipoli and I've just seen your film and I saw it at school and I just had to tell you.'

While I had been paying attention to Hanifi's concept of an Anzac Disneyworld, Tom had fallen into conversation with a young woman who had arrived fresh in Çanakkale after flying London–Frankfurt–Istanbul and taking the bus. One look and I knew she was a Queenslander—sun bleached hair, open face and confident enough to travel alone. Her name was Philippa Holmes, and she was in town on her own form of Anzac business. She opened a large bag she was carrying and produced an item that proved beyond doubt that she was from Queensland: a neoprene stubby-holder. The thing was emblazoned with the Australian and New Zealand flags and the words Anzac Day–Gallipoli–Turkey.

Hanifi lost interest in our conversation. It was obvious he knew instinctively that this strange object was an addition to the Gallipoli industry, but had no idea what it actually was.

Tom strode to the drinks fridge and pulled out a small bottle of Efes beer. He took the stubby holder from Philippa and fitted it to the bottle. 'See, keeps it cool,' he said. Hanifi burst into a wide grin and introduced himself to Philippa. He wanted the rights to any stock she could provide, before anyone else got the same idea.

Philippa, it soon transpired, was no easy mark for Hanifi's tilt at empire. She had built herself a business as an events organiser around Britain and Europe for the past two years, and her brother Andrew was a wetsuit manufacturer back on Queensland's Gold Coast. Using wetsuit material, he also designed stubby coolers, which had become a sideline for his sister at large events, from Wimbledon to major soccer competitions. The Anzac–Gallipoli coolers were a new idea, she said, and she figured they might pay for her tour to the peninsula for Anzac Day.

While Hanifi set to the business of trying to persuade Philippa to agree to a deal giving him retail rights to the stubby holders (an arrangement that he never managed to pull off), Tom and I made plans for our first excursion to the battlefields. We approached the receptionist and booked seats on a Hassle Free mini-bus tour for the following morning.

I had not come to Gallipoli for a guided bus tour, but it was included in my pre-paid package deal and it seemed a shame to squander the opportunity to experience what, for many visitors, is the feature of their journey.

We left next morning in the care of Captain Ali Efe, a former skipper of a Turkish naval submarine who is a military historian at Çanakkale's university. A pixie of a man given to chuckling merrily at his own obscure jokes at every opportunity, he has gained a reputation as one of the more entertaining of Gallipoli's battlefield guides.

'Do we have any English on board?' he inquired before we set off. When he established that his passengers were six

Australians, two South Africans, an American and a New Zealander, he seemed deeply relieved. 'Oh, very good,' he said. 'We don't need the English coming with us, do we?' It was Ali's view that the British had led the colonials into a disaster. He knew his audience, and he didn't want his theatrical view of events constrained by the presence of Britons. I wondered whether he had an alternative script at the ready for a tour that included British travellers, who had lost many thousands more of their ancestors on the peninsula than had Australians and New Zealanders.

Ali handed out lunchpacks as a ferry took us from Çanakkale across to the peninsula. He told us he lost a grandfather and a great-uncle in the battles of 1915 and that, as a child, his father had taken him on hundreds of walking expeditions around the old battlefields. 'This was very much a local army, and thousands and thousands of families around this area lost one, two, three or more men. This is still a place of pilgrimage for them, just as it is for you,' he said.

We bounced between fields of tomatoes, sunflowers, watermelons and groves of olives as we crossed the peninsula, and shepherds stood by the road with small flocks of sheep. We stopped briefly at a new war museum near the old village of Kapatepe. The building sits on a rise with a view along the coast to the north and a Turkish artillery unit once sat nearby, terrorising the Anzacs a couple of kilometres along the beach. The museum was so packed with Turkish schoolchildren we found it difficult to catch a glimpse of its displays of war relics torn uniforms, weapons, two bullets that had hit each other mid-air and had fused together and, grotesquely, the skull of a Turkish soldier with a bullet lodged in the forehead.

We set off on the coastal road to Anzac Cove. Shortly before the cove, Ali pointed to a valley disappearing into the hills rising from the beach. 'Shell Green,' he said. The valley floor there is one of the only level pieces of ground on the whole Anzac battlefield, and as the secret evacuation was being arranged at the end of the 1915 conflict, officers arranged a cricket match to be staged in an effort to feign nonchalance. It wasn't much of a match—shrapnel burst overhead and no one kept score during the few minutes the game lasted, although war historian Charles Bean managed to snap a photo of the event. In May 2001 Steve Waugh and the Australian cricket team visited Gallipoli and restaged the match at Shell Green. Ali was their guide.

'They were huge men,' said little Ali. 'But I didn't understand their game. They were throwing the ball so fast and trying to hit it and running in every direction.' He wheezed with laughter at the memory.

We drove past Anzac Cove on our left, the entrance to Shrapnel Valley on our right and along North Beach to the Anzac Commemorative site where the Anzac Day dawn ceremony has been held since 2000. A long white stone plinth stretched immediately above the beach, and a lawn spread between the plinth and the road above. Set immediately below the road was a stone wall inset with panels depicting the events of the Anzac campaign. The whole site was a natural bowl backing on to the most captivating natural feature of the battlefield, The Sphinx. A massive outcrop of weathered yellow rock and soil reared into the skyline. From the top jutted a shape that instantly reminded the Anzacs who poured on to the beach below on the morning of 25 April 1915 of the Sphinx of Giza. Every one of them was familiar with the Sphinx—they had trained beneath it on the Giza plain in Egypt.

Rain began falling as our little tour party clambered around the commemorative site. I didn't mind—I had been here before and I could return to the battlefields any time I wished over the next week to explore at my own pace. But I felt a bit sorry for the other travellers on the bus. Apart from Tom, this was their one chance to see Anzac, and the rain was getting heavier. As we drove along, it sheeted the windows, obscuring the view. But Tom and the other passengers appeared to have entered a state of grace—they leapt from the bus at every stop and hurried around, ignoring the rain and halting reverently before every site, every sign, as if each held the key to an inner truth.

We began climbing towards the plateau of Lone Pine, and stopped at a statue of a Turkish soldier cradling a wounded man in his arms. The Statue of Respect of the Turkish Soldier honours one of the more extraordinary events of the Gallipoli campaign, which was witnessed and detailed by a young Australian lieutenant, Richard Casey, who later became Lord Casey, an Australian Governor-General. Casey's account of the event is etched at the foot of the statue:

At Chunuk Bair on 25th April, 1915 there was heavy trench fighting between the Turks and the Allies. The distance between the trenches was between eight and ten metres. Cease-fire was called after a bayonet attack and the soldiers returned to their trenches. There were heavy casualties on both sides and each collected their dead and wounded. From between the two trench lines came a call, a cry for help from an English Captain who was very badly wounded in the leg. Unfortunately no one could leave their trenches because the slightest movement resulted in the firing of hundreds of bullets. At that moment, an incredible event occurred. A piece of white underwear was raised from one of the Turkish trenches and a well-built, unarmed soldier appeared. Everyone was stunned and we stared in amazement. The Turk walked slowly to the wounded British soldier and gently lifted him, took him in his arms and started to walk towards our trenches. He placed him down on the ground near us and then straight-away returned to his trench. We couldn't even thank him.

This courageous and beautiful act of the Turkish Soldier has been spoken about many times on the battlefields. Our love and deepest respect to this brave and heroic soldier.

Ali, for once, had nothing to say. An Australian had said it all for him, on the first day of the Gallipoli campaign.

Ali's view of the campaign was unashamedly patriotic. At each of the major sites we visited—Lone Pine, the heights of Chunuk Bair—he gave a lecture offering differing viewpoints of the campaign from the Anzac and the Turkish perspectives. Unsurprisingly, these were diametrically opposed.

The Anzac view of the evacuation from the peninsula at the end of 1915 has always been that it was a cunningly conceived, immensely successful operation that totally fooled the Turks. Not an Australian or a Kiwi was killed as thousands of men crept to the beaches, their feet muffled with torn blankets and hessian bags, to be rowed out to waiting ships. Rifles were rigged to fire through the night, triggered by water dripping into buckets, to mislead the Turks into believing the Anzacs were still in the hills.

Ali snorted at the very idea. 'Can you imagine that thousands and thousands of men could just walk away with the Turks, not 20 metres away with a perfect view from the top of the ridges, not being aware?' he demanded. 'It is ridiculous. For centuries the Turks have had a policy that you do not harrass a retreating enemy. In this case, they did not want to shoot the enemy in the back. The Turkish men wanted to go home to their wives. They were happy to see the Anzacs go home to their wives, too.'

Ali's view has little official historical backing and there is much evidence to the contrary, but it was certainly shared by a Gallipoli veteran from Queensland, Robert Ellwood, who spent his time at Anzac as an unmounted trooper from the 2nd Light Horse. He died some years ago, but in his later years he gave a fascinating, extended interview recorded by the Professor of History at Townsville's James Cook University, Dr Paul Turnbull. Ellwood, who Turnbull told me was a sharp observer with an extremely detailed and lucid memory, was in no doubt that the Turks knew in advance of the evacuation and chose to look the other way.

> *Ellwood:* Did I ever tell you what my opinion of the evacuation was?
>
> *Turnbull:* No, you didn't.
>
> *Ellwood:* Do you mind if we digress?
>
> *Turnbull:* Not at all.
>
> *Ellwood:* I am of the opinion that it was not as it is written, that we escaped from the Peninsula by magnificent strategy or tactics or whatever you like to call it. There isn't the slightest doubt in my mind that the Turk knew every movement that went on in our part of the line. And as for saying that we got away without loss and without the Turk knowing about it and all this paraphernalia that attached to the evacuation—in my estimation it is all baloney. Personally . . . it may be of value, it may not be—[my belief] is the Turk was just as pleased to see us go off the peninsula as we were to go off. And as for saying that he didn't know we went off was all my eye and brother Murphy. That's my candid opinion, probably destroying a very nice fanciful piece of warfare, but that's my opinion of it.

Ellwood told Turnbull he had good reason for his belief: he had a friend named Harry Stone, a signaller who was seconded to the ship being used as headquarters of the Gallipoli campaign about a fortnight before the evacuation began. When Harry Stone returned to his unit on Anzac, he said the 'GOC' (General Officer Commanding the expeditionary force) had been in wireless contact with 'Kemal Pacha'. The full name of the Turkish commander who would late become Ataturk was Mustafa Kemal Pasha. 'You can put your own interpretation on it,' Ellwood told Turnbull.

As our little bus continued through the rain on a high ridge road that had been the front line in 1915, I looked down to the sea and imagined Turkish soldiers doing the same thing. Perhaps some of them saw the Anzacs creeping away, perhaps not. It seemed not to matter, anyway, after all these years.

The other travellers on Ali's tour were moved and impressed with the day's outing, and a young couple from Tasmania seemed close to tears when Ali solemnly handed to each of us tiny boxes containing a bullet and a piece of shrapnel. He had collected thousands of these, he said, during his walks on the peninsula with his father as a child.

I had not bothered to detail much of the trip in my diary. My real exploration of the battlefields was ahead, but now I had a clear idea of the main route in my head.

Naturally, the rain stopped as the bus rocked back across the peninsula, and a weak sun appeared.

We had a bit of time in Eceabat before the ferry left for Çanakkale, and I watched a young man hopping speedily across the town square. He appeared to have a club foot, or perhaps his ankle had been broken and hadn't mended properly. He approached several travellers waiting at the wharf and inquired whether anyone needed accommodation. 'Come, I will show you,' he implored, but there were no takers. I nodded to him, and he began his routine. I told him I was staying at Anzac House and he shrugged. 'That's okay,' he said. 'If you have friends who want a room, tell them to see me. I am always here.' He pointed to a building overlooking the Dardanelles. 'Hotel Ece,' he said. 'Clean rooms, a view across the water, very cheap.'

His name was Paul, and over the next few days, I would recognise him as an expert hustler. A traveller couldn't approach the wharf without meeting Paul.

Back at Anzac House, Tom and I popped a beer and discussed the day's journey as a small group of young Australians gathered. Gradually, we introduced ourselves and pulled tables together.

Philippa, the stubby-holder girl, had been out checking business opportunities, and she arrived with a young bloke from Melbourne, Ben Chapple, in tow. Ben, who had spent months travelling around India, had met Philippa at Frankfurt airport on their separate journeys to Turkey, and already they were mates.

Chris Landsdowne, from Brisbane, had drifted to Turkey from Cairo. Another Queenslander, Gregg Sonnenburg, had met Chris up the coast a week before after flying in from Hong Kong having spent months in Asia. Matt Moffatt, a surfer from Coffs Harbour, had found his way to Çanakkale alone through Bulgaria.

Over a few beers, we recognised in each other the comfort of company at the end of a long road. Someone suggested food. I knew from my first trip to Çanakkale of a kebap house up the street, and we trooped off as if we had known each other since school.

Over spicy lentil soup, Turkish pizzas cooked in a wood-fired oven, flat bread hot from the same oven and plates of kebaps and salads, our conversation slipped hazily and a bit self-consciously around our reasons for coming to Gallipoli, the strangeness of commemorating a defeat and what Anzac Day meant.

Chris had the strongest claim of our little gathering to a familial link to Gallipoli. Both his great-grandfathers had fought on the Anzac battlefields—one from New Zealand, the other an Australian.

He said he had always felt a bit guilty for sleeping in and missing Anzac Day dawn services in Australia. But he had vowed to go to Gallipoli after he arrived in London in 1998 and his best friend had told him: 'things ya gotta do while you're here—run with the bulls in Pamplona; Paddy's Day in

Dublin; Munich beer fest; Anzac Day, Gallipoli'. Four years later, Chris had finally taken the last bit of advice, and was trying hard not to be overwhelmed by his physical presence at Gallipoli. Anzac Day, if it was to remain relevant, had to be dedicated to every Australian who had been in a war, he maintained.

'We shouldn't get bogged down in Gallipoli,' said Chris. 'This is where it all started, and that's why we're here, but I reckon it has to be for all conflicts.'

Ben didn't like the sound of the word 'conflict'. 'It ought to be about putting war behind us, and remembering what damage war causes,' he said. 'Do you think humans could be capable of evolving out of violence?'

Philippa thought defending your country was important. She had, she said, seriously considered joining the Army Reserve, but her family had talked her out of it. She had wanted to visit Gallipoli for years, and she seemed slightly surprised to find herself there.

Matt confessed that he didn't know enough about the Gallipoli campaign and had come to learn about it. He felt he had missed out on something that an Australian was supposed to know, and he wasn't sure whether he just hadn't listened properly when he was younger, or whether teachers had let him down.

I wondered whether any of them thought the surge in enthusiasm for making the trek to Gallipoli was limited to a particular section of Australia's community—the children of an older, less complicated country that existed before World War II, before it had embraced immigrants from Europe, Asia and the Middle East. The last time I had been at the Anzac Day ceremonies, the crowd appeared to display a uniformity rarely seen in a big Australian city these days.

Could it be, I mused, that Australians of predominantly Anglo-Celtic backgrounds were feeling a bit insecure about their place in multicultural Australia, and were seeking a distinctive niche all the way over here in Gallipoli with their great-grandfathers? And in doing so, could we be creating a new twist on old-time cultural exclusivity?

The suggestion provoked heat, as if I had accused the lot of us of some esoteric form of racism. The reaction felt right—these were people with a bit of passion about them, prepared to confront and challenge ideas. I wasn't surprised—everyone at the table was travelling independently, and that took confidence. We would all be in town for days until the big crowds began turning up shortly before Anzac Day. I felt comfortable with these people, but if we were to be companions would we bore each other silly or would there be a spark?

Matt, whose intense focus on the discussion was beginning to alter my initial impression of a free and easy surfer boy, mulled over what I had said and decided that perhaps there was something to the theory about the predominance of Anglo-Celtic Australians at Gallipoli. 'I mean, look at us,' he said. We all laughed, but I noticed most of us looked surreptitiously at each other.

Somehow, Matt thought, Anzac Day had to be broadened to include everyone, whether they had a link to an older Australia or not.

No one had a clear idea how that could be done, although someone suggested that if Australia Day was abandoned—on the basis that hardly anyone knew or cared much about what it was supposed to represent—then Anzac Day would become the country's real one day of the year, and it would naturally belong to everyone.

Eventually we agreed that it was hardly surprising that a lot of the people who considered Anzac Day important enough to attract them all the way to Gallipoli were likely to be descended from families that might have had a boy out here in 1915.

It was becoming a dry argument. The restaurant served no alcohol, but Tom had noticed a bottle shop down the street.

We paid a few dollars for our humble banquet, bought a few bottles of Turkish red wine and wandered back to Anzac House, which seemed all but empty. A lone young Australian sat at a table, writing a letter. His name was Angus Hall, and he joined us as we pinched glasses from the kitchen for nightcaps.

Angus was a Customs officer who had spent time on patrol boats intercepting people-smuggling vessels off the northern Australian coast. He said it was a job that required respect for those arriving as asylum seekers, and there was a barely perceptible flicker of admonition when I inquired what he thought of the government bringing in the Navy to keep such people off Australian shores. It was a subject, I gathered, that he wasn't about to discuss.

Angus was travelling solo, and he had his own story about coming to Gallipoli. He had known vaguely, he said, that three of his great-uncles had fought in World War I.

'But I really took no interest in the family story until I told my mother I planned to travel to Gallipoli,' he said.

'She told me there was something I should see. She pulled an old box from underneath a bed and opened it, and inside were all these letters, diaries, postcards and photos of three boys, all brothers, in their Army uniforms. There were pebbles from the campaigns they had been on, and I suppose there were pebbles from Anzac Cove. The box had been left to my family by my grandmother.

'But what really hit me were three pieces of white silk, each with a red cross on it. When a boy was killed in the war, a piece of white cloth with a red cross was sent to his mother, so she could put it in the window and everyone would know she had lost a son. And here were three of them, one for each son. It meant that in a small place in South Australia, this poor woman, my great-grandmother, had lost three sons. I don't even know all their names, even though they were my great-uncles. One of them was Angus McNeil, because I was named after him.

'It was an amazing thing, complete disbelief, seeing all these things for the first time and reading the letters and the diaries. It was very hard to come to grips with what the mother of three boys must have gone through. So being here is pretty special.'

Angus the Customs officer had a calm gentleness about him, and I was willing to believe he handled asylum seekers with consideration.

His story left our kebap salon chatter scattered in the wind. We sipped our wine, travellers adrift in our own thoughts.

9

A BOAT TO ANZAC

This was the way to see Anzac from the sea, and by the way the Turkish men sheltering with their cigarettes in the lee of the bridge stared curiously at us, it was pretty clear few foreigners found their way on to this deck.

The sea. You have to look at Anzac from the water, because it defines the place as much as the ridges and the gullies. It fits: Australia and New Zealand, islands of immigration, are given their meanings by the ocean.

Homer, whose epic poem the *Iliad* was set hereabouts, mused of the 'wine-dark sea', causing pedants to doubt the accuracy of his imagery. Homer, if he actually existed, was blind and a poet at that, and he was referring to the Mediterranean, but there were fierce days 29 centuries after he was creating his endless tales of love and conflict when the waters of the Aegean, a branch of the Mediterranean, ran dark as the reddest wine.

It was from the water that the Anzacs had come to Gallipoli, and it was back to the water they went when the whole escapade revealed itself, even to the madmen who had set it rolling, to be no longer worth all that blood.

Anzac Cove and North Beach alone on the peninsula gave the men any real pleasure in the months they were there—they would bathe naked, sometimes on horseback, ridding themselves of the filth of the trenches, gaining brief relief from the lice that infested them and reminding them, perhaps, that they came from places where beaches meant blissful indolence and holidays. Young Victorian soldiers with a fine dry wit gave the name Brighton Beach to the long curving stretch around the corner from the Cove, apparently in honour of the strand at Brighton, Melbourne, where bathing boxes line the shore. No bathing boxes at Gallipoli's Brighton, though. Turkish artillery had a clear shot right down its length.

Anzac Cove hunkers between two points—Hell Spit shielding it from the south, Ari Burnu a few hundred metres to the north—and so offered some protection from direct gunshot. Its waters beckoned the soldiers down from the ridges and blessed them, even though the young swimmers died or were wounded with depressing regularity as they frolicked beneath showers of shrapnel from shells bursting above.

'A good deal of shrapnel during the day,' wrote great-uncle George Moore on 21 June 1915. 'One of the boys killed while in swimming. Big mail arrived.'

The following day, George wrote: 'Shrapnel fairly warm all day. Two 5th Battery boys wounded while in swimming. Zeppelin reported in the vicinity. Carried boxes from the base.'

Reading these laconic notes from 87 years ago, Tom and I knew that we must swim at Anzac Cove. The commander of the Australian and New Zealand Army Corps, Lieutenant-General William Birdwood, himself had been an enthusiast of the water, and when a photographer caught him bare-bummed in the sea, flashing a cheeky grin over his shoulder at the camera, the picture caused a sensation when it was published in the Australian newspapers. Readers, apparently shocked by the idea of an unclad general enjoying himself in brief respite from all the real obscenity of young lives wasting around him, sent parcel after parcel to him, all of them containing bathing togs to conceal the body in which he was born. The fact that not a woman was within Cooee of the cove, or that the men of Anzac by then could not give a hoot about the sight of another man's body so long as it was still breathing, seemed not to have entered the minds of all those good souls back home who felt the need to rummage around for swimming costumes for the unchaste general.

But for days after we arrived at the peninsula, the weather was shitty, persuading Tom and I to postpone our desire for a dip. A keen wind swept the straits, and the Aegean sulked beneath a sky of slate. Swimming would have to wait. Still, we knew we had to peer at the cliffs of Anzac from the sea. We needed a boat.

Late one afternoon, Tom and I wandered the pretty sea-front of Çanakkale as little fishing boats, shaped rather like Persian slippers with their toes curled high, came putt-putt-putting into the harbour after a day rolling about on the restless surface of the Dardanelles, dodging the scores of freighters that ply the straits ceaselessly.

Old men, and men not so old but whose faces had been weathered beyond their years by wind and salt and sun, gaffed ropes and buoys and stepped ashore in the dainty way of fishermen, as if it were the land and not the water that could not be trusted as a secure platform. From buckets they took handfuls of small, silvery fish and placed them on the wharf in shallow containers where they splashed about, waiting for buyers. The locals, parochial as locals anywhere, claim with an abandoned logic that if all the waters of the world dried up, you could still get the freshest fish at Çanakkale.

The fishermen stood in their rubber boots, smoking, stroking their whiskered cheeks and tossing jokes into the wind. We felt foolish as they chuckled among themselves because we couldn't understand a word. They couldn't understand a word from us either, even though we made dunderheads of ourselves inventing extravagant hand signals suggesting that wealth would fall their way if they were prepared to negotiate the hire of one of their craft.

The manager of the nearby marina wasn't much more help. He seemed to have some understanding that we wanted to take out a boat, but kept telling us we had to go to a nearby building and hand over our passports. We investigated the building and discovered it was the office of the harbour master. It was locked. We were left wondering about the need to leave our passports. Perhaps if we were to take out a boat, the authorities feared we might defect to the Greeks, just across the horizon.

Defeated, we beat our way back to the hostel through evening chill and the kebap hawkers, roast chestnut barrows, young men offering Chanel perfume very cheap, trucks and buses lining up for the ferry, tour company touts and furtive men insisting they simply wanted to ask a question. 'Excuse me, gentlemen,' they cried as we tried to brush past. 'Could I ask you a question?' The question would be the old one. 'Where are you from?' followed by the knowing 'Ah, you an Aussie, eh? How you going mate?' Followed by the offer to drink tea and meet a brother who, naturally, owned the finest carpet shop/pottery/ night club in town. We kept walking. 'You break my heart,' one of the shifty fellows called in our wake.

It was good fortune that we had failed to hire a boat. Gavin told me so. Gavin, I had already been informed, is the oracle of Çanakkale. His real name is not Gavin, of course. It is Guven Pinar, but he knows English speakers can't remember it so he has settled on the ocker Gavin.

He is a bear of a man, of indeterminate age, who would, if he were Greek, undoubtedly be called Zorba, though no one with regard to a healthy future would call a Turkish man by a Greek name. Gavin, who worked for years for American oil companies and speaks perfect English, acts as chief adviser to Hanifi in matters business, runs the Down Under tour company across the Narrows in Eceabat and is himself a tour guide of some note. He was at Anzac House to take care of some business and to have dinner—a great spread of rice in vine leaves, salads, meatballs, yoghurt dips and piles of flat bread prepared by Hanifi's sister.

A boat, declared Gavin between mouthfuls of the feast, would have to be a substantial craft to make the journey from the Dardanelles to Anzac Cove. It would have to round Cape Helles and beat into the Aegean Sea, and the waters at the Cape were turbulent. A suitable craft could, of course, be obtained. It would cost maybe US$400 for the trip. Even Gavin, a businessman, recognised this was out of the question. We began to feel even more dejected.

'There is a much cheaper way,' Gavin said, as if drawing me into a conspiracy. 'You can take the ferry from Kabatepe to Gökçaeda.'

I had no idea what he was talking about.

'The Australians knew Kabatepe as Gaba Tepe,' he said. 'And Gökçaeda is Turkey's biggest island. It was called Imbros. The English general Hamilton had his headquarters there.'

I felt like dancing.

Gaba Tepe is no more than 2 kilometres south of Anzac Cove. The Turks had artillery pieces in a grove of trees on a rise there that rained hell on the Anzacs. The men of Anzac coined a name for the gun in the Olive Grove that bothered them most. Beachy Bill they called it, as if such a breezy appellation could strip the thing of its terror.

Imbros was directly to the west, 24 kilometres out in the Aegean Sea. The troops on Anzac would find their souls soothed in the evenings as the sun sank into the ocean between Imbros and its sister Samothrace, home of the Great Gods, the Kabeiroi, wreathing the islands' craggy heights in gold and shooting the sky with every shade of red, from pink to ruby. I had thought often of finding a way to visit Imbros, but had all but abandoned it as too difficult. I knew I must see Gaba Tepe from the water and here was old Gavin offering a way for us to join both these places, and to look directly at Anzac from the sea while doing it. The ferry, in steaming out of Kabatepe and in returning from the island, would provide a perfect vantage point.

Gavin made a phone call and announced that the ferry still ran, that it left at 10.00 a.m. and returned late in the afternoon. Best of all, the journey would cost 1.5 million Turkish lira each way, which is about two-fifths of stuff all. Hardly any tourists knew about it, or if they did, they rarely used the service, Gavin said.

Tom and I could have kissed the old fellow's grizzled visage.

And so, a couple of days later, Tom and I found ourselves bustling about the corridors of Anzac House in the early morning gloom before most of our new friends had thought of rising from their beds after a night of mild revelry involving red wine.

After the ferry ride from Çanakkale to Eceabat, we needed only to find the dolmus across the peninsula to Kabatepe. A dolmus is nothing but a mini-bus that goes nowhere until every seat is filled and there is not a square centimetre of standing room left.

The dolmus was there by the ferry terminal in Eceabat, but no one was aboard. We could have stayed in bed another hour.

Paul, the boy with the club foot, called us over to his side of the street to take coffee. He introduced me to his friend, a handsome young man in dark sunglasses. 'He has been to Australia,' said Paul. 'He is going back to get married.'

This was true, said the sunglassed one. He was going to live on an eel farm in east Gippsland, Victoria. The family of his future wife owned the eel farm. He looked very pleased with the arrangement.

I told Paul we had advised several other travellers, unable to find accommodation, that they should seek him out and stay at his hostel, the Ece Hotel. The boy with the sunglasses took a sudden interest. 'How much commission is he paying you?' he inquired, nodding towards Paul, who was hopping across the road at speed, searching out new customers. When I told him I wouldn't think of seeking commission, he peered at me as if I were touched by the sun. 'Really?' he said. 'You should. That's the way things are done.' And then he turned away. There was, clearly, no point talking to someone who didn't understand business principles.

The dolmus began filling as the next ferry docked. Men with flapping overcoats stood on the ship's landing ramp, leaping to the concrete wharf before it had lowered, and ran for the little bus. We had seen this coming and already had seats. The machine grumbled away, squatting on its haunches, its suspension wrecked by a thousand over-loaded journeys.

A dolmus driver does not take your money when you climb aboard. Instead, money is shuffled between the passengers while the driver does what he is paid to do: drive. Fast. Change is negotiated and by the time all the transactions have been completed, everyone has paid, the driver has his money and not a moment has been lost. Tom and I had no idea how this worked, but a fellow passenger standing in the aisle assisted, taking our money, tut-tutting at the 10 million lira note we proffered, swapping it with others and returning handfuls of change as we bounced along, crossing the Gallipoli Peninsula.

Kabatepe proved to be nothing but a wharf and a seawall enclosing a bay beneath a headland, with a few fishing boats harbouring from a stiff breeze sweeping the Aegean. Trucks and cars were already loaded on the ferry's lower deck.

We sauntered aboard. Considering we were about to tackle a stormy ocean, we inspected the lifeboats. The winches holding them were rusted. Ropes necessary for a successful launching were frayed or non-existent. Men stood about drinking tea and butting their cigarettes into the boats. If they were no use for the task of saving lives, the boats at least made useful ashtrays, and it would take a lot of years before they needed emptying, even considering the amount of cigarettes Turkish men smoke.

The cigarette fumes joined a great oily belch of diesel smoke from the ferry's funnel, and we shuddered off into the Aegean.

Shortly, we understood the seawall of the little harbour. The wind came scudding from the northwest, building a swell on the surface and whipping a mist into the air as we cleared the shelter.

Tom and I stood on the after deck and allowed the scene to unfold. To the north, the long arc of Brighton Beach stretched away to the point the men of Anzac called Hell Spit. The white stone of Beach Cemetery was Hell Spit's punctuation mark.

Behind Brighton Beach, the inland was gentle, leading to a long gulch the Turks called Wolf Valley. It was perfectly possible to imagine what might have happened if the Anzacs had landed on Brighton Beach. Even if they had made it to the beach, they surely would have been cut to pieces by the artillery that once stood above and behind us in the olive grove of Gaba Tepe. Those who survived and dragged themselves up from the beach, past Turkish trenches and barbed wire, might have found it easy going in Wolf Valley; they might have been able to stream around and behind the cliffs above Anzac Cove and they might have been able to get to the high ground a bit quicker. But how many might have survived Brighton Beach? From this vantage point, the prospect didn't look at all attractive.

All the stories of the botched landing at Anzac Cove began melting away. Beyond Hell Spit, Anzac Cove was invisible. It was as sheltered as any beach might be along this coast from the Gaba Tepe guns. From the point of view of a landing, it actually made more sense than a small armada of little boats and their cargoes of young men getting shredded on Brighton Beach.

But then we looked at the cliffs rearing in the distance above Anzac Cove. Less than 180 Turkish riflemen were in those hills and along the coast when the boats came out of the darkness on 25 April but each of them had a perfect view of the beach, and they had the advantage of peering down the barrels of their rifles from the heights. It was, in the dawn, a shooting gallery.

The ferry took on a crabbing roll as the swell picked up. We could see now the whole of the southern side of old Anzac. Only the curve of North Beach, tucked around beyond Anzac Cove and Ari Burnu, remained hidden. There was the Lone Pine Memorial, and above and beyond, Chunuk Bair. We took photographs, but the driving sea mist and the gloomy sky could never imprint this view satisfactorily on to a strip of negative.

This would engrave itself only on the mind's eye. We could sketch it all out, and the sketch of Anzac was nothing more than a postage stamp on a canvas. The area of battle was ridiculously small, a pocket of the landscape, and growing smaller as we drove out to sea and the peninsula stretched itself out behind us. The hills flattened until they were nothing more than a bit of an uneven bump on a long grey horizon.

Old Gavin had been right. This was the way to see Anzac from the sea and, by the way the Turkish men sheltering with their cigarettes in the lee of the bridge stared curiously at us, it was pretty clear few foreigners found their way on to this deck.

Tom and I took shelter in the ferry's big galley. A few old women dozed on the wooden slat seating, wrapped in black robes, and a couple of young men stood bored behind a counter, tea urns bubbling away behind them and plastic-wrapped sandwiches wilting. The sandwiches looked dodgy, but out of the freezing wind, hunger hooked in. I took a glass of tea and a packet of Negro biscuits and one of the boys tossed a sandwich on a griddle, heating and flattening it. It contained some sort of pink paste, and I knew I would spend the day worrying about botulism. Still, it was food, and I fell asleep afterwards, my head rolling with the swell.

I awoke to the sight of Gökçeada, old Imbros, thrusting out of the ocean ahead. This was no insignificant hump—it was a genuine mountain, and a rough, tough mountain at that. Our old tub lurched alarmingly as waves, whitecapped and muscular, marched into its side and the captain jockeyed it around to line up with the harbour's entrance.

An ancient bus, its springs long gone, carried us from the harbour up a steep, winding road to the island's main township. Gökçeada the village turned out to be a picture from the Greek isles—cobbled streets, whitewashed cafés and homes, an open market.

Indeed, it was a Greek village, and a Greek isle too, until a third of the way through last century, although it had been under Ottoman control until the very early 1900s. Greek water carriers and wood getters of Imbros contracted themselves to Hamilton's forces during the Gallipoli campaign of 1915, supplying the troops across the Aegean.

But in 1923, after Turkey's war of independence (largely against the Greeks), Imbros was declared under the Treaty of Lausanne to be part of the new Republic of Turkey. Within a few years, Greek schools were closed (later to be reopened, then closed again during the 1950s), and Greek monasteries were seized and razed. The real end of Imbros began during the 1960s. Most of the old farms were expropriated by the state, churches were destroyed, and Greeks began leaving in their hundreds. The Turkish military and settlers of Turkish origin moved in. The military established large bases all over the island, and open prisons for the exiled were established. The Turkish Air Force now operates a radar installation at the highest point of the island's mountain. Greeks who have moved away charge the Turkish government with human rights violations and claim the demographic make-up of the island has been reversed in the past 50 years. They estimate that, in 1950, the Greek population of the island was more than 6000, and there were only 200 Turks in residence. The figures now, they say, are 300 Greeks and more than 7000 Turks.

The Turkish authorities say the island has been developed under their control, with a new harbour, new roads, dams and other public works taking place. Victors always write the history.

Tom and I were largely ignorant of these recent uncomfortable events and anyway, we weren't keen to engage the locals in a debate about fraught Greek–Turkish relations or the subject of human rights, even if we could have spoken Turkish. Still, we could hardly ignore the presence of dozens of young men swaggering through the streets in their splendid Turkish military uniforms and startling white helmets. The existence of the under-utilised ferry became clear. If you are to declare that you own a disputed island, you must keep up the appearance of attachment. Anyway, the military needed a link to the mainland and a nice safe harbour too.

We approached a taxi in the village square and found ourselves confronted with an ancient driver who gurgled at us through a tracheotomy in his throat. Smoking cigarettes in the ceaseless Turkish manner has its price. We had a map, and the driver seemed perfectly delighted to take us to an area of the coast we had identified as the headquarters of Sir Ian Hamilton, commander in chief of the British Expeditionary Force to the Dardanelles. He drew with a finger on his hand a figure that appeared to be 1.5 million lira.

We sped off into picture-perfect mountain country, rocky crags towering above us, streams falling through green hillside pastures. The taxi lurched around bends and began plummeting towards the sea. The driver gurgled a bit, pointed excitedly at a lake behind sandhills and drew up next to a decrepit taverna and what appeared to be the central attraction—an empty caravan park by a beach. He was very proud, but it didn't accord with my directions on the map. We were the wrong side of the lake, and there wasn't anything around that looked the least bit like the country where Hamilton had established his camp, complete with tent hospitals and dressing stations, a prisoner-of-war corral and a harbour for his warships.

Tom and I stood on the beach, tramped up the hillside to a broken down stone hut barely big enough for a sheep, and decided to try again. We produced the map, pointed at the place we originally wanted to go and urged the driver to do better.

We zipped back up the road and came to a gate. On the other side, a rough road led down to the sea. This accorded with all the information I had gathered about Hamilton's headquarters and, after consulting the excellent *Gallipoli: A Battlefield Guide* by Phil Taylor and Pam Cutter, it certainly appeared to be the right place. A wide harbour sat way below us, known in 1915 as Kephalos Bay. Somewhere around here, we were pretty sure, would be a two storeyed stone cabin that had been home to the war correspondents who did most to foster the legend of Gallipoli and the Anzacs—Australia's C.E.W. Bean (who soon revolted and demanded the right to quit the island and live among the men in a dug-out above Anzac Cove) and Ellis Ashmead-Bartlett, the British journalist who kept a French chef, a store of fine wines and a splendid silk dressing gown among his comforts on the island.

The driver would not drive through the gate. He would not even approach it. On the fence was a sign bearing a skull and cross bones. This was Turkish military land. Trespassers, presumably, could be shot, or at least treated with inhospitality. It seemed a long way to come to be cheated of this bit of historical land. But then Hamilton had failed at his task, too.

The driver perked up enormously when we told him to head back to town. He gurgled happily, gunned the motor and startled a family of ducks in a pond by the road. The mother duck took off, flying crazily in front of the car for hundreds of metres, perhaps imagining she was drawing us away from her ducklings. She was fooled, but so were we.

Back in town, we discovered the taxi-driver had quite different ideas about what we had imagined was a 1.5 million lira fare. After much hand waving, he extracted 20 million from the wad in my hand.

We drifted around the cobbled streets, looking at old men watching us as they sipped tea outside cafés.

Tom needed a toilet. Urgently. Perhaps it was the strange pink paste from the ferry sandwich. Gökçeada did not appear to run to public toilets.

Tom disappeared inside a small restaurant. I walked up the street, trying to appear interested in window displays of lanterns, garden implements and elderly radios. I walked back down the street, drawing sidelong looks from soldiers. I walked around the corner, admired whitewashed walls, kicked my heels, stared intently at a rooster strutting across the road. Tom did not reappear. I strolled across the square, nodded at the newly rich taxi driver, and noted that two young soldiers were following. I stopped. They stopped. I turned around and said hello. They grunted and went to stand under a tree.

I had settled on the idea of entering the restaurant on the pretext of buying a glass of tea when Tom emerged. It was the only time in my life when I felt entitled to describe someone as ashen-faced. He was a wreck. And his trousers were wet.

'Mate,' he gasped. 'Mate. That was the worst experience.'

Turned out the tiny cubicle he had entered had two bricks on the floor for his feet, a hole in the ground and a stink that would strip the lining from a bloke's nose.

'It's a hard business trying to hold your pants in one hand while you're squatting,' said Tom, 'and then the knees started to shake so I put the other hand against the wall behind me to balance. Then some bugger tried to come in, and when he pushed open the door it banged against my head and things started to go bad. That's how my pants got wet. Lost my balance. Then I looked around for some paper and the only bloody thing in there was a jug of water. I got panicky until I remembered those sandwiches we had this morning were wrapped in tissue, and I still had some of it. I had to forage around in my pack one-handed.'

The sun, happily, had broken through the clouds. Tom said his trousers were guaranteed to be quick-dry. We took a long, thoughtful stroll to assist the quick-dry process and found a nice little café which we quickly discovered had a western-style toilet, complete with paper, a basin, hot water and soap. Tom was angry as a cut bully calf. He would have been angrier if he had known I had a roll of toilet paper in my day pack. I'd forgotten to tell him.

Later in the afternoon, we caught a dolmus back down the mountain road to the harbour. The dolmus driver ignored the road and carried on an animated discussion with some of his passengers, all the while drifting along at no more than 5 kilometres an hour until we got to the steep section, when he let the old bus have its head. We rocketed towards the ferry.

The wind was still blowing, but it had shifted and the ferry had to push directly into it. Still, the clouds had been blown away.

We crawled, but once again Gavin was right. We were pushing slowly straight towards Anzac Cove.

With the mist gone and the sun sinking behind us towards Gökçeada, the terrain and the memorials of the Gallipoli Peninsula were bathed in the loveliest golden light.

Once again, we could trace an imaginary line around old Anzac, and this time it was clearer. It described a wonky triangle: the Cove at the bottom, up to the right to Lone Pine, along the ridge to the left, all the way up to Chunuk Bair and back down to the beach. As the land got bigger, all the hills and ridges and gullies of the battlefields looked pathetically tiny. A useless hilly paddock set into an expanse of land that outside that triangle hardly felt the step of an Anzac boot and within it gave spring to a river of mothers' tears. A notable example of Anzac boots that tramped outside the triangle of old Anzac were the thousands of men from Australia's 2nd Brigade and the New Zealand Brigade who were thrown into a suicidal charge in the second battle Krithia, far south near Cape Helles, in the early days of May 1915, when 1000 men of the 2nd Brigade alone were cut down.

We stood in the biting chill of the wind on the ferry's for'd deck, transfixed. Tom began to mumble something. It had a rhythm to it. I asked him to repeat it.

'It's my old school prayer,' he said. 'It was the only thing that I could think to say.'

Tom was only a few years out of St Ignatius, Riverview, a big Catholic Rugby school above Sydney Harbour.

The Ignatian prayer, he told me, is this: 'Teach me to be generous; teach me to serve you as you deserve; to give and not to count the cost; to fight and not to heed the wounds; to toil and not to seek for rest; to labour and not to ask reward; save that of knowing that I do your holy will'.

I shut up and stood beside him in the frigid Aegean wind as Anzac Cove disappeared around the corner of Hell Spit and the ferry docked behind its breakwater beneath Gaba Tepe.

10

THE BOOMERANG BAR

*'The really good thing about travelling is you can move around
and no one knows who you are, where you're from, what you do,'
he said. 'It doesn't matter—none of it. You're just another person
and you don't have anyone to answer to. You just have a good
time. You know?'*

A sign on the wall at the funky Boomerang Bar in Eceabat told
us everything we needed to know: 'Yes, we do serve alcohol
to intoxicated persons'.

The music told us the rest. Cold Chisel's 'Khe San' blasted
from the speakers. Just inside the door, a knot of travellers sat
around a giant hubble-bubble pipe desultorily sucking in the
fumes of apple tobacco. Down the back, windows offered a view
of the wind-whipped Dardanelles tossing small white capped
waves against a stone embankment.

There was a trans-Tasman party underway in a nook tucked
in against the windows. Our new mates Ben, Chris and Gregg
had found a couple of New Zealanders, Perran Berry and Robert
Hinton, and a Sydney girl, Renee Haynes. They lounged on
pillows and Turkish carpets on a raised platform with a table in
the centre covered in beer cans and glasses. The cans made me
smile: first the Vegemite Bar and now another copyright knock-
off. The green cans appeared to be Victoria Bitter until you

looked closer and discovered the logo was BB, rather than the familiar VB.

'Come and join us,' called Gregg. He and Chris had quit Anzac House a day or two previously and had set out in search of a job. I was interested to hear what had become of their quest.

Gregg had been to a Turkish barber and his head was shaved clean and startlingly white. The Turkish barber experience looks death defying. It involves great amounts of lather, a cutthroat razer, hot water, hot towels and a stinging astringent at the end. I had watched a barber at work through his window during the morning, a customer on his back in an old leather tilt-chair and a cigarette pointing ceilingwards from within a face of foam. The barber waved his razer around, evidently discussing soccer, the subject that gets Turkish men more animated than any other. I thought of the Heywood barber of my childhood, a fellow named Nightingale, his shop on a Saturday morning full of men, a wireless tuned to the horserace station and the scent of Brylcreem mixed with some vile chemical in which he sterilised his combs. Nightingale, it was said, ran the local SP bookmaking operation, which was handy because his shop was right across the road from the pub.

'Chris and I have found work,' said Gregg. 'We're going to be serving behind the bar here. We get t-shirts, food and grog and we can sleep here. Bargain.'

'Where do you sleep?' I asked. The place was nothing but a down-at-heel barn. There didn't appear to be a bedroom anywhere.

'Right here,' said Chris. 'Anywhere. On the floor, on a couch, where we drop. It's great.' Chris and Gregg were Queenslanders and they had that who-gives-a-stuff-the-sun-will-shine-tomorrow attitude that seems to be born into those happy souls from sub-tropical latitudes. Good luck to them—a bar job with food and lodging seemed a pretty good deal even if there was no pay attached.

I got chatting to Perran. A big square-jawed bloke, he wore a sweater with the New Zealand flag plastered across it. He bridled at my questions about where he was from and where he had travelled.

'The really good thing about travelling is you can move around and no one knows who you are, where you're from, what you do,' he said. 'It doesn't matter—none of it. You're just another person and you don't have anyone to answer to. You just have a good time. You know?'

I took it as a warning not to dig. It wasn't. He was just telling me to relax. Stop being a journalist. Join the party.

His new friend Renee, long blonde hair swept back and wearing sunglasses that remained perched on her nose even at 10 o'clock in the evening, was plugged into headphones attached to a mini-disc player. 'This is awesome,' she said. To a certain age-group of Anzac travellers, everything is awesome.

'New Zealand music,' said Perran. 'Maori band. Check it out.' He handed me the disc player and the headphones. I chugged a beer and listened to fine chugging Maori rock as the evening wore on into night on the Dardanelles.

Matt, the Coffs Harbour surfer boy, wandered in. I hadn't seen him since our evening at the kebap restaurant. His hair was all a-tangle and he wore no shoes. He had the same far-away smile he'd probably wear to his grave.

'Gonna put up a tent,' he said. 'You reckon they'd let me put it up there?' He pointed to the dusty carpark separating the bar from the sea. He drifted away to ask the manager.

'No worries,' he said when he returned.

'You'll be pretty uncomfortable sleeping on the ground,' I told him.

'Nah. Got a roll-up mattress,' he said. 'There was this woman in Spain and she was going to throw it out. Can you imagine that? A perfectly good camping mattress. So I got her to give it to me.'

He was wide-eyed at the thought that anyone would toss away a used strip of thin foam. I offered to buy him a beer.

'No worries,' he said. 'But I can't shout you back. I'm on a budget.' It was nice of him to tell me, I said.

'Yeah, I'm a hard-core tight-arse,' he laughed. 'I can make a couple of bucks go a long way.'

His last job had been in a delicatessen in Storling, Scotland. Since then he had travelled to Morocco, to Italy, across Eastern Europe and on towards Gallipoli. He was still angry that 'gypsies' had tried to steal his pack on a train in Bulgaria. His arm was tender. He had thrown a punch at the robber, who had slammed a carriage door on him, almost breaking the arm. Matt was nineteen and he travelled alone. He'd already been through Central America.

He provided the night's entertainment as he struggled to erect his pup tent in the wind outside, the bar's lights spilling across him and casting dancing shadows. The thing blew down three or four times as we sat warm behind the windows, laughing. But Matt was patient and committed and refused all offers of assistance. Ben and Gregg eventually couldn't stand it, went outside and insisted they help.

When the show was finished, the tent's opening faced directly into the wind scudding off the Dardanelles.

'No worries,' said Matt when I pointed out he would freeze every time he opened the flap. 'I haven't used the tent for a few weeks and it was wet when I wrapped it up, so it needs an airing. Anyway, I've got a sea view. For nothing.' No detail could faze this optimistic boy.

Tom wrote in his diary later that night, 'Matt is a cack.'

I had left my own diary on the table in the bar and invited anyone to write their thoughts.

Perran, who had said the wonder of travelling is that no one knows you, proved the most revealing. Here is what he wrote:

> Perran Berry. Private. 1st Battalion, Royal NZ Infantry Regiment. Gallipoli! I am a soldier. Since I was knee-high to a grasshopper I have participated in Anzac Days and the last two days have been the culmination of my life's perception of the legend of Anzac. I feel closer to this barren coastline of a strange country than any other place I have visited in my, or any other, country. I have served two tours of East Timor and can with an unnerving clarity appreciate the superhuman achievements of the Kiwi and Aussie Diggers during the campaign. I take my hat off to them and salute them.

I did not read his words that night, and I was not to see him again.

Matt the surfer also put pen to the paper of my diary:

> The reason I came to Gallipoli for Anzac Day was to pay my respects for those who died and fought on the peninsula. The more I learn, the more I realise they were just young fellas out for an adventure not knowing what they were in for. To be here and knowing they were my age, just looking for excitement, a lot like myself, is so touching and inspirational I can't describe.

As Matt strolled off barefoot to the bar to try to cadge another beer, Ben chewed at a pen and tried to get hold of his own thoughts:

> This trip here to me is about learning, commemorating and respect. I do not respect the cause of the soldiers who died here but rather their bravery, camaraderie and mateship. Aggression is an emotion that I have felt that scared me. To do things you regret is not possible in war. To be able to understand and learn from past mistakes is an obligation

I have to each soldier that died. Hopefully evolution is a word of meaning to me. Anzac Day is a day to commemorate all soldiers as any war, Turkey or otherwise, is an ugly thing and no one is more significant than the other to me. The Anzac spirit can be grand in any walk of life—'to be brave in the face of adversity'.

Then Ben sat back and stared out the window, wearing his signature quiet smile that suggests he knows something secret. I never was able to break quite through his 25-year-old reserve. Later I asked him about what sort of aggression he had felt that scared him. 'Oh, it was just a few fights when I was younger,' he said. 'Nothing serious, but you know you can get to the point where your anger can overtake you, and it's not something that you want to know.'

Philippa arrived bearing her bag of Gallipoli stubby holders. There had been some incomprehensible fall-out with Hanifi at the Vegemite Bar, and she had decided to cancel her plan to sell her souvenirs through his business. She was angry, but the mood dissipated as she discovered that just about everyone in the Boomerang Bar wanted to part with their money to get their hands on a genuine hand-made Anzac–Gallipoli beer-can pullover. She disappeared among the travellers who had descended on the place as the night grew longer.

The crowd around the hubble-bubble pipe was getting larger and rowdier. Tom and I joined the circle and drew great lungfuls of the sweet-scented smoke. It tasted like nothing at all and, cooled by the bowl of water, it felt like nothing at all, either. Midnight Oil was whooping it up over the loudspeakers: 'How can we sleep when our beds are burning?' screamed Peter Garrett, a long way from the Australian desert.

In the middle of the room Matt was risking his dodgy arm in an attempt to win a little extra travelling money. He was seated across the table from a giant Maori, sweat pouring down their

faces as they arm-wrestled. Matt's slight frame was deceptive—
he was giving the Maori a tough time. Perhaps it was all those
hours paddling through the waves of the New South Wales mid-
north coast. Sinews stood out on his forearm, and his teeth were
gritted. We hooted encouragement, never believing young Matt
had a chance. Unbelievably, the Kiwi cracked first. His arm
began a trembling descent towards the table, and Matt was
unmerciful, forcing his advantage until the thing was done.

There was one round of the Boomerang Bar arm-wrestling
contest to go before Matt could hit paydirt, and the management
wasn't keen to hand over money. The establishment's bouncer,
muscles rippling, was called from the front door, and Matt's run
of fortune was soon over.

Tom and I decided to call it a night. We had a big day
planned—a walk on the Gallipoli Peninsula. The Boomerang
Bar would still be there tomorrow night.

We found a gypsy cart outside the bar. The driver's wife suggested we pay 10 million lira to ride to the ferry terminal. We
drove her down to 1 million, the driver grinned a mouthful of
gums and we leapt aboard, our behinds cushioned by carpets and
our legs dangling. The driver flogged the poor bony pony and we
clip-clopped into the cold night. The streets were empty, and
the sound of the horse's hooves on cobblestones echoed off the
worn-out buildings lining our way.

On the midnight ferry, we met a lonely man standing on the
deck smoking a cigarette. He was, he said, the First Mate on a
merchant ship. A month and a half previously, he had set sail
from Çanakkale, his home, to Rotterdam. And now he was
coming home to see his wife and the baby daughter who was just
six weeks old when he last saw her.

'I will soon be made a captain, and it will take me away
more,' he said mournfully. 'But what can I do? I must make

money to give my daughter a future. I want to see her growing. But I must go away. I know only ships.'

When his daughter was six or seven, he ruminated, he would try to become a pilot, perhaps guiding ships through The Narrows of the Dardanelles. That would be ideal. He could stay at home and still have an income from the sea.

All along my journey through Turkey I had heard the same story: young men and women planning their lives through the narrow opportunities available that might balance how they wished to live and what was available.

We wished the First Mate luck as he flicked away his cigarette, shouldered his sea bag and strode off the ferry on the last leg of a long way home.

Anzac House was quiet. The endless video spool of *Gallipoli* and the *Four Corners* episode was no longer running, and most of the lights were switched off. Only Sibel, the receptionist, was in attendance, and she was tapping away on the computer.

'I am doing my homework,' she said. Another Turkish receptionist swotting late into the night. Sibel was studying English Literature at Çanakkale's university, and worked nights at Anzac House to support herself.

She was a rare beauty, all high cheekbones, coal-black eyes and cascading jet-black hair—a Persian princess from a Mills and Boon cover—and stopped most of the young men with their backpacks clean in their tracks. But she was haughty and would have little to do with the lodgers.

She planned, she said, to train as a pilot so she could fly big passenger planes for Turkish Airlines where she had worked as a stewardess. She had gained a scholarship to travel to the United States of America some years before to undertake the training. But then the disastrous earthquake of 1999 had struck Istanbul, where she had lived with her parents. In a single night her

dreams fell apart. The scholarship disappeared as the govern-
ment redirected money for earthquake relief and to rebuild
Istanbul. Her parents did not have the funds to send her to
America.

So there she was, working as a receptionist in a backpacker
hostel, attending a university she could afford, studying English
Literature. 'Hamlet,' she said. 'A good knowledge of the literature helps me understand the language better, so when things
improve, who knows?'

Sibel returned to tapping the keys of the computer, and I
took the stairs to my little room to write up my diary and to
sleep the sleep of the privileged.

11

A WALK ON OLD ANZAC

It was the light that swept us home. The sun blazed from a sky fried almost white, and the sea had the blue all but wrung from it. It was a relentless light, honest and shimmering.

We hitch-hiked to Anzac. Tom, Ben and I took a dolmus to the Kabatepe museum, prepared to walk the next 4 kilometres to Anzac Cove if we couldn't flag down a ride. We were self-consciously independent travellers and the idea of riding in a taxi or a tour bus seemed soft.

The first vehicle that came along clattered to a stop. The driver, a young man with a heavy stubble, stuck his head out and motioned for us to climb aboard. He drove a Toyota ute. Perfect, really, apart from the fish scales that lined the tray. He was a fisherman off for a day's work on the Aegean. 'Shit, this is all right,' said Tom. We sat balanced on the tray's sidings, hailing our fortune and the morning sun on our faces.

The clouds had gone, the wind had blown itself away, and the first flawless day welcomed us to the peninsula.

Tom and I had awakened at dawn. Ben, who was sharing the small dormitory with Tom, had opened his eyes at all the stirring and declared that bugger it, he couldn't sleep any more and he wanted to come on this adventure too.

The ferry from Çanakkale to Eceabat was, for the first time

since we had arrived at the Dardanelles, heavy with Australians and New Zealanders. Tour buses crowded the lower deck, and knots of travellers fresh in from London and Sydney and Auckland chattered and moved restlessly around, eager for the best view of the approaching peninsula. Tom, Ben and I felt smug as old hands.

Ben grew angry as he listened to an Australian tour guide declaiming to his middle-aged charges that soon the peninsula would be overrun by young backpackers.

The tour guide wore grey slacks and a blue blazer, a name-tag identifying him as Ron and a greying moustache that, we decided, pinned him as a Vietnam veteran.

'The problem with all these kids is they come here for a couple of days, get pissed in the bars, take a quick tour of Anzac, go to the ceremonies and then they go, thinking they know something about it all,' Ron lectured. 'They don't learn anything, really.'

Ben fumed. 'I really hate it when people like that stereotype us,' he said. 'They might have the money to take longer, more expensive tours, but they get around in big buses and I bet most of them see nothing more than us and a lot of the time, heaps less. If it wasn't for people like us, Gallipoli would have hardly any people coming here. We come here with respect and people like him ought to respect that.'

It was a long speech for Ben. I felt amused. Here was I, a 50-year-old backpacker, caught in a generational divide, and I couldn't help but come down on the side of 25-year-old Ben. And yet I didn't think Ron meant any harm. He was doing no more than talking of the Gallipoli experience from his lights. Everyone who travels there seems to claim possession of the place. Ron, if he was a Vietnam veteran, probably felt more proprietorial than most. Besides, as a guide, he undoubtedly had a superior knowledge of the fine points of Anzac history, and I bet those who travelled with him loved the stories he would tell. Perhaps he felt aggrieved that he couldn't leave his charges and wander off to get pissed in the bars, where he might have gained new knowledge of the views of younger travellers. He was, of course, correct in his statement that the majority of young people travelled to Gallipoli for no more than a day or two, and that plenty of them got goat-faced in the bars—it would be absurd to imagine that thousands of young Australians and Kiwis would gather anywhere without doing so. But he was wrong in his view that they didn't learn anything. You can't go to Anzac and fail to learn. The place reaches out and teaches you.

The ute driver dropped us at the Ataturk memorial stone at Ari Burnu, right above Anzac Cove. He waved away our offers of money and ground off north along the beach.

I had two maps. Both were drawn in 1915 from a map taken from a Turkish prisoner. One gave the lay of the land according to the Australians, the other interpreted it from a New Zealand perspective. I had also packed Great-uncle George's diary. Thus I was tour leader.

First, like every Australasian visitor to Anzac, we stood before the large white-stone plinth above Anzac Cove and read the words chiselled on it that cause most visitors to fall silent. The words are those of Mustafa Kemal Ataturk in an address he made to a group of Australian and New Zealand officials who visited the peninsula in 1934. It was, in truth, an address to the mothers of young men who never made it home from Gallipoli:

> Those heroes that shed their blood and lost their lives . . . You are now
> lying in the soil of a friendly country. Therefore rest in peace. There is
> no difference between the Johnnies and the Mehmets to us where they
> lie side by side here in this country of ours. You, the mothers, who sent

their sons from far away countries, wipe away your tears; your sons are now lying in our bosom and are in peace. After having lost their lives on this land they have become our sons as well.

Ben, who had never seen the thing before, simply stood there. Tom and I took photos, but we tiptoed about.

To the right of this generous memorial lay the Ari Burnu cemetery. It is a little place, meaning Bee Point—or, more colourfully, Bee's Nose—pushing into the sea, and most of its graves contain the remains of men who lost their lives on the first day, 25 April 1915, when they came ashore either side of it. To the north is North Beach, curving away until it becomes Ocean Beach, and to the south, Anzac Cove. Until 1999, the Anzac Day ceremony was held within the graveyard, and young Australians and Kiwis slept among the gravestones and the ghosts, waiting for the dawn. But the numbers of pilgrims outgrew the little place, and the ceremonial site was moved a couple of hundred metres up North Beach in the year 2000. We could see workers moving around the new memorial place, tending the turf and carrying timber trestles about. Above, the Sphinx loomed, and the hills rose yellow and tangled with scrub.

We wandered among the gravestones with perhaps two dozen other visitors, most of them young, all of them stepping quietly and thoughtfully, the sea lapping beach pebbles below. Unlike upright Commonwealth headstones elsewhere, all the gravestones on the Gallipoli Peninsula are stone tablets laid on their side, out of respect for the Turks, the victors, most of whom are Islamic.

We stepped off the Ari Burnu lawn on to the sand of Anzac Cove and strode south along it. There is not much you can say about the cove, because it is a state of mind way beyond its unimpressive geography. It is a small curve of a beach between the headlands of Ari Burnu and Hell Spit, which is known also as

Queensland Point, because Queenslanders were the first to step from the boats in the Anzac dawn. There is a sand cliff and a road above it, built originally by Anzac engineers in 1915. Close to the water, the sand becomes small rounded pebbles. The water itself on this windless day was turquoise and perfectly tranquil. The only signs of the past were a couple of shadows that were the foundations of Watsons Piers, where stores and men and mules were once loaded.

It was a serene place, and we had it to ourselves. Tom, always the hopeless romantic, paused on the sand and proclaimed we should say something. 'We shall not grow old,' he intoned, 'as those who are left grow old. Age shall not weary them, nor the years condemn. In the morning and the evening we will remember them.' Ben and I shifted from one foot to the other, but we knew Tom was in the mood for something grand, and anyway, the cove had infected us too.

But it was still early—we tucked the beach away for another visit later in the day, rounded its southern promontory, Hell Spit/Queensland Point, and clambered up a small cliff to Beach Cemetery. Gravestones spilled below a white stone memorial across a lawn towards the sea. A lone woman sat beneath a shade tree, sketching. A busload of Australian school students in matching jackets drifted among the graves.

Simpson, 'the man with the donkey', lay beneath the ground in Beach Cemetery. His grave was identifiable from all the others only because visitors had planted a miniature flag and scattered poppies beside the headstone which reads: 'John Simpson Kirkpatrick served as 202 Private J. Simpson, Aust. Army Medical Corps. 19 May 1915. Age 22. He gave his life that others may live'. He had survived precisely 25 days on Anzac.

Great-uncle George claimed always that on one of his walks

up Shrapnel Valley on 19 May 1915, he was among the first to come across a little man called John Simpson (Kirkpatrick) lying dead with a smile on his lips, a donkey grazing nearby. I never quite believed the story, because almost every soldier who came home from Anzac claimed at some stage to have known, or seen, the almost mythical Simpson. Many of them had not even arrived at Gallipoli before Simpson died.

Indeed, George's diary of 19 May has nothing about such an event save this cryptic entry: 'Poor Scottie found shot in Scrapnel [sic] Valley.' It made no sense to me until, trawling through old records, I discovered something that made me ashamed of my doubts.

Simpson, it turned out, was rarely called Simpson by the men who shared his daily path up Shrapnel Valley and Monash Gully. He was known to them variously as 'the bloke with the donk', or Murphy (the name he gave to some of his donkeys, which is unsurprising, because as a child he had worked donkeys with an English seaside entertainment known as Murphy's Fair) or, good Lord, Scottie. George and his mates apparently referred to Simpson as Scottie because of his accent. Simpson's parents were Scottish, though he was brought up in the northeast of England before he drifted to Australia. George, born in the Australian bush, would hardly have known the difference. It is worth paying close attention to old diaries—the men had no reason to make things up.

Not far from Simpson's headstone, another grave bore a much gruffer inscription: '80 Trooper E.W. Loundes, 3rd Australian Light Horse. 28 May 1915. Age 30. Well done Ted'.

We pressed on, crossing the road and heading inland a bit through the mouth of Shrapnel Valley to its cemetery, the tablets of the dead lying beneath a spreading Judas tree in violent purple bloom.

Three graveyards already, in a stroll of no more than half an hour. In fact, there are 31 Commonwealth War Graves on the Gallipoli Peninsula, each a small oasis of carefully tended green within a landscape of drab scrub and bare hills. Nineteen of them are on that patch of land known as Anzac. There are 22 000 Commonwealth graves on the peninsula, but only 9000 are identified. The names of the 13 000 who lie in unidentified graves, and the 14 000 other Commonwealth soldiers who died but whose remains were never found are commemorated at memorials at Lone Pine (Australians and New Zealanders), Chunuk Bair (New Zealanders), Helles and Twelve Tree Copse.

Each day, Great-uncle George would load up his ammunition cans at the depot on Anzac Cove and step out for the long walk up Shrapnel Valley, or help pull guns up to the batteries in the hills or back down for repairs. Somewhere above the beach around the mouth of the valley, he lived in a hole in the ground. '14th June, 1915', his diary reads. 'Heavy fire on beach in early morning. Two boys shot in dug-out next to me. Piece of cordite came through into my dug-out, but I escaped without a scratch. Carried ammunition up to base.'

I would never know precisely where the dug-out was, or even to where George carried his ammunition. He wrote often of carrying ammo 'up to Holgates', but there is no Holgates on the map. The men had their own names for places all over Anzac, and there are plenty of mysteries to the casual visitor still in the hills above the cove.

First, though, I wanted to get out of the lowlands of the valley and climb for the first real view of the terrain that the soldiers of 1915 had gained.

Preparing to scramble into the hills, I began to understand something about George's diary. He was not a descriptive writer, and he was not introspective either. You cannot easily learn much about what he was thinking or even a great deal about what was going on around him. It is all matter of fact. But almost every day he ended his entries with the words 'carried ammunition'. I had skated over these repetitive words, yet here in Shrapnel Valley it dawned on me that these were the most important entries in the diary. They defined his existence here.

I pulled out Eileen's copy of the diary and looked at it again. I chose a page at random. '7/6/15: Carried ammunition up to base. Heavy shrapnel fire on the beach 11am. Attack by Turks about 11.30.' '8/6/15: Quiet day—gunners from column go to the 5th Battery. Carried ammunition up to Holgates.' '9/6/15: Quiet day. Carried ammunition to Major Caddy's guns and carried boxes to base.' '10/6/15: Very heavy shrapnel fire at about 5pm. No casualties. Carried ammunition to Holgates.' '11/6/15: Heavy shrapnel fire on the beach at about 1pm. One killed, six wounded. On guard at base. Bombadier McGibbon (4th Battery) killed.' '12/6/15: Few shots in the morning. Pack of mail arrived. Carried ammunition to Holgates.' And on and on.

And there it was. George was a boy from the bush aged 21, required to tramp up the hills with boxes of ammunition. There was not the comfort of one of his loved horses. His first thought was about how much death was whizzing through the air. You could read his life at this time as one of drudgery and a fear he tried to bury beneath terse scribbled lines. Climb out of the relative safety of the dug-out, listen for the sound of an incoming shell and its spray of shrapnel, shoulder the ammunition and begin the long walk. The diary had seemed a monotonous thing when I had read it in Australia. Here, it gained eloquence.

We walked along the seaward side of the cemetery and found a track behind the graveyard heading upwards. A sign informed that the trail led to Plugge's Plateau and warned that it was a stiff climb of 570 metres.

Tom, Ben and I were soon gulping for air and sweating. The narrow dirt foot-track quickly became stony, winding up through the scrub at a fierce angle. We stopped for a breather as two men came down. 'It's worth the walk,' one of them said encouragingly, and we weaved on, shallow trenches appearing among the shrubbery.

At the top lay the smallest cemetery on Gallipoli. Plugge's Plateau was named after the commander of the Auckland Battalion, Colonel Arthur Plugge, who set up his headquarters on this perfectly beautiful vantage point above Anzac Cove. The Anzacs had an artillery battery here, too, and I imagined the fierce effort it must have been for George and his mates to drag ammunition up the hill to it. On the first day of the landing, the men had been screaming for artillery cover, but by the end of the day, there were no more than two Indian Mountain batteries and a single Australian 18-pound gun ashore. The Australian gun was no use at the beach, because the trajectory of its shells was flat— it couldn't clear the cliffs. There was nothing for it but to drag the artillery piece up the hill. It took days, and required hundreds of men hauling on ropes. When the battery was finally in position on Plugge's Plateau, it proved so effective the Turks called the place Treacherous Hill and rained fire on it, often damaging the guns.

I had barely been able to make the walk up the hill with nothing more than a small daypack on my back. Dragging a heavy gun, even with the assistance of a hundred or so mates, would have been close to intolerable.

Only 21 graves lie within Plugge's Plateau cemetery, and the headstones gaze out over the Aegean. The view was inspiring, and we began to think we could understand the battlefield topography. In fact, we had only begun, and most of what we would learn lay way ahead of us.

The track continued behind the little graveyard, stopping above a precipice. Ahead and to the right, the land fell sharply away to the floor of a branch of Monash Gully, itself an extension of Shrapnel Valley. To the left, there was nothing at all save a bare perpendicular cliff. Beyond this reared The Sphinx, a high sculpture of yellow soil that bears a peculiar resemblance to the name the Anzacs, fresh from Cairo, gave it.

Directly ahead and below us was a sight that set our hearts pumping. A ridge so narrow that you could hardly imagine could accommodate at its top a mountain goat's hoof stretched from our plateau several hundred metres across a deep valley. It was named by the 1915 soldiers with perfect accuracy the Razor Edge. Tantalisingly, this high thin membrane of land joined Plugge's Plateau with the next substantial hogback of Anzac, Russell's Top.

The only sensible thing was to turn back, take the track back down to Shrapnel Valley and to choose a new route to the heights, just as most of the troops were forced to do all those years ago.

Yet I had read of soldiers running across the Razor Edge from Plugge's Plateau to Russell's Top in the first hours of the scramble from the beach. In the early light after the dawn, they would have presented perfect silhouettes for Turkish snipers.

The three of us stood at the edge of the cliff and imagined what a wild mad escapade that might have been.

'Whaddya reckon?' I asked. Ben had read my mind. He inched his way to the edge and found a path of sorts leading down. He jammed one foot beneath his bum, stuck the other out ahead to act as a brake and began sliding, setting scree tumbling into the valley. I followed, using my pack as an extra brake behind. We slid, almost out of control, for perhaps 10 metres, whooping. Tom followed.

In a few seconds, we found ourselves standing on the Razor Edge. It was no more than 25 centimetres wide. To the left, there was nothing but a vertical cliff falling away. Ben, a Melbourne boy, used the length of an Australian Rules football field to estimate the distance to the bottom. Eighty metres, he figured. I had no argument—I could barely bring myself to look at the drop. To the right, the fall-away was almost as deep, but not quite vertical. If we were to lose our footing and topple that way, we might just tumble, but we wouldn't stop until we reached the bottom of Monash Valley—an area once known as Rest Gully, where troops from the front line were given the mercy of relaxation. Either way, a fall wouldn't leave us in dancing trim.

We began to inch our way across. Suddenly, I was disabled by a rush of vertigo. Everything seemed to be spinning. I couldn't move. Tom wasn't keen on the situation, either. I decided this was impossible, and said so, loudly. Beneath our feet the soil was crumbly, and clods fell into space. We turned back to the cliff above us. But we had miscalculated our escape—the slippery slide down which we had come was too steep to climb. I remembered a line from Les Carlyon's wonderful book *Gallipoli*—only those willing to flirt with suicide would consider crossing the Razor Edge. May I urge readers to take Carlyon's advice.

Having got ourselves into this predicament, our only option was to cross this absurd wall of dirt suspended in nothingness, and Ben urged us on. We turned to face the task and Ben slipped. His sunglasses flew off his face and bounced once on the slope to the right and snagged on the branch of a bush a couple of metres down. 'Are they expensive?' I called. 'About 80 bucks, but we'll have to leave them there,' Ben replied.

For some unaccountable reason I felt this would be a defeat. I jammed a foot into the loose soil below, grabbed a spindly branch of a tough little shrub and leaned down, hooking one finger around an arm of the sunglasses. The tiny victory shook me free of the incapacitating dizziness.

Ahead, the knife-edge path disappeared over a rise. Ben took my pack, slung it on his shoulders, gulped a deep breath and ran over the obstacle, one foot perfectly in front of the other. He disappeared. 'It's better over here,' he yelled.

I got down on my hands and knees and crawled over the narrow hillock, feeling ridiculous. The ridgeway was hardly wider on the other side, and Ben laughed. Tom scuttled behind me.

'How the bloody hell did anyone run over here in Army boots, carrying a rifle?' Tom demanded. 'It's like trying to balance on a tightrope without a net.'

To our left, across the deep valley, The Sphinx ignored us, gazing careless and ageless out to sea.

We got the idea that if we rammed our feet into the loose earth on the right-hand slope, we could stomp our own path, balancing with one hand against the top. It worked, and we proceeded slowly until the track began widening.

We started climbing again. The path was so steep we had to pull ourselves up, grasping any bit of vegetation our hands could find.

I remembered a lazy Saturday afternoon from my youth. A mate and I drove out to a place on the Victorian coast known as Yellow Rock. It was named after a sandstone outcrop above a wild sea at the foot of a cliff, a place much loved by surfers. My mate and I scrambled past the golden rock and wandered along the pebbly beach. Eventually we decided to climb the cliff. We had to drag ourselves up, clinging to the scrub. Everything about that long-ago day bore a spooky similarity to what I was experiencing on Anzac: the pebbles on the beach, the yellow rock, so like a sphinx, the difficulty of the climb and the vegetation.

I was about to remark on this when Ben stopped, looked around and said: 'You know, this could be Australia.'

Tom agreed. We began comparing places we knew. Mt Martha, outside Melbourne, Ben ventured. Tom had in mind headlands above Sydney Harbour and areas along the central New South Wales seaboard. I thought of my own territory in southwest Victoria, and Margaret River in the southwest corner of Western Australia.

In fact, the monotonous yet subtle colours of the earth and the heath, the old loose soil, its substance weathered away, could have been almost anywhere on the Australian coast. But it was the light that swept us home. The sun blazed from a sky fried almost white, and the sea had the blue all but wrung from it. It was a relentless light, honest and shimmering.

Soon we gained firm ground on a flank of Russell's Top, a solid hump between two deep valleys, yet still part of what the Anzacs called First Ridge, which began on Plugge's Plateau.

Tom and I pulled bottles from our packs and we stripped off our pullovers and poured water down our throats. I thought of the Anzacs, thirsty most of the time. The first of them had trained for long days on the island of Lemnos, south of Imbros, forced to practise leaping from small boats to the shore and running up the hills, all the while limited to 2 litres of water a day. Perhaps it was what saved them when they got to Anzac Cove and North Beach: the knowledge of thirst and strong legs to drive them.

We looked back at the Razor Edge and in the distance, perched at the lip of Plugge's Plateau, ant-like figures waved to us. Later we would discover the little group was led by Australian documentary film-maker Harvey Broadbent. He had filmed us as we crawled across to Russell's Top, but was too canny to replicate the effort with his friends. Broadbent was the producer of *The Fatal Shore* and he was making a follow-up documentary.

Tom, Ben and I allowed ourselves the brief indulgence of feeling like conquerors. But what had we done but strolled over a tricky path in our hiking boots, with little daypacks on our backs? The Anzacs had done it infinitely tougher.

Charles Bean wrote of soldiers scaling the cliffs to our perch soon after dawn:

> Odd parties of the 11th and 12th Battalions were scrambling up these gravelly and almost perpendicular crags by any foothold which offered. One of this party, Corporal E.W.D. Laing . . . clambering breathless up the height, came upon an officer almost exhausted half way up. It was the old Colonel Clarke of the 12th Battalion. He was carrying his heavy pack, and could scarcely go further. Laing advised him to throw the pack away, but Clarke was unwilling to lose it, and Laing thereupon carried it himself. (Laing and another trooper, named Margetts, continued climbing until) Margetts . . . reaching the top, found to his astonishment the Colonel already there. (C.E.W. Bean, *The Story of Anzac*, Sydney, 1924, Vol. I, p. 272)

Colonel Lancelot Clarke was 57 years old. He was shot dead a few hours later, and lies now in Beach Cemetery. It seems likely, from Bean's description, that this oldest of soldiers had climbed the bare gorge between The Sphinx and the Razor Edge to the very spot where we three stood guzzling water.

We picked our way up to the summit of Russell's Top, hiking between weathered trenches that were still clearly visible. At the top, we gained an entirely new view of old Anzac, which made what we had seen from Plugge's Plateau seem hardly anything at all.

Ahead and below us to the east lay a deep valley and its far wall rose steep as a wave on a big day at Bondi. The top of this cliff was once terraced and riddled with tunnels and closed trenches: Quinn's Post, Courtney's Post and Steele's Post. Men had to use ropes to climb the cliff to these posts. A few metres over the lip of the cliff had been the trenches of the Turks. Quinn's Post was the most exposed and dangerous of all the rotten places at Anzac, and Bean recorded that soldiers in the valley looked up to it as a man might look at a haunted house. Looking at it from Russell's Top made us feel the same way, even though most traces of the terraces had been taken by the wind and the rain.

To the southeast along the same ridge was the white cenotaph marking Lone Pine. Sweeping our eyes back to the northeast, past Steele's and Courtney's and Quinn's, the land rose towards a hill known as Baby 700, and above that it continued rising over Battleship Hill (also known as Big 700), all the way up to the high ground of Chunuk Bair. Between Quinn's and Baby 700 sat the nasty end of the valley overlooking Monash Gully, known as Bloody Angle. Beyond that, at the foot of Baby 700, was the thin spit of land known as The Nek.

In short, we could see almost all of what was known as Old Anzac—the battlefields of the first weeks of the Gallipoli campaign for Australians, New Zealanders, a scattering of British marines and the Indian mule-team drivers.

All those place names make it sound like a vast theatre. But you would be hard-pressed to get all the place names on a map without over-writing, because the entire area would fit inside a few paddocks of a reasonable-sized Australian farm. Add it all together and it would make little more than 3 square kilometres. You could just about lob a rock from Quinn's to Courtney's, which were joined by tunnels, and the Turks and the Anzacs could lob hand-grenades and jam-tin bombs at each other with the greatest of ease—the trenches at some spots were no more than 10 metres apart. These days, a road runs the length of the front line from Lone Pine up to Chunuk Bair and the distance between the opposing trenches—no man's land—was precisely the width of that road.

Back across the valley from the front line, high on our ridge, we dallied among the trenches on the eastern side of Russell's Top. Dust rose from our boots as we wandered about, and the trenches were shallow, worn away by 87 years of wind and rain and fractured by hard summer sun and the bite of winter snow. Tom and Ben walked bent over, searching for spent shells and shrapnel balls among the dust and the gravel. They looked like mushroomers. 'I've got a bullet here,' cried Tom, and Ben chimed in: 'There's a cartridge here.' The earth was littered with misshapen lead and brass, and it was no stretch to imagine the air alive with shot. The fire would have come from the Turk entrenchments across the valley's corner above Bloody Angle, from a network of trenches known as the Chessboard, and from the slopes of Baby 700. In mid-May 1915, Russell's Top took on the appearance of a slaughter yard after New Zealanders and Australians repulsed a suicidal charge by thousands of Turks.

But this day we were alone, apart from an occasional lizard rustling through the undergrowth. We had seen no soul since the waving figures atop Plugge's Plateau, though we knew there must be hundreds, perhaps thousands, of people travelling the roads around Anzac.

'This is what I came for,' said Ben. You could see his personal claim on the place settling on him.

We tramped on, tracking behind The Sphinx, below us now, heading around to Walker's Ridge, the main path for the Anzacs up from North Beach. Way below was Mule Valley, where the Indian regiment had its camp and where the mules of Gallipoli sheltered. A communications van sat at the top of the cliff, a satellite dish perched alongside and its generator humming. We resented the intrusion of modern technology's noise. We hurried past and the sound receded. The van would be used on Anzac Day to broadcast the televised ceremonies back to Australia and New Zealand.

Around the corner, another cemetery waited. Walker's Ridge Cemetery sat at the edge of an escarpment that gave us a tableau quite unlike the tough land behind us. We sprawled on the lawn in front of the graveyard, a breeze cooling us. We looked out at a flat coastal plain far below, and the whole of North Beach and Ocean Beach sweeping north to the horseshoe of distant Suvla Bay. Inland a bit from Suvla Bay lay its salt lake, a wavering mirage. Way out to sea, Imbros and Samothrace thrust out of the ocean.

'It's probably not right to lie down at a cemetery,' Tom said. He was a worrier, concerned to do the right thing by this place.

'I don't think the blokes here would mind,' I murmured, the sun on my face. 'They're all lying down, too.'

'At least we've come here to be with them,' said Ben. 'How many other people come here?'

Tom became restless, and drifted among the gravestones. 'Oh, shit,' he said. 'Listen to this: Private R.H. Robertson, 20th Australian Infantry, 7-11-1915. Age 16.' Sixteen. A child, the age of my youngest daughter, Georgina, in Year 10 at school, carefree, her life ahead of her. The boy had died only a bit more than a week before the Anzacs had finally walked away from this bit of land. We could not laze there anymore.

A short distance up the slope we came to the cemetery of The Nek. It sat before a glade of trees. Nearby, a few old trenches had been dug out and lined with pine logs to give visitors some idea of what might have been here once. The effort had failed, simply because what had happened at The Nek was all but unimaginable to those born towards the end of the twentieth century.

A bronze plaque set into the stonework at the front of the cemetery likewise failed to grasp the enormity. 'In this cemetery there were buried 321 soldiers of the British Empire,' it said. 'Of these the names of five are known and their graves are marked. The names of five others are also known but their graves are unknown and they are therefore commemorated on the headstones facing the cross.' There is a little more detail: 'Most would have been of the Third Australian Light Horse Brigade killed on 7th August, 1915'.

Yes. On 7 August 1915, hundreds of good young horsemen from Victoria— the 8th Light Horse Regiment—and Western Australia—the 10th Light Horse—were fed on foot to the Turkish machine guns, no more than 40 metres away in what now is a peaceful copse of trees. As dawn broke, wave after wave—four of them, each of 150 men—were ordered to leap out of the trenches and run into the bullets. It was a monstrous cock-up from start to finish. A naval artillery barrage stopped seven minutes early, leaving all those empty minutes for the Turk defenders to shake the dust from themselves and prepare their guns for the first charge. When the first surge of Light Horsemen, their horses a world away, were mown down, the next young souls were lined up and ordered out of the trenches and into the next world. And then another. And then another. The film *Gallipoli* reaches its climax at this moment, but the film has played with the horror of it, blaming British fools for the slaughter. The truth of it is that Australian fools commanded it. The Nek was so exposed that the bones of more than 300 of those dismounted horsemen lay in the open until 1919, when a party of Anzacs came back to bury them properly. Thus the vast majority of those buried there are unnamed.

'How could these blokes just keep obeying stupid bloody orders like that?' Ben demanded. 'How could they? It was just suicide.' He was deeply, deeply upset.

It is a question that has haunted historians and the families of the men for 87 years. It has never seemed enough to explain it all away with the claim that men from that era were trained to follow orders without question.

My friend Michael McKernan, the historian, had given me a task when I had told him I was going to Gallipoli. 'When you get to The Nek, look back over your right shoulder. You will be able to look all the way down the ridge to Lone Pine,' he had said. He was right.

'I have a theory that those men at The Nek had been watching what had been happening at Lone Pine—men fighting hand to hand in the Turkish trenches, dying, going bloody mad.

'So I think the men at The Nek had become pumped up with the idea that if their mates could do that down at Lone Pine, well, they became fatalistic and decided they would just have to do it, too. I can't find any other explanation.'

I explained this theory to Tom and Ben. We stood on the bridge of land that gave The Nek its name, a neck between Walker's Ridge and the slope of Baby 700. It was apparently spelled the Afrikaans way by men who had already fought in the Boer War. We gazed south across the valley and along the front line to Lone Pine, less than a kilometre away. We tried to imagine what it must have been like, watching the carnage which had begun at dusk the previous day at Lone Pine. The sound of it would have continued all the long night. And then the dawn, and the command to leap out of the trenches.

'Your mate could be right,' said Tom. 'I can't think of anything else, either.' Ben was dubious, but conceded there seemed no other sane reason.

We were a bit shattered, but we pushed on around behind the cemetery and found a park at the edge of the escarpment. Its lawn was clipped, and we lay in the shade of a tree unfamiliar to our eyes, but similar to an olive. The park once was ploughed with Turkish trenches, and there is a marble obelisk dedicated to an Ottoman warrior, Mehmet Cavnes. The obelisk stands where Turkish machine guns bristled. It was as peaceful as the garden of a Mediterranean villa and we were still alone.

Tom had been to the supermarket back in Çanakkale and had packed tuna, tomatoes and fresh bread rolls. We built large sandwiches, carved them with my pocket knife and wolfed them, surprised at our hunger.

'You know, it's really hard to get your head around the idea of being here in a hostile environment with a view like that across the sea,' said Tom. Cypress pines reached towards the sky, the Suvla plain shimmered below us, and the Aegean lay torpid.

We talked about the land we had tramped and its undeniable similarity to the Australian environment. Ben felt it might have been some comfort to the Anzacs, finding themselves in familiar surroundings. It went some way, I felt, to explaining the gravitational pull that Gallipoli exerts on a new generation. Half a world away from Australia and New Zealand, in a nation as exotic and strange as Turkey, lies this corner of a peninsula that is not only soaked in Australian and New Zealand sweat and blood, but which has a physical presence that welcomes the traveller with an easy acquaintance. The light and the scent breathed home.

We snoozed a bit in the midday heat and eventually struggled to our feet, shouldering our packs. This day's journey was less than half done.

12

LONE PINE AND A BAPTISM AT THE COVE

How could any of these young men without women who knew the song or the story not feel a tug of the heart at the idea that some-where, a sweetheart might be waiting? 'For I know she's waiting there for me 'neath that lone pine tree.'

Reluctantly, we walked out from beneath the trees of Sergeant Mehmet's memorial park. We were rejoining civilisation. We stepped on to the road a few metres up from The Nek cemetery, and were confronted by a tourist bus edging its way along the narrow strip of bitumen. Passengers stared down at us with what looked like pity as we trudged along, and we looked back, feeling sympathy for them because they were not experiencing our free ramble.

The road led a few hundred metres from The Nek towards an intersection with the road that stretches along the Second Ridge front line, all the way from Lone Pine in the south up a relentless rise to Chunuk Bair.

The intersection is on the slope of Baby 700, which is actually a little less than 600 feet [180 metres] above sea level, but was given that name to distinguish it from Big 700, which rises a bit to its north, and which is almost 700 feet [210 metres]. To

complicate matters further, Big 700 was later given the name
Battleship Hill, because the big ships out in the Aegean used it
to train their guns on the peninsula.

Baby 700 was in many ways the key to the Anzac campaign—the key the Anzacs never quite got to unlock. On the
first day of the battle, Australian and New Zealand forces
seemed to have it within their grasp, but they lost it, regained it
and lost it again. By late afternoon, the Turks got it back and
never gave it up again.

We could see clearly how the hill gave the Turks a commanding position over Monash Gully, making it virtually impossible
for the Anzacs to move along the valley during daylight hours.
Snipers had a clear shot right down the gully, and any man who
raised his head above the trenches of Quinn's Post, immediately
above Monash and at Baby 700's foot, could expect to have it
shot off.

Yet Baby 700 seemed hardly more than a pimple on the landscape as we traipsed along its flank. Anzac, where the walk is not
so steep it causes you to gasp, rises almost imperceptibly. You
know you are on a high point only when you get there. We
crossed the intersection and marched along for a bit as buses
swept past before we found a dirt track leading east to the Baby
700 cemetery. It led us only a short distance, but once again it
was as if we had left the world behind. No buses stopped, no
travellers came down the path. They missed one of the most
moving of the Anzac graveyards.

The cemetery holds 493 souls, but only 33 Australians, ten
New Zealanders and one British marine are identified. The
remaining 449 bodies are those of soldiers 'known unto God'.
Most of them died on the first day of fighting, and their bodies
lay around the spot—behind what became the Turkish lines—
until some of them were buried by Turkish soldiers on 24 May,

when the Turks and the Anzacs agreed to cease shooting each other for a day in order to dispose of the stinking, fly-blown piles of bodies.

I pulled out Great-uncle George's diary and found a short, confronting entry from that day, when enemies mingled and swapped cigarettes:

> An armistice from 7am till 4.45pm to bury the dead. Was up in front of the trenches and saw about a dozen of our fellows that fell in the first charge about a month previous. They are in a terrible state of decay, beyond all recognition, almost skeletons. Carried sandbags to the 8th battery in the evening, dug two gun pits 4th battery.

His diary entry did not say where he was in front of the trenches, but it could not have been far from Baby 700.

In fact, most of the bodies buried were those of Turks, who had made a furious charge five days before the armistice in an attempt to sweep the Anzacs into the sea. Thousands of Turkish bodies had piled up in front of trenches where hundreds of Australians and New Zealanders had died, creating a stench that was unbearable, depending on which way the wind blew, and a serious health hazard. George's diary mentions something of it, in the same entry in which he recorded that 'Scottie', the man with the donkey, had been found dead.

> 19/5/15: Very determined charge by Turks at about 12.30 in the morning, but was repulsed by infantry after hard struggle. Turks lose very heavily, a good number taken prisoner. Our casualties about 500, very heavy artillery fire on the beach about 6am; two of our fellows wounded. Put two guns in position and carried ammunition. Met a train of mule carts with fifty dead Australians and one Turk coming down from trenches.

From this forlorn spot we had a clear view east across to the Third Ridge, which remained out of reach of the Anzacs, apart from a handful of determined men who fought their way across to it and perished there on the first day. Beyond the Third Ridge lay a glimpse of the Dardanelles, the prize they never reached. The distant water looked to us like a small bay of a lake.

A breeze blew softly over the silence, a bed of irises nodding by the gravestones. Nearby, along another walking track behind the cemetery, we found a solitary artillery piece, known as the Mesudiye gun, squatting in the scrub. It came from a Turkish ship torpedoed by a British submarine in late 1914, and had been used in the defence of the Dardanelles before being dragged up the slope of Baby 700.

We returned to the road and began plodding up the long hill, sweating, when two Turkish labourers from the Commonwealth War Graves Commission pulled up and offered us a lift in their work truck. We accepted gratefully and cruised a kilometre, cramped together on the back seat, over Battleship Hill and up to Chunuk Bair, unable to converse with our benefactors because we had no shared language.

Hordes of travellers milled about the summit of Chunuk Bair. Enterprising locals had set up stalls selling soft drinks and ice creams and trinkets beneath a grove of big old pine trees, and children ran through a maze of trench lines and among rows of buses parked beneath a lawn sprouting giant concrete monuments.

Chunuk Bair, from an Anzac point of view, is sacred ground for New Zealanders. It is equally revered by the Turks, because it is the site of Mustafa Kemal Ataturk's most decisive and strategic victories. On 25 April 1915, the then young commander Kemal created his own legend by ordering his panic-stricken troops to defend the slope of Chunuk Bair. Though outnumbered by the Anzacs and out of ammunition, Kemal demanded that the Turkish 57th regiment turn and face the enemy. His command on that first day has entered the realm of myth. 'I do not order you to attack, I order you to die. By the time we are dead, other units and commanders will have come up to take our place,' he is generally recorded as having said.

In his ground-breaking biography of Ataturk, the Istanbul-born writer Andrew Mango related that the actual order had greater flourish. According to papers found on a dead Turkish soldier, the order was: 'I do not expect that any of us would not rather die than repeat the shameful story of the Balkan war [in 1912–13, when the Ottoman empire lost vast tracts of its territories]. But if there are such men among us, we should at once lay hands upon them and set them up in line to be shot.'

Whatever he said, the men of the 57th heeded Kemal's words and died to a man keeping the Anzacs from the heights. Three-and-a-half months later, Kemal led his troops on another crucial defence of Chunuk Bair.

The British forces began mounting massive assaults along the Gallipoli Peninsula on 6 August, most of which were 'diversionary' attacks to mask the real intention—an attempt to take Chunuk Bair and the higher point another 1.5 kilometres north-west of it, called Hill 971. The main Anzac diversions included the disaster at The Nek at dawn on 7 August and six days of furious hand-to-hand fighting at Lone Pine.

On the night of 6 August, Anzac forces set off to march from Ocean Beach north of Anzac into the hills and valleys leading to the heights known as the Sari Bair Range, intent on surprising and outflanking the Turks. Australians were supposed to take Hill 971, known as Kocacimentepe, but it never happened.

The assault turned to a shambles as troops (including those under the command of Australia's Brigadier-General John Monash, an engineer by profession) became lost in the impossibly dark and confusing country below the heights, and the New

Zealand Brigade hesitated when required to advance. A great force of 20 000 British troops landed much further north at Suvla Bay, under the command of a 61-year-old Lieutenant-General, Sir Frederick Stopford. Stopford apparently had no idea what he was doing and simply failed to move inland when he had the chance. The cemeteries around Suvla hold more than 5000 bodies largely because of his indecisiveness.

It was not until the morning of 8 August that New Zealand forces managed to claw their way on to Chunuk Bair, but by then Kemal had reinforced the high ground. By then, too, all those Australian horsemen down at The Nek were dead or wounded. The plan had been for the New Zealanders to come down to The Nek from Chunuk Bair and to attack behind the Turkish machine guns. But the Kiwis did not reach Chunuk Bair until two days after the fury at The Nek was over.

The Auckland Battalion was ripped apart before the New Zealand Lieutenant Colonel William Malone finally captured the summit with the Wellington Battalion. The New Zealanders, if they had managed to get far out of the trenches that filled with bodies, and if they had had a moment to spare for sightseeing, could have looked down from the hill to the glittering water of the Dardanelles, the British goal.

Among the Kiwis' tribulations was a devastating assault of 'friendly' shellfire that fell short of the Turkish positions, and which probably came from Australian howitzers down near the beach. It is likely these were guns that had been supplied with shells carried by Great-uncle George. Despite massive loss of life, Malone's force held on until the following night, when it was replaced by British troops from the 6th Loyal North Lancashires and the 5th Wiltshires. The following day, 10 August, Kemal's soldiers drove the British from Chunuk Bair, and the last real hope for the Gallipoli campaign was gone.

Kemal had won. During the battle, Kemal was struck in the chest by a bullet or a piece of shrapnel. He was saved when the projectile hit his pocket watch, and the incident became part of the Ataturk myth that is told and retold in Turkey.

Colonel Malone, who led several bayonet charges on Chunuk Bair, was killed beneath a misdirected shell fired either from the Australian artillery down near the beach or possibly a British naval gun. He left behind a letter to his wife: 'I am prepared for death and hope that God will have forgiven me all my sins.'

Thus both New Zealand and Turkish monuments vie for space on Chunuk Bair. Both are massive. The New Zealand memorial is a stone plinth visible for kilometres around. It bears the transfixing words: 'From the uttermost ends of the Earth.' Right across the lawn is a bronze statue of Kemal, complete with a floridly written account of his escape from death thanks to the pocket watch.

Tom, Ben and I stood above one of the trench lines on the lip of Chunuk Bair and gazed down upon the tangled ravines and black gullies that had so beggared the navigational skills of Monash and exhausted Malone's men. Beneath our feet, Rhododendron Ridge provided a sort of scrubby bridge from Chunuk Bair to the lowlands above the beach. Immediately below our perch, a small plateau known as The Farm—there was a shepherd's hut there once, apparently—sat as the single patch of flat land on the snarled and baffling terrain. The Farm has become yet another cemetery.

The previous day, one of our fellow guests from Anzac House, a New Zealander called Ron, had scrambled all the way down Rhododendron Ridge to the beach, hardly caring that the tough undergrowth ripped his legs. He was ill-advised enough to wear shorts on his expedition (there are poisonous snakes in the undergrowth, though we never saw any) but he was determined to tackle Rhododendron Ridge because it was the route used by those long-ago New Zealand troops. Ron eased the pain when he reached the beach by sharing a bottle of spirits with a couple of old Turkish fishermen still occupying Fishermen's Hut, a landmark from the first day of the Gallipoli campaign. A Turkish machine-gun nest at Fishermen's Hut had met an Anzac boat on the first day of the landing, and within minutes the beach and the sea were littered with bodies.

'You know,' said Tom, 'the word "if" just hits you here. If Kemal hadn't been able to stop the Australians getting here on the first day, they would have gone right to the Dardanelles. If he hadn't stopped the New Zealanders in August, it would have been all over for the Turks.

'If that had happened, and the mines were cleared from the Dardanelles, the British would have taken Constantinople. And that would have changed history.'

Tom was hardly the first to stand at Chunuk Bair and ponder all the ifs. Historians have been doing it for decades and they are split widely on their theories.

It is a mind-twisting exercise. If the Anzac and British expeditioners had managed to break through the Turkish lines and held the high ground, the campaign above Anzac Cove would have been shortened dramatically and many thousands of Turkish and Allied lives would have been saved. If Constantinople had been taken, it probably would have been handed to the Russians. If that had occurred, it is possible the Bolshevik Revolution would not have occurred (the Tsar's reign would have been bolstered and at least have been granted a stay of execution). If Russia had been supplied with British weapons, ammunition and stores through the Dardanelles and the Bosphorus, the Russians might have mounted a successful eastern front against Germany, bringing World War I to a swift close and saving millions from ghastly doom in the trenches and the mud of the Western Front in France and Belgium. So no communist empire (perhaps), possibly no World War II, maybe no Cold War.

And what of Australia and New Zealand? When I was a boy in the 1950s and 1960s, almost every family had a maiden aunt. These were women whose dreams of motherhood had died on the battlefields of Gallipoli and Europe. They sat as wallflowers at country dances and city social events in the years after the Great War, or they simply sat at home, their hopes of finding a suitable partner withering into resignation. Not enough men had come back to go around. All those children who would never be born, who might have been great leaders or scientists or artists or dreamers or plain workers, parents themselves in time, left an invisible hole as big and empty as the desert in the young hearts of Australia and New Zealand. In Britain and Europe and Turkey, too. I thought of Ömür's great-grandmothers waiting in their village for the return of men who would never come, and not so much as an official letter to relate what might have become of them.

To the Turks, though, if the battles of Chunuk Bair had not occurred it would have meant that Mustafa Kemal did not transmogrify into Ataturk and build a new Turkish nation. Indeed, there almost certainly would be no Turkey now—Russia and the European nations would have carved its territories away.

You could think yourself into decreasing circles, juggling all the ifs. None of the argument is worth a can of bully beef, though, because Kemal and his troops held Chunuk Bair and restricted the British forces to less than 2 per cent of the Gallipoli Peninsula. All the rest is a long daydream, wistful as the days and nights of maiden aunts.

Tom, Ben and I, wearying of the crowds, bought ice creams and cold drinks from a stall beneath the trees and prepared to continue our trek. We noticed the Turkish labourers packing up their truck, and signalled we'd like another ride. The two men grinned, motioned us aboard and we barrelled back down the front line road, 3 kilometres to Lone Pine.

On the way, we passed a Turkish cemetery and memorial to the men of the 57th regiment of the 19th Division who gave their lives at Kemal's order on the day of the Anzac landing. The memorial and cemetery, which is treated by Turkish people as a mosque, is built on what was The Chessboard, a maze of trenches that gave the Turks such a commanding position above Monash Gully. Busloads of Turkish schoolchildren and a scattering of Australasian travellers wandered through the cemetery, though few bodies are actually buried beneath the headstones. Women placed flowers in the outstretched hand of a giant sculpture of a Turkish soldier.

We passed Quinn's and Courtney's and Steele's Posts cemeteries on the right, and Johnston's Jolly cemetery on the left, but I knew I would be back to these places in a few days, so felt no guilt at failing to stop at places that lie at the heart of the Anzac story. Besides, the day was advancing.

We had to spend time at Lone Pine. It is impossible not to. It grabs you and holds you. More Australian men lie beneath the ground at Lone Pine, or are commemorated on its stone roll of honour, than at any other place on the Gallipoli Peninsula.

And yet its name has nothing at all to do with Australia, beyond the memory of a song the homesick soldiers might have heard on a gramophone or a pianola. Its genesis is to be found in a remote locale that few Anzacs had ever been: the Appalachian mountains of Virginia in the United States of America.

On the 1915 map I carried with me, the place we call Lone Pine was called Lonesome Pine. It got the name from a song popular in Australia in 1914, though I had never been able to find out much about it. A bit of digging revealed a winsome tale.

The song was called 'On the Trail of the Lonesome Pine'. It was written in 1912 by US songsmith Ballard MacDonald, with music by Harry Carroll. American culural imperialism was well underway in Australia even then. It was a jolly little ditty, yet full of longing: 'On a mountain in Virginia/ Stands a lonesome pine/ Just below is the cabin home/ Of a little girl of mine/ Her name is June/ And very very soon/ She'll belong to me/ For I know she's waiting there for me/ 'neath that lone pine tree.'

The song, though, was not the start of it. In 1908, the American author John Fox Junior wrote a novel called *Trail of the Lonesome Pine*. It was a love story set in the Appalachian mountains, beginning and ending with two lovers, June Tolliver and Jack Hale, meeting at the base of a large pine tree at the top of a mountain. Fox spent his writing years in a mountain town called Big Stone Gap in Virginia, and his book made such an impression that three movies of the story were made—the first in 1911, the last in 1936. It remains a cherished part of American mountain culture: every summer since 1964, a stage adaption of it is played by Virginia's Official Outdoor Drama in Big Stone Gap, though I doubt many who attend the event would be aware of its connection to a hilltop on the Gallipoli Peninsula.

When the Anzacs climbed from Shrapnel Valley and Shell Green to the plateau the Turks called Bloody Ridge, they found a single Aleppo pine tree standing above the low scrub. All the other trees on the plateau had been cut down by Turks intent on using the logs to buttress the trenches they had dug into the land.

Perhaps someone, struck by the sight of the single tree, began singing 'On a mountain in Virginia/ Stands a lonesome pine', or perhaps some romantic had read John Fox Junior's love story, or perhaps a few of the boys had seen the silent movie of 1911. How could any of these young men without women who knew the song or the story not feel a tug of the heart at the idea that somewhere, a sweetheart might be waiting? 'For I know she's waiting there for me/ 'neath that lone pine tree.'

Something altogether less idyllic awaited the Anzacs beneath the lone pine on Bloody Ridge.

If Chunuk Bair is sacred ground to the New Zealanders, Lone Pine is Australia's holy place.

In the five-and-a-half days of the August offensive, from dusk on 6 August to the weary, mind-numbing morning of 12 August, the men of the 1st Australian Infantry Brigade tore away logs covering the Turkish trenches and went at the business of killing with bayonets and bare hands. The Turks counter-attacked and counter-attacked, but the Australians would not relent. The Turkish trenches, which lay under what now is the Lone Pine cemetery, were captured, and seven Victoria Crosses were awarded for bravery. The equation was this: for a piece of land not much bigger than a football field, 2000 Australians and 5000 Turks were counted as casualties. Casualty is the easy, lying word the military uses to strip emotion from the reality of death and maiming. Many of the captured trenches were used as mass graves.

The lonesome pine, like so many other living things on that ridge, was blown to bits, and a bit of its trunk was later found in the remains of a tunnel. Australian soldiers gathered cones and took them home, where the seeds were propagated. A tree grown from these seeds stands in the grounds of the Australian War Memorial in Canberra, and others can be found at memorials and schools all over the place.

One such tree, grown from just such a seed, spreads shade in the Lone Pine cemetery. When bushfires raged across the Gallipoli Peninsula in 1994, destroying pine forests and returning Old Anzac to the sort of hardy environment that greeted the

Australian and New Zealanders in 1915, the tree inside the Lone Pine cemetery escaped untouched by the flames.

Commonwealth War Graves Commission workmen had erected stadium-style seating around the cemetery for the coming Anzac ceremony, and travellers sat silently on the bleachers while others combed the headstones, some searching for ancestors. We joined them.

The rows of headstones and their epitaphs struck us dumb. '2195A Private N.W. Clarke, 3rd Bn Aust. Infantry 7–12 August 1915. Age 18. God took our Norman. It was His will. Forget him No. We never will.'

'365 Private G.F. Preston, 3rd Bn, Aust. Infantry. 7–12 August 1915. Age 22. Gone Before.' Before everything a life might hold, one imagines.

'1393 Private H. O'donnell, 11th Bn, Australian Infantry, 12 May, 1915. Age 16. He sleeps where Anzac heroes came to do and die.'

'75 Driver W. Bergin, 10th Bn, Australian Infantry, 6 August 1915. Age 21. A mother's thoughts often wander to this sad and lonely grave.' We stood a bit longer before W. Bergin's grave. His mother's grief compelled us to do so.

I thought of mothers and wives across Australia and New Zealand sitting through long nights, a candle guttering or a lamp hissing, chewing on pencils and choking on loss as they struggled to find a few final words for the sons and husbands who would never walk through their doors. In 1919, the Imperial War Graves Commission was established to give every fallen soldier a decent burial or a memorial. Every family of a dead soldier whose remains could be identified received a letter inviting them to write a few short words for a headstone that would stand in the sun and the rain and the snow, far away. The words could add up to no more than the space of two lines on the little stone:

68 characters, including spaces. How does a parent sum up the love for a child, his body beyond reach, in 68 characters? Mrs Bergin, I thought, had done as well as might be imagined.

And then there were the graves of the unidentified dead, who will never have an epitaph: 500 of them. At least they had graves.

On a long, long memorial wall of stone were chiselled the names of 3268 Australians and 465 New Zealanders who died during the Gallipoli campaign and who have no known grave, and another 960 Australians and 252 New Zealanders who were buried at sea.

Above this stood the Lone Pine obelisk, which Tom and I had seen from the deck of a ferry far out in the Aegean Sea. It contained a small echoing chapel, with visitors' books open. I took refuge in the little chamber and flicked through the books. Most visitors seemed unable to write more than 'rest in peace' or 'lest we forget', but I found myself unable to speak after reading a little message from Ian and Bron Lukowigk of Townsville. 'May we never forget you,' they had written. 'RIP Great Grandpa, wish we could have known you.'

The obelisk was throwing a long shadow into the dust beyond the cemetery. We set off to find a path back down to Shrapnel Valley, crashing around among old Australian trenchlines until we returned to the road and walked back past Johnston's Jolly cemetery a few hundred metres from Lone Pine. A sign informed us of a steep pathway into the valley and to the 4th Battalion Parade Ground cemetery. We plunged down through thick bush, heading west. Once, this would have been Bridges' Road, a route for soldiers moving from Shrapnel Valley up to Wire Ridge—named for its tangle of barbed wire—between Johnston's Jolly and Lone Pine. The road was named for the commander of the 1st AIF, Major-General Sir William Bridges, who tended to upset his men by recklessly strolling about above ground, often bringing sniper fire down on men who knew enough to keep themselves hunkered in the trenches. An officer of the old school, he seems to have been intent on leading by exemplary courage. He was shot in Monash Gully on 15 May 1915, reportedly while actually taking the advice of his men to be careful running between cover. He begged the men to leave him where he lay, so the stretcher bearers would not be placed in danger. He was ignored, and the Turkish snipers resisted taking a single shot at the bearers as he was carried to the beach. Bridges died while being transported by ship to Alexandria. His was the only Australian body to be returned to Australia from Gallipoli, and his grave sits on Mt Pleasant above the Duntroon Military College in Canberra, where he was commander from 1910 to 1914. While Walter Burley Griffin designed the city of Canberra, few know that Bridges' grave is the only building Griffin designed in Australia's national capital.

The pathway down from the heights proved very nearly vertical. At the bottom, we burst out of the scrub to be confronted by one of the loneliest and loveliest cemeteries on Anzac. The 4th Battalion Parade Ground cemetery, a small raised patch of the most perfect green with a view straight down Shrapnel Valley to the sea, was deserted. We felt as if we had found a secret place—the feeling that had infected us for much of our walk earlier in the morning before we reached the Second Ridge road. There are 117 graves at the 4th Battalion Parade Ground—three British, 107 Australians and six unidentified. Private S.C.O. Matthews, who died on 11 May 1915 aged 23, has been given the epitaph: 'Someday, sometime, our eyes shall see the face we keep in memory'. Private Phillip Lush, also of the 4th Battalion and who died the same day as Private Matthews, is remembered thus: 'He made good'.

The afternoon was disappearing fast. We walked up behind the graveyard and found a footpath heading further uphill to a spur between the extension of the head of Shrapnel Valley to our left and Monash Gully, to our right. As we wound higher on the spur, the wall of the Razor Edge formed a silhouette half a kilometre to the north, and we wondered aloud at the madness that had tempted us to crawl across it.

Eventually, the track led us down towards the junction of Shrapnel and Monash Valleys—and then disappeared. We found ourselves confronted by a wall of head-high entangled vegetation and thorned bushes that snagged our clothes as we tried to beat through. We took off our packs and held them in front of us, trying to ram a path, but it was futile.

Tom and Ben settled on a new strategy, veering left and downhill. It worked, and we discovered a rough track running alongside a small creek. It was slippery, but we were heading in the right direction—towards the sea. Tom pointed to a white object beneath a bush and I recoiled. It looked like a skull. Ben investigated and found it was nothing but the shell of a long-dead tortoise. I was relieved, and Tom clowned around with the thing, tossing it about and chuckling at my initial horror. A minute later, the laugh was on him as he leapt from one side of the creek to the other, lost his footing and hit the muddy bank with a thud.

Suddenly, the scrub opened out and we were back at Shrapnel Valley cemetery and its Judas Tree. We had completed a great triangle of a walk, covering much of the original battlefields of old Anzac.

It was time for a final ritual.

A busload of tourists stood above Anzac Cove in a soft light, listening reverently to a guide explaining the detail of the first landing. We recognised some of the travellers—Renee from the Boomerang Bar and three young blokes we had met on the ferry during the morning who were from Canberra's Marist College.

The sun was an orange ball hovering a degree or two above the sea between Imbros and Samothrace.

There was no path down from the road to the beach of Anzac Cove—there was just a 6-metre cliff, created when the road was built, carving more than half the beach's original width away.

Ben took a look and declared, 'Piece of piss.' He leapt over the edge, slid, gained a foothold and danced down the face. Tom and I followed as best we could.

Tom stripped to his jockey shorts. I had Speedos beneath my jeans. We had known for days that we would swim at Anzac Cove. Had to.

Gingerly, we waded into the water, leaving Ben sitting on a rock on the beach. The chill was a shock after the day's heat.

In the shallows, beach pebbles quickly turned to larger, smooth rocks covered with slippery lichen. It was difficult to stand upright, and I thought of the Anzacs jumping out of their boats, their Army boots sliding on the rocks, bullets churning the water. But it was a hard reach, this imagining, for this was no pale dawning, and there were no rifles above in dark hills. We were alone, and the hills were lent a soft glow by the sinking sun. The water was golden.

I waded until the rocks gave way to sand in deeper water. I dreaded the thought of submerging in the refrigerated sea, but we had come so far there could be no getting out of it. I took a breath and plunged, emerging with such a bellow that a group of heads from the bus tour popped over the cliff to see what the fuss was about.

Tom was splashing about happily a bit further out, but I felt alone.

I dived underwater and cruised along the bed of the sea, cocooned within a green, endlessly silent world. It felt like a baptism. I held my breath until my lungs began a revolt.

The urge to swim at Anzac Cove captures many travellers. In 1990, the man who would become Australia's deputy prime minister, Tim Fischer, couldn't resist. To the delight of accompanying journalists, he raced unexpectedly into the water, and the reporters hurled pebbles so he might experience a little of what it meant for the Anzacs to swim beneath shrapnel fire. I remembered a scene from the film *Gallipoli* where swimmers heard underwater the sound of shrapnel as dull fizzes and pops, disembodied, as if they were far away—even as a swimmer was hit and his blood turned the water red.

Soon, we were back on the beach, dressed and damp and in search of a trail back up to the road. Ben and Tom each pocketed a pebble from the beach. For many who come here, it is an instinctive thing, this urge to take away a piece of the Cove.

I skimmed George's diary, searching for something suitable with which to connect experiences at this place. It was there in the entry for 15 June 1915. Twenty days earlier, George had written of the sinking of HMS *Triumph*, a large battleship. 'Submarine amongst the Allied fleet in bay,' he wrote on 25 May. 'Sunk HMS Triumph about a quarter of a mile out. Saw the explosion and watched her sink. Sank in about 10 minutes, 50 hands lost.'

Then, on 15 June, came the sequel: 'Shell fire on beach in evening. Ninety gallon of wine washed up from Triumph. Great rejoicing.' Finally, a contented day at the Cove. It must have been a brief blessing, that wine, bringing a crooked smile to a battalion of lips as the shells screamed in.

The bus had gone, and twilight was descending, the sky violet, as we marched along. It was likely, we thought, that we would have to walk the 12 kilometres back to Eceabat. It didn't matter. We felt as if we could walk all the gentle night.

Within a few minutes, though, an ancient four-wheel-drive vehicle came chugging along and stopped. The driver was going home to Eceabat. He was a gardener with the Commonwealth War Graves Commission, and asked what graves we had visited. He expressed delight and surprise as we reeled off our list.

'Oh,' he said. 'Many, many. Not so many people see all these graves. And are they nice?'

We told him the cemeteries were beautiful, and the gardener was flattered. 'Thank you, thank you,' he said. 'Must be kept nice for all those men from your country.' It was a touching thing to hear from a Turk, and we pointed out that thousands of his countrymen lay up on those ridges, too.

'Yes,' he said. 'War is no good.'

He dropped us at the Eceabat terminal just in time for an evening ferry.

Both Eceabat and Çanakkale had been transformed while we had been away. Young Australian and New Zealand faces were everywhere, and backpacks disappeared into every doorway where there might be a bed for the night. The ferry was low in the water with big coaches. Newcomers, young, old and in-between, swarmed the decks. Tea waiters weaved among the crowd.

Anzac House was in tumult. The place crawled with new arrivals, many of them seething because the hostel was booked out. Staff were scurrying and a pile of essentials had been dumped at the front door by delivery truck—sacks of rice, boxes of vegetables, cartons of beer and, yes, jars of Vegemite. The two computers were in impossible demand, would-be emailers lined up. Every chair was occupied down the back of the hostel, where the audience couldn't possibly hear the soundtrack of *The Fatal Shore* playing on the TV.

I felt off-balance. We had emerged from a silent world of land and sea and gravestones, and the racket was too much.

I grabbed my backpack and escaped. My time as a guest of Anzac House was over. The Anzac Day hordes had arrived and

I strode up the street to the two-star Anzac Hotel, booked four months previously over the Internet. A polite young man from reception insisted on carrying my pack and showing me the way to a private room with its own bathroom. In the lobby sat a group of tourists with nicely pressed trousers and shirts, and a couple of women in frocks. Two or three of the men were sporting brand new Akubra hats. I gave them a wave, and one of them nodded and almost tipped the brim of his hat.

I sat on my bed, for which I had paid 285 British pounds to guarantee a roof for the next three nights plus a bus tour to Troy and across the battlefields in what is perhaps the tightest period of accommodation anywhere in the world, and felt disconnected.

Scribbling in my diary for half an hour offered no settlement. I tucked the diary away in my pack and walked back around the corner to the hubbub of Anzac House. It felt like home. Tom was standing amid the uproar with a beer in his hand.

'Wrighty,' he called. 'You're back. They've given me a bunk in a dormitory of twelve and half of them are sheilas. What do you think we go to the Boomerang for a beer and talk about what we did today? It was great, wasn't it?' He had a grin that was as cheerful as an Irish bar.

'No worries,' I said. 'Ninety gallons of wine. Great rejoicing.'

We caught the 10.00 p.m. ferry back across the Dardanelles to discover the Boomerang Bar packed to the rafters. The sound system was cranked up to about 12 with AC/DC roaring. Chris and Gregg were flying up and down the bar, trying to deal with a hundred orders at once. Kids from Contiki and Fez tours stood on tables and the room heaved with dancers. Tom and I fought our way through the bedlam, grabbed a couple of drinks from Gregg and headed for the back door. Outside, the carpark had become a camping ground. A convoy of big troop-carrier trucks was lined up. Their trays were fitted with rows of armchairs bolted to the floor beneath canvas canopies. Barbecues welded to the sides of these giant vehicles had been swung down, and hungry travellers were throwing steaks on the hotplates. These trucks were the mammoths of the overland trails from London through the Middle East and across Africa.

Nearby, every inch of ground was covered with tents. Travellers sat around on little aluminium chairs, playing guitars and yapping. We searched for Matt's tent and found it a metre or so from a truck wheel. Other tents had stolen his sea view. He wouldn't be happy, particularly because the new tents had been erected along a strip of new turf he had been told to avoid. Still, he had not been squashed by a troop-carrier.

We fought our way back inside and found Matt wedged against the bar, refusing to give up his spot to anyone and not amused by the turn of events. His eyes were glassy—he had just finished a Boomerang special, the 'funnel of love', perhaps the least sophisticated drinking game known. Beer is poured into a funnel attached to a long corrugated hose and the drinker simply guzzles the contents at speed.

Something other than camping arrangements was tearing at Matt, though.

'I'm glad you're here,' he said, grabbing me by my shirt. 'I really need advice. I just don't know what to think.'

Matt was as intense as I could imagine him to be.

'This bloke just came up to me and showed me an old bullet he'd taken off the battlefields,' he said. 'It's not right, is it? Forgive me, but I'm a bit upset about it. I mean, what are the ethics of this?'

That dishevelled, carefree Matt, the Coffs Harbour boy who looked as if nothing mattered but the next wave or the next open road, could be so troubled by the ethics of a stranger removing a single bullet from the Anzac battlefield was intriguing.

'I mean, I don't know if I had a grandfather or a relative here. I'm going to have to ask my mother, and I can't believe I've come all this way without knowing that,' he said.

'But it can't be right for anyone to be taking things from a place like that. It's like stealing from a cemetery, isn't it?'

I hardly knew what to say. He was right, of course. The battlefields have become a peace park protected by law, and no artifacts are allowed to be removed. But so many visitors pocket a shell or a ball of shrapnel that it has become a kind of ritual. Tour guides regularly present a bullet and a shrapnel ball to each of their guests, neatly packaged. And the fact was, I had a couple of these very items burning a hole in my pocket, taken from Russell's Top during the day. I intended to take them back to Heywood for George's sister Eileen.

I made soothing noises at Matt and told him his instincts were right, and that I was not well positioned to advise him on ethics. He had a good heart, that boy, which is why no one could help but like him. He seemed mollified.

The Boomerang party was beginning to steam. Outside, an English bloke with blond hair and dead eyes was rumoured to be making a small killing unloading ecstasy tablets on young travellers. The funnel of love was bobbing around the room and I couldn't get through the crush to order a drink from Chris or Gregg.

It seemed a good time to catch the last ferry back to Çanakkale.

13

ANZAC EVE

*He sprinkled my hands with a lemon perfume, handed me a towel
to wipe my face, and wrapped me in a bear-hug. 'Happy Anzac,'
he said. I couldn't manage a word.*

Anzac Day at Gallipoli is a marathon. It begins the day before,
and you cannot expect any real sleep for 36 hours. On the
morning of 24 April, I allowed myself a sleep-in.

At least, I tried, but it didn't work. The hotel was strangely
quiet, and I missed the sound of slamming doors, the flushing of
toilets, the hiss of water from the shower block and the cheery
calling of young travellers that had become the signature of
morning at the hostel around the corner. I tossed and turned in the
genteel silence of my hotel room and eventually gave up. Pulling
on a pair of jeans and a t-shirt, I laced up the hiking boots that had
accompanied me on every step of this journey and strolled to
Anzac House. The place was in uproar. During the night, a couple
of urchins had scaled a wall three storeys high and had broken
through a window to the dormitory Tom was sharing with a dozen
newly arrived travellers, who had all been at the bars of Çanakkale
and Eceabat when the burglary occurred. A couple of passports,
travellers' cheques, cash and clothing had disappeared back down
the wall with the young intruders. Police had been called and had
taken about 30 minutes to roust the suspects from a back alley.

There had been a scene at the police station. The alleged burglars, aged twelve or thirteen, were given a few backhand cuffs and a kick in the pants to persuade them to confess and their parents, also called in by the gendarmes, were mightily unimpressed. The parents, unwilling to challenge the police about this rough justice, began threatening the backpackers who had laid the complaint. It was a fraught night, but the stolen passports, money and the rest had not materialised. As far as I know, nothing ever did.

Tom had been too travel-savvy to leave any of his valuables in the dormitory, so had slept through much of the kerfuffle. I felt a little smug about the webbed money belt I wore under my jeans, containing passport, air tickets, travel insurance papers and cash. It never left my body, and had proved its worth through years of travel to some of the dodgiest countries on Earth. It was not entirely foolproof, but I figured that if someone was going to take the trouble to rip off my pants to get at the money, then I was in so much strife that the theft of passport and dollars was a secondary consideration. Anyway, I always had a small wad of walking-around money in my pocket to hand over in the event of a mugging.

Tom and I quit the upheaval in the dormitory and ordered an omelette and tea for a leisurely breakfast downstairs. We had a day to kill, and there was no point travelling to the battlefields just yet. The peninsula, we knew, would be crawling with new arrivals. The road from Istanbul was a long trail of coaches and mini-buses, nose to tail, all bouncing along to Anzac Cove. Some of the bigger tour companies had convoys of a dozen or more buses crammed with Australians and New Zealanders on package tours. By midday, it would be just about impossible to move at the better known cemeteries of Anzac.

Ben and Philippa, who had not made reservations at Anzac House during the high-priced three days of Anzac, had moved out and found rooms in private houses around Çanakkale. They dropped in for a cup of tea, grumpy with the morning. Philippa needed to transfer money from her stubby-holder sales back to London, but was having trouble making herself understood at either the local banks or the post office. Ben decided to help and enlisted the support of the Anzac House manager, Serif. They set off to a bank as Tom and I jumped on a ferry bound for Eceabat. We wanted to see how Hanifi was faring with his renovations at the Vegemite Bar.

Hanifi wasn't around, and the Vegemite Bar was quiet. It was set up as a restaurant, with long rows of tables next to picture windows right above the waters of the Dardanelles. It was clean and ordered and Tom and I agreed it would never attract back-packers. It was built for a more civilised clientele. The wharf and the motel suites and the private launch were yet to come. Visions take time. We wished the absent Hanifi luck and wandered outside. Across the road, an empty lot had been transformed into a sea of silver. Fez Tours, from London, had erected 300 tents, all of them silver. A couple of days before we had chatted to a couple of young Australian blokes, stripped to the waist, as they laboured to create this flimsy city. We bought them a beer and they told us the job was paying their way to Gallipoli.

Tom sauntered off to seek out Chris, Gregg and Matt. None of them had booked a bus to Anzac for the Anzac Day ceremonies, so they had to make plans. I returned to Çanakkale, restless and—for a few hours—purposeless.

Along the seafront from the Çanakkale ferry wharf is the town's only first-class hotel, The Akol. The official parties from Australia and New Zealand take over entire floors of the hotel each Anzac period, and the Australian deputy prime minister, John Anderson, and the Governor-General, Peter Hollingworth, were expected. The New Zealand government had sent Conservation

Minister Sandra Lee. I decided to drop into the hotel and see who I could find.

In jeans and t-shirt, I felt out of place in the cavernous foyer, but found a small group of Australians gathered in a conversation pit by the bar. Among them were Piers Akerman, a well-fed columnist from Sydney's *Daily Telegraph*, and the Australian artist Tim Storrier. They were planning a sailing trip along the Aegean coast after the Anzac Day ceremonies, and I was welcomed into their company. Drinks were bought, and I found myself sipping a vile concoction of vodka and fizzy orange. Akerman and Storrier wanted to know where to find a decent meal, and I told them of the kebap salonu No. 2 that had become second home to Tom and me. They looked mildly interested, but I had a feeling the humble cuisine that satisfied us wasn't quite what they had in mind. I was seized by the realisation that I was going budget class, and for once I didn't really belong around the lounge chairs and the mahogany bar of The Hotel Akol.

Another journalist, Peter Wilson, joined us. I had known him for years, and he was now the London-based European correspondent for *The Australian*. He was a little harried because his Internet connections weren't working properly and he had stories to file. He already had his Anzac Day story in his head. He was outraged at all the drinking that was going on among the young travellers coming to Gallipoli. The night before he had been to a bar south of Eceabat called The RSL Club. Kids were falling down drunk, he reported. This seemed no revelation at all, and I was amused: put 10 000 or so young Australians and Kiwis together in a small town, and rowdy behaviour was hardly unlikely. But Wilson, a fine reporter, felt it was an appalling indictment and sacrilegious to the memory of the Anzacs. C'mon, Pete, I said, the original Anzacs were hardly angels and they were the same age as a lot of these kids who had travelled the world to pay homage to their memory. Plenty of the long-gone soldiers were wilder, too. Why, the very first action a lot of the original Anzacs had seen was the Battle of the Wazza.

In fact, there were two 'battles of the Wazza', both of them inglorious. The first was on Good Friday, 2 April 1915, and the second was on 31 July 1915. Both took place in Cairo's red light district, the Haret al Wassir. Australian and New Zealand troops training nearby took to the dubious delights of the 'Wazza' with great enthusiasm, but things got out of hand. Apparently unimpressed by prices for watered-down liquor and the fact that many of the troops caught the clap from the women of the brothels, rioting broke out. In both 'battles', Egyptians' houses and shops were set on fire, chairs, tables, wardrobes—and, in one case, a piano—were thrown out of second-storey windows and general drunken uproar occurred. Military police and other troops had to be called to restore some sort of order.

Compared to that sort of behaviour, the young people cramming the bars of Çanakkale and Eceabat were lambs.

Besides, I told Wilson, wait until tomorrow: when the Dawn Service began at North Beach, and later at the ceremony at Lone Pine, he would see nothing but quiet respect on display. But Wilson had made up his mind, and his Anzac Day story in *The Australian* appeared under the headline 'Beer-swillers invade sanctity of Cove'. Virtually every line of the piece concerned young Australians and New Zealanders guzzling grog in the eight bars of Eceabat, which is about 12 kilometres from Anzac Cove. The following day, his report of the Anzac ceremonies was headlined 'Ban the boozy bacchanalia at Anzac Cove'. It painted an alarming picture of 'hundreds dancing and boozing near the graves of those they were there to honour'. The stories caused such concern back in Australia that the government ordered an inquiry. The Office of War Graves, which was asked by the Minister for Veterans'

Affairs, Dana Vale, to investigate, described Wilson's report as 'greatly exaggerated' and 'misleading'. 'Despite the large crowd, both the dawn and Lone Pine services were marked by exemplary behaviour,' the inquiry found. It also pointed out there were no war graves on the Anzac commemorative site where the dawn service was held.

The truth, as usual, lay somewhere between these widely divergent points of view. Wilson saw what he saw and reported it, through the focus of a tight deadline. The Office of War Graves was unlikely to respond that an event it had organised was, as Wilson reported, in danger of becoming 'an embarrassing drinking tour which pays little respect for the dead'.

In fact, there have never been any easy truths about Anzac: it is about as valid to say that all men who came to Gallipoli were heroes as it would be to say they were all the sort of scoundrels who were happy to burn down homes and businesses along the streets of the Wazza.

The verities of the Anzac Day services on Gallipoli, anyway, were before us. It was mid-afternoon and the dawn service was still fourteen hours away. The vice-regal figure of Peter Hollingworth, jaw jutting, breezed through The Akol's foyer, trailed by a flurry of officials, on his way to open an art exhibition down the street.

I farewelled my companions at The Akol and strolled along the waterfront. The sun shone and I bought an icecream—a Turkish treat made of goat's milk and sugar mixed with the pulverised root of a plant named saleph. The result is a compound that stretches like rubber, and the vendor played up to a small crowd, twisting and tugging and tossing his icecream as if it were silly putty. Children grinned and danced from one foot to the other, tugging at their parents' clothes and begging for a taste. I chose a cone of mulberry-flavoured icecream and felt a lightness of the heart that, in the age of TV, a simple street vendor could entertain whole families. The air was scented by the sea and artists had set up easels along the pavement. A theatre group had colonised a stretch of the seafront walkway, and a large crowd gathered as painted actors roared at each other and brandished swords in a play of homage to the military glories of the Ottoman Empire. For the Turks, Anzac Eve was a festival. It was impossible to imagine that the great-grandparents of these people, laughing and carefree, had suffered so much beating back an invasion of my ancestors.

I wandered, the sun on my face, watching old women sitting on the seawall, cackling among themselves, and their men sipping tea at nearby cafés. A young fellow swaggered past, looked me in the eye and declared, 'Anzac, hey?' and gave me a thumbs up. We shook hands and continued our separate promenades.

Eventually, I retreated to my hotel, considering a nap. Two Australians—a tall young man and a young woman with blonde hair bleached almost white—were at the reception counter, immense backpacks on their shoulders. They appeared exhausted and frustrated. The receptionist was explaining there were no rooms available. There were no rooms anywhere, he said.

'We just want a shower,' the woman said. 'Isn't there somewhere we could shower?'

I introduced myself. The couple said they had travelled by bus from Syria. They couldn't remember their last decent sleep. They had simply wanted to get to the Anzac ceremonies, but they hadn't figured on a total lack of accommodation when they arrived. The tall man's name was Grant. He was an Australian soldier on leave. His girlfriend was Gabrielle, a nurse from the Canberra hospital.

'I have a room,' I said. 'It has a shower.' I gave them my key and they disappeared with their backpacks into the hotel lift.

It seemed a good opportunity to check my travel arrangements for the night. I mooched around to Anzac House and was told I was booked on Hassle Free Tours bus number three. The guide was a Turkish woman named Sandra, who was on the pavement outside, looking out for her charges. Yes, she said, we meet at the ferry wharf at 11.00 p.m. The bus would be waiting across the strait at Eceabat. Don't worry, you will not be left behind, she promised. It seemed simple enough, but crowds of travellers, fresh in from their day's tour of the battlefields, were already beginning to fill the streets. Within a few hours, searching for a tour guide would be similar to hunting for a needle in a haystack.

Something else was happening on the street. Turkish hawkers were hauling barrows along the pavement, jostling for position near restaurants and hostels. Each barrow was loaded with items of clothing. Clotheslines of Anzac souvenir t-shirts were erected and a brisk trade began. However, the bulk of the items were the sort of thing one might purchase for winter: woollen scarves, gloves, mittens, beanies and balaclavas.

The sun was almost gone, and the breeze from the Dardanelles was turning cold. Scarves and beanies began to make sense.

I had come prepared for a cold night. Back in my room I had lightweight thermal gear—long johns and a long-sleeved singlet. I had also packed a medium-weight fleece pullover, Gortex jacket and thermal-lined gloves and beanie. A New Zealand couple peered at one of the barrows and wondered aloud whether they would need cold-weather gear. I exhorted them to purchase everything they could carry. The clothing was so cheap they could jettison it the next day if they did not want to haul it around for the remainder of their Turkish tour.

Tom was nowhere to be found and I began worrying that he might not make it to Anzac for the ceremonies. I called him on his mobile phone and he told me he had been chasing around after John Anderson to get an interview for his radio network back in Australia. How are you getting to Anzac, I asked?

'Oh, mate, no worries,' said Tom. 'You're not going to believe it. Chris and Gregg have talked the owner of the Boomerang Bar into lending us his truck. We're going to drive.'

The truck was famous around Gallipoli. It was a big 1963 Mercedes-Benz troop carrier painted bright yellow. It looked a bit like a wartime Blitz if you were prepared to ignore the outlandish paint job, and it usually had a load of hollering backpackers bouncing around on the tray. It sounded the ideal vehicle for a rollicking ride through the night across the peninsula.

'If I get there first, I'll reserve a spot for you at the site,' I said. We agreed to send messages on the mobile phones to ensure we found each other later in the night.

Back at the hotel, Grant and Gabrielle were showered and sporting decidedly brighter spirits. They hoisted their packs and set off, damp-haired, to book a bus for the trip to Anzac.

My chance for a nap had come and gone. I worried that if I lay down now, I would sleep for hours and miss my rendezvous with bus number three. Evening was advancing, so I set off up the street to the familiar eating house, the kebap salonu No. 2. Everything seemed to be coming by numbers. The restaurant manager greeted me like an old friend and I sat alone, filling up on Turkish meatballs and gritty salad. When I finished my feast, the manager wouldn't give me a bill. 'Is Anzac,' he said. 'My gift to you.' He sprinkled my hands with a lemon perfume, handed me a towel to wipe my face, and wrapped me in a bear-hug. 'Happy Anzac,' he said. I couldn't manage a word.

Down by the ferry wharf, the crowd was building. Coaches stretched in a line down the street, belching diesel fumes. Travellers milled about and guides called for their groups to stay together. A boy selling pistachios was doing endless business and the chestnut vendor's cart seemed to be afire. I hurried to my hotel to don thermals and to pack a sleeping bag, jacket, gloves, beanie, chocolate bars, pastries, fruit and water for the night and day ahead. I tossed in a bottle of wine, having failed during the day to find a single bottle of rum, which seemed the thing to take to Anzac.

Burdened with a heavy day-pack, I returned to the wharf and managed to find Sandra the tour guide looking anxious. 'I thought you were lost,' she said sternly. 'Stay close.' The others in our group were mainly middle-aged and elderly New Zealanders and several of the men wore service medals.

The ferry, running every half hour to cope with the crowds, came bellowing to the pier and we trooped aboard. Every seat was taken and I stood at the rail, watching Çanakkale's lights recede. All around, excited conversations filled the night. 'I've wanted to do this all my life,' an elderly woman said to no one in particular. 'My father was here, you know.' I turned to her and she began sobbing. Her travelling companion, a younger woman, took her by the shoulders and walked her towards a packed bench, and several young men got to their feet, offering their seats. If this old lady was overcome on the ferry, I thought, it would be a long night once she reached the peninsula.

Eceabat's main street was jammed with buses. Tour guides held signs above their heads, trying to draft the crowds disengorging from the ferry into designated groups. I stuck to the heels of Sandra, and members of our little mob called to each other in a vain attempt to cling together. It was pandemonium. Perhaps a thousand people filled the wharf and the street. Somehow, we found Hassle Free Tours bus number three and I dropped into a seat. Almost instantly, I fell asleep. When I awoke, the bus hadn't moved and, apart from the driver and me, it was empty. 'Road is blocked,' the driver said. 'Too many buses.' My fellow travellers had disembarked to go in search of coffee. As I stepped off to do the same thing, Sandra, followed by her passengers, returned. 'We will move soon,' she promised. 'You must return to your seat.'

Eventually, we began moving and I fell asleep again. I awoke to discover our vehicle inching through a tiny village, white-washed walls almost brushing my window. We appeared to be taking a great arc across the peninsula and approaching Anzac from the north. A trip that normally took no more than 20 minutes was taking more than two hours. We had left Çanakkale at 11.00 p.m., and now it was after 1.00 a.m.

I figured Tom and the boys would have found their way to the ceremonial site and I dialled Tom's phone. It was engaged.

The bus began slowing and, outside the window, hawkers' barrows lined the edges of the road. Pistachios, Efes beer, kebaps, t-shirts, scarves and gloves, trinkets . . . the streets of Çanakkale appeared to have moved to Anzac. Travellers traipsed beside the bus, weighed down with packs. We had, I decided, arrived. Our conveyance, anyway, was stopped. The traffic was jammed. I bid farewell to Sandra and the other passengers, grabbed my pack and jumped off, into a stream of pedestrians. Ahead and to the rear, the lights of buses seemed endless. A few hundred metres away I could see three floodlit flagpoles rising into the night. It was the ceremonial site. But how was I to get there? Each side of the road was choked with people, and the further I walked, the thicker the crowd became. Rock music boomed from big speakers somewhere up in that crowd. Searchlights waved around and the mass of bodies ahead seemed to be heaving, casting strange shadows. I had a sudden feeling that I was watching one of the more surreal scenes from *Apocalypse Now*. Good Lord, how were elderly folk to cope in that mess?

There seemed only one sensible thing to do. I quit the road and pushed through undergrowth, stumbling on uneven ground until I reached the beach.

I was almost alone. A full moon hung red in the sky, and the Aegean stretched flat before me. Pebbles crunched beneath my boots.

I dialled Tom's phone again. I could hear singing in the background when Tom answered.

'Where are you?' I asked. Tom laughed.

'Mate,' he said. 'If I gave you a million guesses, you'd never even get close. You can't imagine what's happened.'

14

DAWN AT ANZAC

At 4.30 a.m., the moon slipped behind the island of Gökçeada, old Imbros, and a deep darkness settled, just as it had exactly 87 years previously. The loudspeakers fell silent and the crowd hushed. Soon, a military band swung into a medley of tunes and the bitter chill of the night seemed to drift away.

I had a sinking feeling. Tom and the boys had surely got themselves into some sort of jam and weren't going to make it.

'We left the Boomerang Bar about midnight in the yellow truck,' Tom said. 'We got about 600 feet down the road and it blew up. Smoke and steam started coming out of the motor and it wasn't going any further.'

'So where are you now?' I asked.

'That's the best bit. We pushed the truck back to the bar and we found that bloke with the horse and cart. So we paid him a lot of money.

'Now we're all on the cart and we're on our way. We're more than halfway there. It's fantastic.' He roared with laughter, and the singing in the background became louder. It was the lilting Queensland version of 'Waltzing Matilda'.

'I've just done a live cross to 2UE and they reckon they've never heard better radio. Listen to this.'

Tom stopped talking, the singing died away and I could hear horse hooves on bitumen. It sounded like a brisk trot.

'Every time we come to a hill we all get off and walk. We're a bit worried about the horse,' Tom said.

'Then every time we're going down a hill, we get off, too, so we don't have the cart pushing the horse along. We're doing a fair bit of walking.'

There were, it transpired, seven people aboard the little cart, including Tom, Chris, Gregg and Ben.

'So far the police have let us through all the roadblocks, but I don't know if we are going to be allowed to go all the way on this contraption,' Tom said. 'But it doesn't matter. We'll be there soon, even if we have to walk a bit. It's a beautiful night.'

I told him I'd stake out a decent patch of ground amid the crowd and would get back to him with directions. Amused at the thought of my friends' little adventure—and envious that I was not with them—I continued walking along the beach towards the floodlit flagpoles. The noise from the crowd above grew louder with every step.

Soon I found myself directly below the ceremonial podium. Above, the crowd appeared enormous. I scrambled up from the beach and discovered there wasn't a square centimetre of lawn that wasn't occupied. Thousands of bodies lay side by side in sleeping bags. Small groups sat around, singing and laughing and yelling to each other. Pretty obviously, all these people had arrived during the day to secure prime positions. Above the lawn, thousands more figures moved around in the darkness, lit weirdly by large spotlights, and buses continued crawling along the road. I skirted the lawn, found a track through scrub and headed up to the road. The noise was deafening. Jimmy Barnes was screaming 'Khe San' from banks of loudspeakers, and big generators roared somewhere away in the bush. Young travellers

stood around the loudspeakers, drinking, apparently unconcerned about ear damage. Inland from the road more crowds
seethed. Tour guides were setting up chairs for their older customers in a natural bowl, and families and school groups were
burrowing into the undergrowth to gain a bit of territory.
Higher still, at the foot of the black ridges that confronted the
first Anzacs, hundreds of people were scattered, intent on
getting a view of proceedings, their jouncing torches suggesting
fireflies in the night.

It all reminded me of an outdoor rock festival from the early
1970s. There was even a bank of Porta-Loos hidden away in
the bush. I hardly dared think what might be going through the
minds of older travellers who had come to pay quiet homage to
the Anzacs. Wait, just wait, I willed them. Come the dawn, the
rock festival will be replaced by something else altogether.

My most urgent task was to find a spot that would accommodate me and my friends. I headed back down to the lawn in
front of the podium, trying not to step on sleeping bodies. The
search for a piece of unoccupied ground appeared hopeless, but
I spotted a small group vacating their territory at the very edge
of the crowd, not far from the podium. I pounced, laid out my
sleeping bag, pulled a coat out of my pack and tossed it a metre
away, threw the pack towards another corner of the unoccupied
ground and sprawled in the middle of my makeshift colony. All
I had to do now was to defend the area.

A bloke lying in a sleeping bag next to me cocked an eye.
'Neat trick,' he said.

'I've got a bunch of mates walking in and I'm trying to save
them a spot,' I explained. 'No worries,' he said, and tossed his
pack into my pile of belongings. 'That might help.' I was grateful, and dug around in my bag for the bottle of wine. My new
friend sat up and declared he'd be happy to toast the morning.

The wine tasted vile, but improved quickly. Despite my thermals, the chill of the night was fierce. I crawled into my sleeping bag and waited for Tom's call.

About 2.30 a.m., my phone buzzed. 'We're here,' said Tom, and I directed him to my patch of turf. Chris arrived carrying a Turkish carpet and tossed it on the ground. Ben had a small flask of whisky and a metal soup plate. He poured a slug of spirits into the plate and handed it around. Gregg's newly shaved head was freezing, so I lent him a beanie. Tom had his tape recorder slung over his shoulder and said he needed to wander around and gather interviews for his next cross to Sydney radio. The rest of us crammed together while Chris, Ben and Gregg recounted the tale of their journey across the peninsula.

It was pretty much as Tom had explained, but Gregg added a bit of colour. Tom had been giving an interview with Sydney radio when the truck blew up, he said.

'Tom gets a phone call on his mobile and goes to a live radio cross saying "I'm in an old army truck and heading up to the battlefields . . . blah blah blah . . . there's a young Australian driving the truck . . ." The vehicle has reached a screaming roar by this stage. I'm surprised Tom could hear a thing, so we turn the truck around to try and drive back. We just keep on accelerating, going nowhere, and just as Tom's saying "we seem to be having some sort of mechanical difficulties" water starts shooting out the dash. The clutch seems to be gone and the truck's overheating so we cut the engine and push the truck back to the bar.

'Chris quickly runs over to the smiley entrepreneurial gypsy horse and cart driver who's been transporting people up and down the 500 metre main street for the last few days and sees if he can take us up for the services—the truck no longer being an option.

'This guy wouldn't miss an opportunity so agreed for a price that was suitable for him. So the seven of us jump on to the back of the cart and start again. Not far in Tom got his next call and says, "You'll never believe it, I'm now headed up to the battle-field on the back of a horse and cart . . . well actually it's more of a donkey and cart . . .". With a very audible clip clop clip clop in the background he pulled off what sounded like a fantastic piece of radio.'

The cart ride had been stopped by the police about 3 kilo-metres from the ceremonial site, Ben said, and the little party had walked the rest of the way.

'It was just perfect,' he said. 'No buses or cars were allowed on that stretch of road, so we walked along beside Anzac Cove all alone, with the moon shining on the water. It was peaceful and still. Everything ever written about that first night, when the Anzacs came ashore, says it was a perfect night, so we got to see it like it is supposed to be seen.'

A young woman came down the track and stood in front of us, shivering. 'Hey,' I said, 'Aren't you Gabrielle? You had a shower in my room?' The boys looked impressed. 'Hello,' she said. 'I can't find a place to sit down.' Chris moved over and pro-vided a tiny spot on his carpet. Gabrielle's boyfriend Grant, the soldier, appeared and plumped himself down, too. Our small piece of Anzac was getting crowded. I shrugged on my jacket and took a stroll down to the beach. Bonfires had been lit and young Turks stood around, laughing and chattering. It was their ceremony too, and their land, and it was good to see them. I stood by one of their fires, but we had no common language other than a history. We grinned at each other and warmed our hands.

At 4.30 a.m., the moon slipped behind the island of Gökçeada, old Imbros, and a deep darkness settled, just as it had exactly 87 years previously. The loudspeakers fell silent and the crowd hushed. Soon, a military band swung into a medley of tunes and the bitter chill of the night seemed to drift away. Bodies began shedding sleeping bags and, as the crowd took to its feet, we discovered there was room to move. We grabbed our belongings, Chris shouldered his carpet and we crept closer to the stage.

A trio of pipers marched through the crowd, kilts swaying and pipes wailing. The hair stood on the back of my neck. A *catafalque* party tapped its slow, ritualised and solemn march. The four soldiers halted, reversed their arms and stood, heads bowed. The revelry of the night was gone. There was not a sound from the more than 15 000 people standing in the dark.

John Anderson recited part of Laurence Binyon's 'To the Fallen', from which the Ode to Remembrance is taken: 'They went with songs to the battle, they were young/ Straight of limb, true of eye, steady and aglow/ They were staunch to the end against odds uncounted/ They fell with their faces to the foe.'

I nudged Gregg and nodded inland. An almost imperceptible pale grey light was sneaking into the sky, and the silhouette of The Sphinx was gradually appearing.

In the other direction, a hundred metres from shore, a Turkish fishing boat sat moored on the still sea. Two old fishermen, bottles in hand, were standing at the stern, watching proceedings.

Governor-General Peter Hollingworth spoke, and the ponderous tone, honed during his years as an Anglican bishop, gave it the rhythm of a sermon. 'Each year we come here in greater numbers,' he said. 'Older people to reflect and rediscover, and to realise long-held dreams and to see first hand a place they have always imagined. Younger people in a bid to understand more about their nations' history and about themselves.'

The first rays of the sun hit the peak of The Sphinx, turning it golden.

Hymns were sung, readings from Psalm 46 and *Ephesians* were given and the 'Lord's Prayer' was spoken. Wreaths were laid and the 'Ode of Remembrance' was recited: 'They shall not grow old, as we that are left grow old . . .'.

As the dawn found its way into the shadows of the commemorative site, a bugler blew 'The Last Post' and its final, trailing note fell away into a two minute silence so deep that every one of us could hear the lapping of the Aegean on the stones below. 'Reveille' brought us back.

The national anthems of three nations were played and flags made their way up the poles. As the Turkish anthem, 'Istiklal Marsi', began, the fishermen on their boat stood straight and bawled the words of their nation's song. Kiwi voices sang 'God Defend New Zealand', and Australians sang 'Advance Australia Fair'. The *catafalque* party slow-marched away and Anzac Day was upon us. The fishermen danced a jig on their boat, fired up the motor and chugged off across the silvery sea. Large gulls soared above the beach.

This was, said Ben, the Anzac Day dawn service to attend. I thought of all the other dawn services at which I had been present: in small towns in Victoria, on a wooded knoll in Arrowtown, New Zealand, in the cutting known as Hellfire Pass built by British and Australian slaves on the Burma–Thai Railway, in the Australian cemetery above the village of Villers-Bretonneux in France, at the National War Memorial in Canberra. Each contained the same elements as the other—night turning to day, the solemnity of paying honour, 'The Last Post' and the Ode. After each, I had to physically shake myself out of the dreamlike state induced by the hour and the ritual.

But this was Anzac, where the day had its birth. Ben was right. This was the one to attend. In a secular age, this was the Australian and New Zealand church. Alone among the nations, we had chosen our one consecrated day not to trumpet a victory, but to remember ancestors who had suffered and died trying. What those we remembered were trying to do is not immaterial, for in the context of their time it was an attempt to take a place in a world beyond their distant shores, and it was an attempt to fight what most of them were led to believe was an assault on a way of life that was their own. That they discovered that the world in which they found themselves was confusing and treacherous, and that they may have come to believe that they were misled and misused by an empire that saw them as mere colonials is not immaterial, either. The acronym ANZAC says a great deal, for its genesis on the beach below us denotes the first time that Australians and New Zealanders had seen themselves in matters international as people separate from the old world. The Australian and New Zealand Army Corps. The very words celebrate a spirit that recognised the pith of independence was strong only within a reliance on each other: the corps, where friendship—what they called mateship—bound men together. They were volunteers, the Anzacs, the only entirely voluntary armed force in the world through World War I.

In choosing Anzac Day as the most important national day of the year—and the first ceremonies were in 1916, only a year after the Gallipoli disaster—Australians and New Zealanders were not celebrating war. They were remembering the shock and the pain that came with giving birth to a couple of little nations in a world gone mad and honouring their children, who did not give up, even in defeat.

The whole crowd was shaking itself awake. The adventurous and the curious set off into the hills, or drifted to the beach, heading towards Anzac Cove a few hundred metres to the south.

Buses began lining up again and tour guides held their signs above their heads, trying desperately to gather their charges.

Tom, Ben, Gregg and Chris declared they would walk up Shrapnel Valley to Lone Pine. It would be another small adventure. Most other walkers continued down the road to Shell Green, where they would head uphill to Lone Pine along an easier path built in 1915 for artillery movements.

The night and age had wearied me and I opted to find bus number three for the trip to Lone Pine. Sandra the tour guide was waiting on the road, and she shepherded me with her other passengers through the milling, confused crowd to the coach. I was asleep almost before I slumped in my seat.

There were seven separate memorial services on the Gallipoli Peninsula each Anzac Day. It was impossible to attend all, simply because they were spread so far apart with too little time between them, and the roads were clogged. Apart from the international dawn service at the North Beach commemorative site, there was a 9.00 a.m. Turkish International service at Mehmetcik Abide (the Turkish soldiers' memorial on Chunuk Bair); a French memorial service at Morto Bay, east of Cape Helles, at 10.10 a.m.; a Commonwealth service at Cape Helles at 10.55 a.m.; the Australian memorial service at Lone Pine at midday; the Turkish 57th Regiment service between Lone Pine and Chunuk Bair at 12.50 p.m.; and the New Zealand memorial service at Chunuk Bair at 1.40 p.m. You would have needed a helicopter to buzz between all these events.

The crush of traffic and bodies has now persuaded the authorities to stagger the services over two days. Shortly after I returned home from Gallipoli, the Australian Department of Veterans' Affairs announced that the Turkish service at Mehmetcik Abide, the French Memorial Service at Morto Bay and the Commonwealth Memorial Service at Cape Helles would, in future, be held on the morning of 24 April.

This still left the four major services to be held on 25 April—

Anzac Day itself—in the Anzac sector of Gallipoli. The schedule for 2003 was for the dawn service to be held at the Anzac Commemorative site at 5.30 a.m.; the Lone Pine ceremony to be brought forward to 10.30 a.m.; the Turkish 57th Regiment Memorial Service to be held at 11.30 a.m.; and the New Zealand Service, at Chunuk Bair, to be brought forward to 12.30 p.m.

Virtually every Australian on the peninsula chose the midday ceremony at Lone Pine as their goal during my visit, and a few took the 3-kilometre trek up the hill afterwards to Chunuk Bair for the New Zealand service, where a couple of thousand Kiwis gathered.

It seemed I had only just closed my eyes when my coach stopped outside the Lone Pine cemetery. Shakily, I disembarked, waving to my fellow passengers—most of them New Zealanders en route to Chunuk Bair.

It would be hours before the service began at Lone Pine, and I decided to stroll up to Quinn's Post. Its cemetery sat almost at the edge of the cliff above Monash Gully and I wandered around it, trying to imagine the maze of tunnels through which the old front line soldiers had once scurried, and the entrenched firing line where they had invented the periscope rifle because they were so close to the Turks they could not raise their heads above the parapet. No sign of the post remains, but behind the cemetery it was still possible to divine the terraces that once gave some comfort to the troops clinging to the side of the cliff. In the early days of the battle, the only way up that cliff to Quinn's was by rope, at night.

I walked across the road from the cemetery—the width of no-man's-land. This side was the Turkish front line, a place the Turks called Bomba Sirte: Bomb Ridge. I thought of hand grenades and jam tin bombs hurled back and forth, and the wounded and the dying piling up and screaming. There was no cemetery here for the thousands of Turkish casualties and I crept in among the scrub, keeping an eye out for collapsed tunnels. The remains of trenches were everywhere, and here and there the soil had indeed caved in. I found a patch of soft grass, laid my head on my pack and closed my eyes. The sun was hot already. But I could not sleep—not properly. Instead, I lapsed into an extended, disturbed daydream. I do not believe in ghosts—never have. Yet there seemed to be ghosts about. They prowled through the undergrowth and they wore ripped and tired uniforms. It was, of course, my imagination, heated up by the sun. I sweated and tossed and turned for two hours, not quite sleeping, not quite awake. Eventually I shook myself free of the trance, stumbled to my feet, slunk off into a shallow trench and removed my thermals, stuffing them into my pack with all the other cold-weather gear that had been so useful during the night, and which had become a prickly torment up here on Bomb Ridge.

Before I travelled to Gallipoli, I had played with the idea of spending a night alone at Quinn's Post. Now I knew I could never do it. The funk of my daydream had given the place a haunted quality, just as old Charles Bean had written of it. Dispirited, my eyes gritty, I traipsed back down the road towards Lone Pine, passing Courtney's and Steele's Post cemetery, built above the tunnels which connected the two posts and which were almost as dangerous and exposed as Quinn's.

A sizeable crowd had built at Lone Pine. Tiers of temporary seating benches which had been built around the cemetery were full, giving it the appearance of a tennis stadium. Within the cemetery itself was an even bigger gathering. Thousands of people, almost all of them young, had taken possession of the rows of graves. Every gravestone had at least three young people standing or sitting around it. Some youngsters had draped

Australian flags over the stones. More draped flags over their own shoulders, or had the flag painted on their faces. I remembered a conversation around a table back at Anzac House with a group of young travellers. They were all republicans, they said, but they worried that a republican leader would want to replace the Australian flag. 'We don't want that—it's ours and it always has been,' one of them said, and the others voiced agreement. I expressed surprise that they would want to keep the Union Jack in the corner, but they weren't having any of it. It was, they declared, part of their country's history. And here at Lone Pine was proof of that attachment.

I couldn't find the boys, but ran into Philippa and two other women who had been staying at Anzac House, Danielle and Belinda. They were standing a few metres behind the lone pine tree, clicking photos. 'Have you ever in your life seen anything like this?' Philippa shouted. As she spoke, a huge cheer rose from the crowd. Australian veterans from World War II, Korea, Vietnam and members of the peacekeeping force of the Sinai were being led to a VIP enclosure at the front of the cemetery beneath the imposing Australian memorial. As each walked in, the crowd applauded and roared. Finally, a bearded Turkish veteran from Korea shuffled in, and the applause was deafening. The old man looked around, bewildered, and raised his arms. The crowd whooped and whistled and gave him a standing ovation.

Soon, I found the boys with the assistance of my phone-messaging service. They were towards the rear, and Gregg, the tallest of the bunch, waved an Australian flag until I spotted him. I waded through the crowd and discovered my friends had saved me a spot in front of a gravestone. It was the grave of Sapper C. Spence, Australian Engineers, who died on 6 August 1915, aged 22. 'Father in thy gracious keeping, leave we now our loved one sleeping,' the inscription read. I had brought with me a sprig of rosemary, and I laid it on the stone.

Our little group had grown. The boys had found Coffs Harbour Matt on their walk up Shrapnel Valley. 'We're walking up through the scrub and the next thing we hear something crashing around among the trees, then the vegetation starts swaying and bending and Matt bursts through,' said Chris. 'It was the funniest bloody thing I'd seen for ages.'

Matt beamed at me and gave me a hug. Tom had caught up with a friend, Kate Blanchford of Sydney, who had flown in from London. Tom's sister had turned up too and he was looking mighty pleased with himself. Another friend of the boys from Anzac House and the Boomerang Bar, a bearded bloke named Craig, had joined our gathering.

Up the front, a band struck up and a young woman from the military sang 'I am Australian' by Bruce Woodley and Dobe Newton. The thing has been done to death, but at Lone Pine it sounded new and not at all corny. Half the crowd joined in. When the music died away, a young man leapt to his feet in the bleachers and hollered, 'Aussie Aussie Aussie!' The entire crowd seemed to lose its head and shot back 'Oi Oi Oi!' I had been dreading something like this, but there was such sharp spontaneity to it that the cry seemed stripped of its usual yobbo essence, and everyone laughed. A Mexican wave rippled around the bleachers and, for a moment there, we could have been at the cricket.

'You know,' said Ben, 'No other crowd in the world could do this in one of their country's most sacred places. I feel as if I should be uncomfortable with it, but I'm not. I think the blokes under the ground here would appreciate what we're doing. I hope so, anyway.'

Chris spread his carpet and we used our packs as backrests as the formal ceremony began and a silence sank upon the immense gathering which numbered, I discovered later, 10 000. Right in front of me a young man wore a t-shirt that had inscribed on its back part of a Banjo Paterson poem: 'The mettle that a race can show, Is proved with shot and steel, And now we know what nations know, And feel what nations feel'.

The young Australian Ambassador to Turkey, Jon Philp, stood and spoke of the mutual respect that had grown between Australian and Turkish soldiers at Gallipoli, a respect that had endured. He told of how Australians had refused the offer of gas masks on the Gallipoli battlefields, because they would not believe the Turks would stoop so low as to use gas—and they didn't.

There were hymns ('The Lord's My Shepherd, I'll Not Want') and readings and prayers and a student from Mackay North State High School, Tara Ward, recited part of Michael Thwaites' poem 'The Anzac Graves of Gallipoli': 'You may not pass this place. Here you must stop. Though all the world's great tides run heedless by/ These quiet graves, where wandering goats now crop/ The thyme and salt bush, under a silent sky'.

What had seemed an exultant day out in the sunshine had taken on the characteristic of a service in a cathedral. Heads were bowed and the lone pine drooped with the weight of its significance. The hush enveloping the plateau brought to mind a cliché: silent as the grave.

Deputy Prime Minister John Anderson is rarely regarded as a great speaker, but his address to the Lone Pine service was a small treasure. He told the story of a relative, Patrick Anderson, who was wounded a day after the 25 April landing at Gallipoli, and died shortly afterwards.

'Patrick made out a simple will on the day of the landings, and gave his money to Miss Eileen Ross,' Anderson told the still crowd, his amplified voice accentuating the stillness of the crowd. 'She must have been very special to him, but all we know about her now is that she lived on a station near Glen Innes.

'Patrick should have lived into the 1960s, married his sweetheart and grown old to play with his grandchildren. Instead, he was taken from us, like so many in this place of death.

'They will never truly die. We have recorded them in stone, and we speak their names with pride. They live on in every town that has a war memorial, and every time our children march on Anzac Day.

'Remember what you have seen here today. Remember how you felt at the rising of the sun. Tell your children about your journey.'

A breeze ruffled the needles on the pine, and it seemed the only breath in the whole quiet place. We were rescued by a hymn: 'O God, Our Help in Ages Past . . .' Wreaths were laid, and the Ode recited.

The 'Last Post' blew away across the ridge and out across the Aegean, and in the minute's silence that followed I thought of Anderson's cousin and Miss Eileen Ross and what might have become of her heart in the years after Gallipoli.

The military band played a dirge as the wreaths were laid, and I snapped a picture of the boys. Their faces were lifted skyward and bathed in sunlight, and their eyes were closed. Like the thousands of people around them, they were burrowed deep inside their own thoughts. The Turkish and Australian anthems were played, and the breeze lifted the flags of the two nations that had fertilised this ground with blood and bone.

If it were possible at this moment to distill the spirit here, I thought, you might be able to solve the problems of the world. The young military woman sang Peter Allen's old song, 'I still Call Australia Home', her voice clear and floating.

The ceremony ended, but almost no one moved. Tom's friend

Kate was weeping and the boys were clearing their throats. Tom admitted he was 'a bit shaky' and Chris volunteered that he had discovered a tear in his eye twice—when Anderson had spoken about his relative and when the Turkish veteran had laid a wreath on the memorial stone. Ben, usually slow to display any emotion, blurted out: 'I've been fighting back the tears for ten minutes. I found it all amazing. I've never felt so proud to be Australian'. Matt thought the experience might have changed his life. He said that during the ceremony, he had suddenly remembered that, as a child, he and a friend had played soldiers on a hillock in his mate's backyard. 'We were re-enacting Gallipoli, and now I'm here and I can't tell you how special it is,' he said, as if he needed to say something and all he could hold on to was a memory of childhood. Gregg just stood there, waving a small flag. In front of me, a young man sat by a gravestone, gently patting it.

Down towards the tree, the official party filed away and a small mob of men appeared with a tarpaulin and rolled it out on the ground. A crowd gathered, and pennies began flying through the air. Tens of millions of Turkish lira were tossed at the feet of those standing around. Two-up was underway, and Chris hurried into the fray. One of the players spotted a Turkish soldier watching from a distance, grabbed him and handed him the throwing paddle. Soon the Turk was grinning and tossing the coins. A few of his friends joined in. Within ten minutes, hundreds of people were gathered, furiously hurling money at each other and watching the pennies fly. I thought of an old World War I story from the deserts of Syria, almost certainly apocryphal. A Turkish warplane pilot lined up for a strafing run above an encampment of Australians. But as he swooped, he noticed the men were involved in a ritual. Their faces turned to the heavens and then they all bent down. The pilot, a Muslim, kept his finger off the trigger. He could not shoot men he thought were praying to Allah. And perhaps two-up is a sort of religious ceremony, albeit pagan, with its formalised, rhythmic movements, the fixed concentration of the congregation, its reliance on the airy flight of symbols of hope and its scattered moments of ecstasy.

'I just love this,' Chris grinned. 'Two-up on Anzac Day. And we're at Lone Pine.'

Down the road a bit, another two-up school was established at Johnston's Jolly cemetery.

Above, Turkish Air Force jets began an aerobatics display, coloured smoke boiling in their wake. They rolled and dipped and screamed and roared through the sky.

Thousands in Lone Pine simply stayed where they were, standing and sitting among the graves as if they did not want this moment of their lives to pass.

At the far end of the ridge on Chunuk Bair, the New Zealand ceremony began with a fierce *haka* performed by soldiers.

New Zealand Conservation Minister Sandra Lee opened her address speaking in the Maori language: 'Nga mata haere, haere, haere. Tatou te hunga ora tena tatou, tena tatou, tena tatou katoa—To the dead, farewell, farewell, farewell. To us, the living, greetings, greetings, greetings to us all.' Australians present could hardly avoid being shamed. Maoris were among the fiercest fighters on Gallipoli, but the Australian military in 1914–15 wanted no indigenous people in its ranks—Aborigines who tried to sign up routinely had their recruitment papers stamped 'not suitable'. Their blood was not considered good enough to spill on a World War I battlefield. Deep in the National Australian Archives resides a record of one John Cubbo, a station hand who enlisted at Charters Towers, in the Queensland central west, on 18 March 1917. He was 21 and it is almost certain he was a splendid horseman, as were virtually all the station hands and stockmen of those vast Queensland station properties. He was sent off to No. 1 Depot Company at Enoggera, apparently destined for the Light Horse.

Almost six months after he enlisted, he had still not left Australia. On 7 September 1917, he was discharged on the advice of the Australian Military Force's Medical Board. He was judged to have a 'permanent disability'. The Medical Board's 'History of an invalid' is so stark and confronting that merely reading it is stupefying. Cubbo's disease or disability is listed as 'Not sufficient European parentage'. The date of origin of disability is given as 'birth'. Required to state 'concisely the essential facts of the history of the disability', the Medical Board's explanation is this: 'Father—dark man; Mother—half caste'. The 'causation of the disability' is once again, that one word: 'Birth'. Cubbo's condition is described thus: 'This man is not absolute black, but shows some signs of white blood'.

He was duly served his discharge papers, inscribed with the reason 'Having been irregularly enlisted'. The camp adjutant who signed the paper offered one small piece of kindness. 'Character good', he scrawled. So a young horseman of good character was thrown out of the Army because he was Aboriginal.

There is a postscript. Cubbo was obviously a determined young man prepared to swallow his humiliation. On 1 June 1918 he returned to the Charters Towers recruiting office and this time he was accepted. His papers describe him as a 'British subject', 5 feet 10 inches tall, weighing 147 pounds, of dark complexion, with black hair and black eyes, with perfect eyesight. There is no mention of any disability, or of his birth. Indeed, his medical papers this time have a single word next to the question of disability: 'Nil'. Perhaps the Army was running desperately short of recruits after four years of war had taken the lives of almost 60 000 young Australian men but, whatever the reason, Cubbo was assigned to the 5th Light Horse Regiment's remount unit. He sailed from Sydney aboard the troopship *Port Darwin* on 14th September 1918 and arrived in Cairo on 19 October—less than a month before the war ended. Cubbo was fortunate enough to return to Australia, unharmed, in early 1919, and he was awarded the appropriate medals for a returned soldier, which is perhaps all he wanted to be when he was first turned away for having the wrong colour of skin.

In this closed attitude to indigenous people, Australia lagged far behind its antipodean neighbour. The official exclusion of Aborigines was not only bigoted and racialist—it was futile. Scores of men of Aboriginal heritage managed to sign up, including a number from Great-uncle George's own Western Victorian district, requiring the Army and other men in the trenches to turn a blind eye. Their blood turned out to be the same colour as that of everyone else, including the Turks. Yet it was not until 1945 that Australia commissioned its first Aboriginal officer, Captain Reg Saunders. He was born at Purnum in Western Victoria, an hour's drive from my own birthplace. I can recall seeing him, snowy-haired and ramrod straight, walking through the streets of my childhood in his later years. He was a hero—shot in New Guinea, where he lost a brother during World War II, he commanded a rifle company in Korea. But he wasn't the first of his family to go to war. Both his father and his uncle served in World War I and his uncle, Reg Rawlings, received a Military Medal for bravery on the Western Front, France, before being killed in action in 1918. So much for Aborigines being judged not suitable as Anzac soldiers.

Up on Chunuk Bair, Lee spoke of the first day of battle on Gallipoli, the bloody ordeal of it, and quoted a soldier of the Auckland Infantry Battalion, who asked the question afterwards:

'Was it worth it? Was it worth your lives?' and who answered himself, 'No, no it was not.'

The Kiwi ceremony was smaller and less formal than Australia's, but the statistics of what it commemorated were proportionally even more dreadful. Of the 8566 New Zealanders who fought in the Gallipoli campaign, 2515 were killed in action, another 206 died of disease or other causes, and 4752 were wounded. In short, 87 per cent of New Zealanders who went to Gallipoli were killed or wounded. 'Almost every family in New Zealand was affected by this tragedy,' Lee pointed out. This is only slightly greater than the percentage of Australian casualties at Gallipoli, though the raw Australian numbers are much higher. In all, Australia suffered 26 111 casualties—8709 fatalities, and 17 402 wounded—according to the figures generally accepted by the Australian War Memorial. And it is true that in Australia, just as in New Zealand, virtually every family was affected by the tragedy of World War I.

It was mid-afternoon before the buses began to file down the hill from Chunuk Bair to Lone Pine. It was an astonishing sight. On the single-lane road following the old front line, 880 coaches snaked along, centimetres separating them. It seemed every tour company in Europe, Australia and New Zealand was represented. There was even a Derryn Hinch coach.

Exhausted travellers slumped by the side of the road, waiting for their ride. Hassle Free Tours bus number three was nowhere in sight. The Lone Pine two-up school had long gone into recess, and the Johnston's Jolly game was winding up. A young man walked into the graveyard and barked, 'Righto, let's clean this place up. It's a cemetery.' Within seconds, the players conjured blue plastic rubbish bags and cleared away every can and food wrapper.

Eventually, with the sun dipping towards the ocean, I spied my bus creeping around a corner. It stopped and I piled aboard.

It took another hour to reach Eceabat, but I didn't mind. I slept all the way.

Tom had expressed a desire to return to Anzac Cove for a swim and had walked off down the hill with a number of our friends, confident they could all hitch a ride back across the peninsula. Gregg and Ben chose a more direct strategy: they began jumping buses and were thrown off a few. Eventually they tried one of the numerous Fez Tours coaches, and told the guide aboard that they couldn't remember which bus number they had been allotted. But they overdid it, telling the guide they couldn't remember the name of the hotel in Eceabat at which they were supposed to be staying, either. 'But we do not have a hotel at Eceabat,' the guide said. Slowly, a grin spread across her face as she realised Gregg and Ben were trying to fox her. 'Ah, so you are lost,' she said, and took the microphone to speak to the genuine Fez Tour clients. 'Ladies and gentlemen, we have extra passengers today. They are lost. What should we do?' Her paying passengers voted unanimously to allow Ben and Gregg to travel free.

A strange, end-of-school atmosphere infected the other side of the peninsula. In Eceabat and on the ferry across the Dardanelles, and in the streets of Çanakkale, travellers appeared stunned and directionless. Most had come not quite knowing what to expect, and now it was over. They seemed lost inside feelings that had overwhelmed them, and they spoke softly, as if afraid to disturb the process of storing away an experience they did not wish to lose. They were drained by a day and a night and a day without sleep.

An enervation sank into me too as I dragged my feet back to my room. This journey was coming to an end, but I could not surrender just yet.

I showered and changed into a clean pair of jeans and a shirt and sat on my bed to read the final entries in Great-uncle

George's Gallipoli diary. He was one of the fortunate few who had arrived on the first day and who were taken off Gallipoli before the long months wore into the horrors of late-summer dysentery and the frozen weeks of an early winter in November, when snow fell on the peninsula, drinking water turned to blocks of ice and men died of the cold at their posts. As an artillery driver, he was taken back to Egypt to be trained for the business of dragging ammunition wagons to the trenches of northern France.

On 1 August 1915, he wrote: 'Left Gallipoli at 11.20am for Alexandria. Was rowed to the Prince Abbott in a horse barge and was awfully sick [He must have been seriously ill, because no boat called Prince Abbott seems to have existed]. Reached Lemnos [a Greek island west of Imbros] at about 7.00 pm and went aboard HMS Aragon about two hours later to await another boat for Alexandria'. For the next two days, he stayed aboard *Aragon* 'as the headquarters is on board of her [and] officers and men are coming and going all day'. A day later, he transferred to the *Annaberg*, 'a captured German boat and a dirty tub at that'.

By 6 August he was 'well out in the Mediterranean, posted submarine guard and having good weather and a calm sea'. On 8 August George wrote, 'Arrived in Alexandria in early morning. Finis'.

There was no looking back in his words, no analysis of what he felt about leaving mates turning to dust beneath the ground, no musing on the dreadful three-and-a-bit months he had spent on Gallipoli. The 'Finis' put it behind him. Whatever it was that he experienced remained locked away in his psyche. For the hundredth time, I kicked myself for having never sought to sit down with George in his later years in an attempt to winkle out the memories that must have bounced around inside his head. But, like all the others of his generation, he was gone before I properly knew him and he took Gallipoli with him.

Now I had returned to Gallipoli with George's diary as a rough guide, and I felt I knew him and his mates a little. It was, I thought, time to have a farewell drink for them, and to farewell the mates I had made too. It was time for a last journey across the Dardanelles to the Boomerang Bar.

The rickety old place was fairly shaking. Chris and Gregg were earning their keep, running up and down behind the bar, fighting a losing battle to meet shouted orders from a tumult of customers. Gregg caught sight of me, beckoned me through the squash and handed me a can. 'What a day,' he said, ignoring the loud complaints of those around me. 'Fantastic, eh? Come back whenever you want. Chris or I will fix you up.'

I agreed, shook his hand and headed out the back. Beside an overland tour truck, Matt had set up his own two-up school. Scores of patrons were tossing lira notes around in the semi-darkness. 'I'm making some good money here,' Matt called, grinning. 'It's not about that, though. This is what the old fellas used to play.'

Back inside, music blared. Ben leaned against a pillar, a contented smile on his face as he watched young patrons dancing on tables and spilling beer on the floor. Everyone in the place seemed in a state of exuberant intoxication. Tom circulated with his friend Kate. I recognised a lot of people and waved and tried to have a conversation or two, but it was impossible to hear or be heard.

The windows had steamed up and someone had climbed on to a window ledge and written with a finger on the pane three words: 'Faith, courage, Anzac'.

I was too weary to try to keep up with the festivities. I elbowed my way to the bar. Chris and Gregg took a moment from their duties and we looked at each other and grasped hands. The two boys and Matt had decided to stay a few more days. 'Catch you later,' we said to each other.

Outside, the gypsy cart and driver waited. I couldn't be bothered trying to whittle down the price and handed over a wad of lira. We rattled through the streets of Eceabat, and I caught the midnight ferry to Çanakkale. It was almost deserted.

Next morning, there were more farewells to be endured. I found Tom and we shared breakfast in Anzac House, hardly talking. 'Some trip, eh?' he said. I nodded. Tom was off on a long tour along the Aegean Coast, and had no idea when he would return to London. I thanked him for his companionship and he gave me a copy of his personal diary.

Ben and Philippa were heading to Istanbul. We promised to catch up there before we all flew away in our different directions. Philippa would return to London and Ben planned to find his way around Europe.

Çanakkale was emptying before our eyes. The staff of Anzac House mooched about, shaking hands. A stream of coaches shunted towards the ferry, bound for Istanbul and ancient cities down the coast. Hanifi was asleep—he had been working almost non-stop during the most profitable few days of his year.

Gregg, Chris and Matt had decided to stay to walk the battlefields, which would be deserted. We knew they would be sleeping-in after an all-nighter at the Boomerang Bar.

My bus for Istanbul was waiting. I swung aboard and waved to Tom.

Across the Dardanelles and leaving Eceabat, I passed the Boomerang Bar. All the overland tour trucks were gone. In the carpark stood a single blue tent, facing the water. Matt had got back his sea view.

15

GEORGE'S TREE

Of the 40 soldiers who have Avenue of Honour trees dedicated to them at Hotspur, fifteen had their young lives blown away in World War I.

There is an old tree, a kurrajong, which stands in a bedraggled row of such trees along a little-travelled road in a hamlet in Australia, and which has outlived George Reuben Moore.

It is Tree Number 40 of the Avenue of Honour at Hotspur on the banks of the misty Crawford River in the far southwest of the state of Victoria. It has been growing since it was planted by relatives of mine in June 1918, even before the Great War was over.

George's tree.

There are such trees all over Australia standing in rows along roadsides, though few of them are quite as Australian as kurrajongs.

Most of the Avenues of Honour, which you may find wherever there is a town, are planted with European species—elms, oaks, plane trees. They all represent the same thing: a memory of men gone from the Earth. But the kurrajong, known to botanists as a *Brachychiton populneus*, is so Australian it has an Aboriginal name meaning shade tree.

I like to think George would have enjoyed the idea that, not far from where he was born, an Australian shade tree sits peace-fully, dedicated to him, which will live on and on.

I think, too, he would have liked all the young people I met and teamed up with on my pilgrimage to the now-peaceful place that had once scared the hell out of him, and which laid such a spell on him he kept the diary of his days there with him until he died.

When I returned to Australia, I placed between the pages of that diary a ball of shrapnel and a spent, misshapen bullet I had found on a ridge above Shrapnel Valley. I hope the authorities forgive me, but I thought George's little sister Eileen would like to have them during the remaining years of her life. She has never been to Gallipoli. Like most women of her generation, she had to imagine the place, and God only knows how deep the imagining clawed into hearts and lives as the lists of the dead and missing got longer and longer.

A couple of weeks after I returned to Australia, the last Anzac, Alec Campbell, died. The nation's flags flew at half-mast, there was a state funeral, the newspapers ran front-page obituar-ies and the country's opinion-makers debated anew the meaning of Gallipoli as if, somehow, there was fresh meaning to be had from this 87-year-old tragedy.

When I think about it all, no new meanings come to mind. We have known all along what it means—the trick is not to allow the knowledge of it to return to dust just as the mortal remains of all the Anzacs are doing now.

George was fortunate enough to have a long time to think about the meaning of Gallipoli.

After he was taken off the peninsula at Anzac Cove, he was sent in 1916 to France and to Belgium to drive his teams of horses into the howling, roaring tumour of the Earth that became known as the Western Front. It is not hard to think that George must have wished he had not got to drive horses at all. My mother's father, John Wallace Malseed, also fought on the Western Front and was wounded twice in two years. The few stories he was prepared to share in his later years made me wonder often how anyone remained sane on those fields of hellfire.

It is beyond amazing that George was never wounded or killed, for he continued his work right through the hideous battles of the war until one month before the whole torment was called off. In October 1918, George was put aboard a ship to return to Australia on what was called Anzac Leave.

It was supposed to be a special treat for those few men who had set out for the Great War at the very start and who had survived all the years of slaughter. But George was ever-after chagrined that he was not there at the finish on 11 November so that he could have gone to England and travelled gaily about, free of soldiering, perhaps with a girl on his arm.

He brought home with him a metal tobacco box that had a large hole ripped into the front of it and a small hole ripped in the back. It had taken a piece of shrapnel meant for his heart on one of his walks at Gallipoli. He had carried the tin in his breast pocket. Many men brought home with them stories of such preternatural escapes, but George's tobacco box still exists. It sits today, with his tattered old uniform, in a private museum run by Mrs Vanda Saville outside Heywood, 20 kilometres from the Hotspur Avenue of Honour.

A World War I obelisk stands in Heywood's main street, outside the little school, Number 279, where I learned to write with chalk on a hand-held piece of slate. The obelisk has George's name on it too. This is a clannish district that remembers its folk. Indeed, Heywood is closer to his birthplace than Hotspur, but I imagine tiny Hotspur needed to set its reach wide to gather its heroes.

Of the 40 soldiers who have Avenue of Honour trees dedicated to them at Hotspur, fifteen had their young lives blown away in World War I. I don't know if George ever saw this little avenue of tragedy. After the war, he left Western Victoria, where the wind blew and where the rain fell so constantly that Heywood was known to the old-time bullockies as the Glue Pot, and went north.

He took himself off to Red Cliffs, near Mildura on the Murray River, where the sun shone all year. Got himself a soldier settler's block, ran irrigation channels into it governed with small waterwheels, grew grapes on it, dried them in the sun and produced raisins and sultanas. He and his wife Elsie had no children, but George couldn't stop thinking about all the children and wives of the men who never came home with him from the battlefields. For years he spent his free hours raising money for Legacy, the organisation that cares for war widows and their children. Elsie died in 1975. Old George couldn't bear to live alone, so he sold his vineyard and returned to the remnants of his family at Heywood. He moved up the coast apiece to Warrnambool and died there in 1979 aged 85, his Anzac diary still with him.

Now there is just a tattered old kurrajong tree in an avenue spreading shade on warm days, a canopy when it rains and its leaves sighing in the breeze.

I believe George might have been content with the thought of that.

POSTSCRIPT
ONE YEAR LATER

Turkey's winter of 2003 was long and bitter. For the first time in memory, the Judas tree that spreads its branches over the neat rows of lost boys beneath the headstones in the Shrapnel Valley cemetery had not bloomed by Anzac Day. Gallipoli guides had to tell their charges that at this time of the year, with spring upon the peninsula, the tree was normally a shell-burst of purple. But the winter of 2003 had been too cold and too protracted, so the Judas tree was withholding its favours for a sunnier day.

Perhaps the times did not suit a wild and joyful spray of colour, anyway. The past year had seen the nation's already-dire economy continue to slide and fewer international travellers were prepared to face their fears about global terror. It was possible to visit many of the ancient hill-top temples along Turkey's Aegean coast and discover you were the only visitor—where there would normally be with thousands of wanderers. The war in Iraq had put the finishing touches to this disastrous situation, spooking anyone who might have imagined visiting any country that could be considered remotely Middle Eastern. The war was surely the last straw . . . until a previously unknown disease was given the alarming name Severe Acute Respiratory Syndrome, and airliners everywhere began emptying.

The oldest of cycles, war and pestilence, was rolling again, and it brought me back to Gallipoli. I had managed to convince the editor-in-chief of the *Bulletin* that Gallipoli could provide the springboard to any number of stories. Maybe after Anzac Day I could find my way to Iraq or one of the nearby Middle Eastern countries. Turkey, after all, shared borders with both Iraq and Syria. Australian troops were part of the Coalition military forces putting an end to Saddam Hussein's regime in Iraq, and there was talk that Syria might be next. The problem was that by the time I reached Istanbul, the attack on Iraq had turned out to be what its planners had meant it to be all along— the swiftest, most technically precise and most overwhelming in history. It was an American lesson to the rest of the world that said: 'There is only one superpower left on this Earth, and if you want to mess with us, this is what you will get'. Once Hussein and his commanders had disappeared in the smoke and debris of Baghdad, the story was over so far as front-page headlines were concerned. The modern attention span is around the length of a movie, and Iraq was coming to the end of its last reel. And as for the 'local angle': what was new about an Australian prime minister sending Australian troops halfway around the world to fight someone else's war? That was one of Australia's oldest stories, as Gallipoli itself attested. As a fall-back, a flight across a SARS-afflicted world might also have been a ripping yarn, but by the time my plane landed in Singapore, en route to Istanbul, the sight of an airport full of people drifting around in face masks was already passé—everyone who watched the six o'clock news had grown accustomed to such scenes. And so, my journey would become little more than a re-run of the well-worn Gallipoli pilgrimage—a story with something of the ageless to it but, this year, with a dark question hovering over it, too. In this age of terror, would Australians ignore all the warnings and still go to pay homage to those who had faced their own age of terror? It was a serious question: the day after I arrived in Istanbul, three small bombs exploded in the streets, though thankfully no one was injured. A day later, news agencies and the *Australian* newspaper reported a security flap: a platoon of suicide bombers, trained by Al Quaeda, allegedly had flitted across the border from Iraq, and were en route to Gallipoli, the blood of Australians in mind. It was, of course, a furphy but, just six months after Bali, it concentrated the mind.

I did however, have another angle of sorts. The Australian government was sending the Treasurer, Peter Costello, to speak at the dawn and Lone Pine ceremonies. I would interview him and I already had the hook to the article I would write—the trip to Gallipoli had become a rite of passage for thousands of young Australians. Was it a rite of passage for Peter Costello, too? He had been on a single political trajectory for so long that he had become a cliche—the prime minister in waiting. It would be interesting to see how Costello handled this most delicate, far-flung part of the Australian soul.

The journey had a deep familiarity to it for me. Having landed in Istanbul, I caught a cab from the airport to the Side Hotel. The staff were unchanged from the year before, and I was welcomed with handshakes and hugs. This time, I wanted to try a new method of travelling from Istanbul to Gallipoli. The Turkish coach system was supposed to be among the world's most user-friendly, so I thought I would check it out. I popped into the little travel agency next door to The Side and asked to be booked aboard a coach from Istanbul to Çanakkale. No worries, said the travel agency receptionist, a New Zealander named Hayden who moonlighted as a DJ aboard 'booze cruises' held nightly in April on the waters of the Bosphorus. The coach ticket cost the princely sum of 20 million Turkish lira (around

$20 Australian) and a mini-bus would pick me up from the hotel and take me to the *otagar*—the huge coach terminal stuck way out in Istanbul's suburbs.

And so, the following morning, I found myself aboard a Truva Tours coach bound for Çanakkale, easing past hundreds of similar vehicles parked in the multi-storey *otogar*, bound for every point of Turkey.

Coaches appear to be the Turkish equivalent of a domestic air service. The seats recline and a steward attends each traveller's needs. We had driven no more than a kilometre before the steward, a carefully groomed young man who spoke a little English, began handing out plastic-wrapped cake and pouring coffee or tea for every passenger. For the remainder of the five-and-a-half hour trip he provided mineral water on request from a mini-bar, and poured refreshing lemon-scented elixir on our hands. The coach floated down the highway, and I slept easily. Having previously hired a car and driver and taken a Hassle Free mini-bus, the coach was by far the most comfortable way to travel this road. Such coaches leave daily, on the hour every hour, apparently.

The magazine's travel company had made reservations at a hotel in Çanakkale called The Helen. I had never heard of the place, and feared it might be one of the numerous fleabags that inhabit the back streets. To my great surprise and relief, The Hotel Helen turned out to be a brand-new establishment in the main street, right next to the Anzac House hostel. It was clean and shining, and my room came with fluffy white pillows and doonas and a splendidly tiled bathroom. At US$45 a night, it was a bargain. I had managed to stumble into Çanakkale's best hotel without knowing it existed.

Sadly, the Kebap Salonu No. 2 had disappeared some time during the year, but I found a new, slightly ritzier place just up the street from The Helen that served almost the same sort of food as the old joint. A slight melancholy crept around my heart as I wandered the street: the old town was changing. Worse, I didn't have a band of friends, nor the time to search out a new mob. I wasn't going to meet a bunch of cheerful backpackers in the Hotel Helen, and when I ventured through the front door of Anzac House, I felt a stranger. Hanifi was absent, off in Istanbul drumming up business. Serif the manager was friendly, but too busy to talk for long.

Across the Dardanelles, the Boomerang Bar was swinging in to action, and I had a couple of beers with a pair of travellers I had met on the coach—a Canadian and an American who had been meandering around Europe for the past two years. A tattered visitors' book lay on the table, and I searched through until I found last year's entries from Matt, Gregg, Chris, Ben and Philippa. Tom's name wasn't there, but he probably didn't need to leave his name—anyone who met him would remember him.

The Boomerang Bar was a pale imitation of itself this time. It was possible, even on its busiest night, to move through the room at a steady walking pace. It seemed the most reliable pre-Anzac guide—the crowd was drastically down on the year before. In fact, this turned out to be only part of the story. The number of travellers prepared to spend a few days in Çanakkale or Eceabat or around the peninsula was significantly less than the previous year. I assumed that only a couple of thousand people would attend the Anzac Day ceremonies.

But that's not what happened at all. On Anzac Eve, almost 10 000 souls barrelled along the single-lane road that swings around the peninsula. Organisers had only 8000 programs setting out the orders of service, and they were all gone by soon after midnight. The crowd hunkered down on the grass and in the scrub to await the dawn service at the ceremonial site above

North Beach, crammed together in sleeping bags, just as they were the year before. This time, however, the vast majority had flown in to Istanbul from London and had caught buses specifically for the Anzac Day services. They weren't staying—they would return to Istanbul by nightfall. But they had come. They had ignored all the travel warnings and the dire stories about Al Quaeda and had come for this one day of the year.

Tightened security—scores of Turkish troops were milling up and down the roads, the beach was fenced off and snipers were on the ridges where, 88 years previously, other snipers had rained death—had another effect. Hawkers were forbidden from setting up stalls along the road to the commemorative site, so no beer was on sale. This, together with official statements banning alcohol and a fiercely cold night, resulted in a noticeably muted crowd. Peter Wilson's stories the previous year about the 'Bacchanalian orgy' at Anzac, though dismissed by a government inquiry, had been quietly heeded. There was no rock music blaring on the loudspeaker system. Instead, at 3 a.m., musician and storyteller Jan Wozitsky—formerly of the old Bushwhackers band—stomped on stage and began an hour-long concert of yarns from Anzac, songs of the period, poetry and jokes. It lent a warmth to the freezing dark. The size of the crowd seemed perfectly suited to the space allotted, and by the time a piper from the Royal Scots Dragoon Guards stood on the Anzac plinth above the sea and wailed into the gloom, the gathering was awake and imbued with the expectancy which always gives the place before dawn a spooky character. The band of the Royal Military College, Duntroon, took over at 4.45 a.m. and, at 5.30 a.m., with the slightest lightening of the sky beginning to reveal The Sphinx behind us, the tap and roll of a drum announced the entry of the *catafalque* party. The old ritual took hold of us. Afterwards, the crowd slowly shook itself out of its reverie and began the march into the hills, up to Lone Pine. I joined the tramp along the seafront, past Shrapnel Valley and its bloomless Judas tree, to the turn-off to Shell Green, climbing the long steep road built by engineers under fire in 1915 to provide a path for artillery. I stopped halfway up the hill and stood in the small Shell Green cemetery. Way below, the Aegean lay grey beneath a cold sky.

Out there beyond the horizon, the world was still fighting. World War I, the Great War, was supposed to be the War to End All Wars. The bones beneath my feet at Shell Green were supposed to have been part of the great sacrifice to gain a lasting peace. Such brave, optimistic naivety.

Still, there is something compelling about guileless intent, the courageous innocence we often confuse with naivety. Something of the sort had been nagging at me for a year, and my return to old Anzac was the opportunity to deal with it.

A year before, late at night in the Boomerang Bar, Matt the surfer boy had tackled me about the morality of removing artifacts such as shrapnel balls and spent bullets from the battlefield. I had offered a lame response to his earnest inquiries about the ethics of the matter, largely because I had pocketed a couple of misshapen rounds of ammunition myself. My too-neat excuse had been that I intended to take these mementoes home and present them to Great-uncle George's sister, Eileen. But I had never sent them to Eileen. The small, mangled pieces of metal had sat in my top drawer at home, digging at my conscience every time I saw them. They belonged where they had lain in the dirt for almost a century, in the Gallipoli Peace Park and, eventually, the echoes of Matt's anxiety wore through every argument I might have had.

And so I had brought these insignificant relics back with me to Gallipoli. As I reached the last hundred metres of the artillery road above Shell Green, I stepped off the track, pushed my way through the scrub, stood at the lip of a deep valley and flung the shrapnel ball and the twisted shell into the void. It was, surely, their slowest and least deadly journey through space. But they were home, and I felt freed of a considerable weight.

Up at Lone Pine, the cemetery was filling. A Mexican wave swept around, and the crowd whistled and cheered as veterans were brought to their seats. I sat upon a grave and for a moment, a year had not passed at all. The lone pine tree shivered with the breeze, hymns were sung, prayers intoned. Peter Costello spoke. 'We stand here to honour sacrifice,' he said. 'We do so because sacrifice is an uncommon virtue and a virtue that we, successive generations of Australians, can take from and learn from and in a much smaller way return. It is difficult to leave those who have paid so high a price. In spirit Australia has never left this site. And we never will.' In a world that hasn't learned where peace might be found, it seemed as good a sentiment as any. The soldiers beneath us had found peace, and each year we go to honour them and wonder at their suffering and their offering of their lives and the dreadful circumstances that brought them to it. On a planet so constantly immersed in turbulence and madness, perhaps that is enough. The hills above Anzac Cove exist for us—Australians, New Zealanders and Turks—as a long frozen moment piercing the story of our nations' being. It can mean, for each of us, whatever we want it to mean.

ADDENDUM—TIPS FOR TRAVELLERS

A journey begins in the imagination. These days, it also begins on the Internet. I planned most of my trip to Turkey by tapping into the virtual world. All you need to do is fire up the Internet, choose a search engine (my favourite is www.google.com) and begin tossing in words. Istanbul, Sultanahmet (Istanbul's old city), Anzac, Gallipoli, Çanakkale, Eceabat—words like these will have you bouncing all over cyberspace. To make things even easier for you, I have compiled a shortlist of the most useful Websites among the hundreds I ploughed through. You will find them below.

To supplement the world of virtual information, you should purchase a guide book or two. I chose just three: Lonely Planet's *Turkey*, Dorling Kindersley's *Eyewitness Travel Guide on Istanbul*, and *Gallipoli: A Battlefield Guide* by Phil Taylor and Pam Cupper (Kangaroo Press). All are excellent.

To actually get to Istanbul in order to begin my journey, I simply phoned a travel agent in Australia. There are plenty of different airlines and routes, but I chose the simplest from Sydney—flying Qantas to Singapore, then Turkish Airlines from Singapore to Istanbul. Turkish airlines has the newest fleet of aircraft in Europe, by the way. This isn't a sponsored plug—I paid my own way, all the way. Anyway, check out your own travel agent. The return flight, economy, is likely to set you back about $2500, including taxes.

Once you arrive, the options are pretty well unlimited. It is a simple matter to hire a car or mini-van and choose your own route. But my advice is not to even think of driving in Istanbul; this is a city of 16 million or so (and climbing), the roads and streets are cluttered and the locals drive like maniacs. Take a taxi or mini-bus to your hotel or hostel and walk around the major sites from there. Walking is a joy in such an exotic city and most of the places you will want to see are in the old city of Sultanahmet (which is where you ought to stay) or nearby in the Bazaar quarter, or along the banks of the Bosphorus, which has a constant stream of ferries.

Outside Istanbul, Turkey's bus system is so good that for a minimal outlay you can go just about anywhere in comfort. Almost every town has a bus station, known generally as an *otogar*. Apart from the main intercity bus lines, you can often catch smaller mini-buses (*dolmus*) to nearby villages. If you only want to get from Istanbul to the Gallipoli area, buses leave every hour. The best idea is to book a seat at a travel agent or the front office of your hotel or hostel—the cost is likely to be around US$10–12—and many of these buses will pick you up in front of the Haghia Sofia, or come to you. The alternative is to choose an organised tour. There are scores of them and, once again, your travel agent ought to be able to arrange one that suits your needs. Most people who travel all the way from Australia or New Zealand take a guided tour that includes a few days in Istanbul, followed by a trip (usually by coach) around the most-visited areas of Turkey: Ankara, Cappadocia, along the Mediterranean–Aegean Coast, to Gallipoli and then back to Istanbul. Such a tour will introduce you to ancient cities and landscapes that will stun you, and you won't have to worry about organising a thing. The cost will depend on the level of accommodation you choose, the route, the length of time you spend and the tour operator. Including airfares from Australia or New Zealand, figure anything from $4000 to $10 000.

Ready to go? A few things you need to know

Before you pack your bag, the most important advice is the oldest advice: pack light. Lay out all the clothes you want to take and halve them. Then reward yourself by doubling the amount of money you think you will need. Seriously. You can always bring home money you don't spend, but it's tough to discover you don't have enough when you are away. Buy, beg or borrow a good-quality backpack, fill it and get it fitted comfortably to your body before you go anywhere. Any good camping or adventure shop will usually sort you out. Make sure the pack has a detachable day-pack. Alternatively, take a shoulder bag that has a strap that you can sling across your body, and which can fit at your side, under your arm (this is about the most secure arrangement in a crowded street).

Think hard about whether you really need a sleeping bag. It takes up a lot of space in your pack, even in a compressor bag, and unless you are camping out, you will probably never need it. If you are staying in hotels or hostels, there will be plenty of doonas or blankets. A sleeping sheet is all you will require in a hostel, and you can almost always hire a clean one on the spot. A silk sleeping sheet, available in all good camping and adventure stores, is an excellent investment—it will be a bit of luxury every night, and it stuffs down into a tiny carry-bag.

Remember that you can purchase most things you will need 'on the road' and, in Turkey, it is likely they will be cheaper than at home. As for clothes, choose carefully and you won't need many items because you can wash them out overnight, or drop them into the laundries that are in every major town; they are cheap and the staff will do the washing, the drying and the folding in a few hours. Take quick-drying materials. My daughter's advice proved right—jeans won't dry overnight, even on a heater, and they will chafe next day. And they are relatively heavy. Lightweight cargo pants are a good idea for men or women and they have plenty of pockets. Whatever you are going to wear on your feet (I would recommend you check out a good climbing store for vented, lightweight but strong hiking or 'approach' shoes) make sure they are well broken-in. Wear them for weeks before you leave.

Before you fly anywhere, remember to pack *anything* metal and sharp (pocket knife, scissors, even nail file or needle and thread) into the bag that is going into the plane's luggage hold. Otherwise, these items will be confiscated at the security gate and you might never get them back. If you must carry medication, make sure you bring the doctor's prescription with you and leave a copy with someone you can easily contact at home for emergency faxing. Some ingredients of medicines (such as codeine) are illegal in some countries, but you will be okay if you can prove they have been prescribed at home.

Your carry-on luggage should include pen for filling in landing cards, a book for long hours with nothing else to do, an extra pair of socks to keep your feet warm once you take off your shoes on board, and a pullover or fleece (it can get cold on board, and in April don't expect a warm arrival in Istanbul). Plus, you will need something warm to wear at Gallipoli while spending the night in the open before the dawn service. Deodorant, a toothbrush and tiny tube of toothpaste, a water-mist spray, moisturiser and, for blokes, an electric or battery operated razor (you can shave with moisturiser) will add to your comfort and help you stay relatively fresh on the plane. An eyeshade and ear plugs are useful, although many airlines provide these, and quite a lot also hand out socks. You might ask your doctor to prescribe Normison or similar sleeping tablets if you want a decent rest. They should send you to the Land of Nod for around six hours, and there is no hang-over. To reduce the effects of jet-lag, work out the local time at your destination and sleep when it is night there (for instance, if you are likely to arrive at dawn or early morning, get to sleep six or eight hours before you are due to land, then stay up all day).

There are a number of good checklists on the Web to ensure you have packed everything you will need. One of the best is on *TNT Magazine*'s Website at http://www.tntmagazine.com/uk/worldtravel/packing_checklist.asp

Money: Stop thinking in Australian dollars when you land in Istanbul. Think in US dollars or Euros and learn the mysteries of local currency, the Turkish lira, as quickly as possible. This takes a bit of practice, because most of the notes are the same colour, and all those zeroes can easily fool you into believing a 10 million lira note is 1 million lira, or vice versa. Have US$20 in your pocket when you land in Instanbul. That's for the on-the-spot visa. Have another US$20 to change into Turkish lira to get you started (a taxi into Sultanahmet costs the equivalent of US$10–12; a shuttle bus is vastly cheaper). Some hotels try to insist that you pay in US dollars, which may be rude and illegal but understandable considering the rate of inflation and the weakness of the Turkish lira. It's therefore not a bad idea to have a reasonable stash of US dollars hidden away in a money belt or sewn into your pants or a corner of your pack or wherever you think it might be safe. It's up to you whether you carry travellers' cheques, though they give you an extra (and secure) fall-back position if you happen to lose your cash or credit card. I didn't bother with them—your Visa card, Mastercard, or Cirrus-linked Bankcard will get you instant cash at ATMs, which are commonplace. In Istanbul's Sultanahmet, there is a bank of ATMs directly across the road from the Haghia Sofia. Around Gallipoli, there is a machine near the entrance to the wharf in Çanakkale; and in Eceabat, head across to the far side of the square from the wharf. Use them early in the day, if possible, as some ATMs run out of cash during the afternoon.

Local customs: Turkey is officially a secular nation, but almost everyone is Muslim. Most are pretty relaxed, but visitors should observe a couple of basic requirements. Dress modestly, particularly when visiting mosques. Bare legs and bare arms are frowned upon, and women should wear a scarf over their heads. You must remove your shoes before entering a mosque and it's a good idea to carry a plastic bag in which you can carry your shoes, although such bags are often available at the door. There is no charge to visit mosques, but a small donation as you leave is appreciated.

Keep connected with home: Set up a Hotmail or similar email address before you leave. Most hostels have Internet access, and Internet cafés are just about everywhere. They are cheap (from about 60 cents per half hour to a couple of dollars) but the Turkish keyboard can be tricky. Get a local to advise you. If you have a mobile phone, remember to request global roam before you leave home, and remember also that if someone calls you from a mobile at home, part of the cost of that call will appear on your bill. However, SMS messaging is cheap wherever you go, because the cost is limited by international agreement to a small set fee per message (usually around 25 cents, Australian).

Have a great journey!

Websites

The following list of Internet sites will get you started. I have limited the hotels and hostels to those I actually stayed in, or which I visited and inspected.

http://www.turizm.gov.tr   Official Turkish Tourism site, which includes links to many Australian and New Zealand tour operators specialising in Turkey, plus most things you will need to know while planning your trip. Interesting use of the English language!

http://www.anzacsite.gov.au   The Anzac Commemorative Site on the Gallipoli Peninsula, a very useful guide to all things Anzac.

http://www.nzhistory.net.nz/Gallery/Anzac/Anzac.htm   A New Zealand perspective on Anzac Day.

http://www.nzhistory.net.nz/Gallery/Memorial/MEMORIAL.htm   New Zealand's National War Memorial, with historical links.

http://www.awm.gov.au   Australian War Memorial site and an indispensable research tool.

http://www.anzachouse.com   Anzac House (Çanakkale, Dardanelles). Here you can make reservations, book Hassle Free tours, learn about the Anzac campaign and check out frequently asked questions about travelling in Turkey.

http://www.anzacgallipolitours.com   TJ's Hostel and Tours (Eceabat, Gallipoli Peninsula). You can make reservations, organise tours, and the site has many other extremely useful snippets of information.

http://www.anzacs.org   Very useful site with epitaphs of soldiers with known graves, plus a wide range of other historical information.

http://www.dva.gov.au   Official Australian Department of Veterans' Affairs site on Gallipoli, with up-to-date info on Anzac Day services.

http://www.naa.gov.au   Research a relative who went to Gallipoli through the Australian National Archives.

http://www.sidehotel.com   Side Hotel, Istanbul: rates US$20 per night (single, no bathroom) to US$70 (four-bed apartment). The site has information about the hotel and Istanbul and you can make reservations online.

http://www.sultanahmetpalace.com   Sultanahmet Saray (Palace) Hotel, Istanbul (36 rooms) for those with an eye for luxury, from US$130 per night for a single to US$230 for a family deluxe.

http://www.starholidayhotel.com   Star Holiday Hotel Sultanahmet, basic budget hotel (US$25 single to US$45 triple, but ask for a deal).

http://www.abone.superonline.com/~orienthostel/index2.html   Orient Hostel, Sultanahmet, Istanbul (US$7–US$9 a night). Gathering point for backpackers. The site includes information on Istanbul and tours to Gallipoli.

http://www.istanbulcityguide.com   Hotels, weather, photo gallery and food in Istanbul.

http://www.tntmagazine.com/uk   *TNT Magazine*. Great, London-based magazine for travellers, with just about anything a young Australian or New Zealander might want to know about using London as a jumping-off point to Turkey, or anywhere else for that matter.

The Hotel Helen doesn't have a Website but it can be found at Kemalpasa Mah, Cumhurivet Meydam # 57, Çanakkale, and contacted on 902 86 2121818, or by fax on 902 86 2128686. Single rooms are US$45 per night, doubles US$65. A bargain for those in search of a little comfort.